History of the
UNITED STATES OF AMERICA

History of the
UNITED STATES OF AMERICA

From Independence to the Civil War

Archana Ojha

Orient BlackSwan

All rights reserved. No part of this book may be (i) modified, reproduced or utilised in any form, or by any means, electronic or mechanical, including photocopying, recording or by any information storage and retrieval system, in any form of binding or cover other than in which it is published, without permission in writing from the publisher; or (ii) used or reproduced in any manner for the purpose of training, development or operation of artificial intelligence (AI) technologies and systems, including generative AI technologies, without permission in writing from the copyright holder.

HISTORY OF THE UNITED STATES OF AMERICA:
FROM INDEPENDENCE TO THE CIVIL WAR

ORIENT BLACKSWAN PRIVATE LIMITED

Registered Office
3-6-752 Himayatnagar, Hyderabad 500 029, Telangana, India
e-mail: centraloffice@orientblackswan.com

Other Offices
Bengaluru, Chennai, Guwahati, Hyderabad, Kolkata, Mumbai, New Delhi, Noida, Patna

© Orient Blackswan Private Limited 2025
First published 2025

ISBN 978-93-6973-841-0

041002

Typeset in
Adobe Garamond Pro 11/13
by Le Studio Graphique, Gurgaon 122 007

Printed in India at
B.B Press, Tronica City, Ghaziabad, U.P. 201 103

Published by
Orient Blackswan Private Limited.
3-6-752 Himayatnagar, Hyderabad 500 029, Telangana, India
e-mail: info@orientblackswan.com

Contents

List of Figures, Maps, and Tables	*vii*
Preface	*ix*
Acknowledgments	*xi*

	Introduction	1
1.	The American Revolution: The Rise of a Nation	18
2.	The Formulation of the American Constitution	52
3.	Thomas Jefferson and Jeffersonian Democracy	73
4.	Andrew Jackson and the Emergence of a New Political Ethos	89
5.	Removal of Indigenous Peoples and Westward Expansion	105
6.	The War of 1812	141
7.	American Exceptionalism: Chattel Enslavement	164
8.	The Civil War: Slavery, Sectionalism, and Economic Interests	223

References	257
Index	266

Figures, Maps, and Tables

FIGURES

1.1	Declaration of Independence, broadside, printed by John Dunlap in Philadelphia	36
1.2	*Declaration of Independence*, by John Trumbull, oil on canvas (1819)	48
3.1	*Hoisting American Colors, Louisiana Cession, 1803*, by Thure de Thulstrup, oil on canvas (1902)	81
4.1	General Jackson Slaying the Many-Headed Monster, cartoon (1836)	94
4.2	King Andrew the First, lithograph (1833)	96
5.1	*American Progress*, by John Gast, oil on canvas (1872)	129
6.1	Engraving showing the burning of Washington, by Warner J. Barber (1827)	152
7.1	A Slave Auction in Virginia, *The Illustrated London News* (1861)	169
7.2	Harriet Tubman, portrait by Harvey B. Lindsley, taken between 1871 and 1876	218

MAPS

1.	Territorial Acquisitions of the USA	xvi

TABLES

I.1	Timeline for the Establishment of the Thirteen Colonies	9
1.1	Important Events: The American Revolution	26
2.1	American Constitutional History	58
8.1	Events Leading to the Civil War	224

Preface

The present volume aims to acquaint the reader with an integrative and interconnected history of the United States of America, which will be of use not only to undergraduate and postgraduate students, but also to all those who wish to understand the rise of the United States as a global power. Some topics have been prioritised over others to provide space for major themes and patterns in the USA's history. In this vein, an attempt has been made to provide more detailed analyses of the aspects of American history that are of greatest significance for students and readers in India. While the settlement and colonisation of North America was intrinsically connected to the European world which, from the fifteenth century onwards, was a significant influence on its polity and economy, the history of the United States has to be studied as a separate continent—one marked by a unique set of circumstances, and indeed a projection of exceptionalism that both intrigues, beckons, and creates a sense of awe in the minds of the people. Economically, the USA has been a dominant power since the end of the nineteenth century and has been a superpower since the end of World War II. Therefore, it becomes essential to study the rise of the United States as a modern nation in the last quarter of the eighteenth century, when monarchies still dominated the Western world. The rise of a modern nation, with a written constitution that, in its very first amendment, incorporated the Bill of Rights to protect its citizens' constitutional rights, heralded a nation that would eventually carve out a distinct path in terms of politics, economy, society, culture, and military affairs.

Acknowledgments

I began working on this book at the suggestion of my guide and mentor, Professor Christopher Sam Raj (Centre of American, Canadian and Latin American Studies, School of International Studies, Jawaharlal Nehru University, Delhi). The idea came to us while I was working on my doctoral thesis, which I submitted to Jawaharlal Nehru University. Since I have been teaching the history of the USA at the University of Delhi for nearly 36 years, this volume is the fruition of that labour. The volumes are based on the distilled experiences of an Indian (the real Indian that Christopher Columbus had set out to find!) who, as an undergraduate student, opted for the History of the USA paper at the University of Delhi, and even during postgraduate studies took a deep interest in American history. An interesting facet of my teaching career, both at the undergraduate and postgraduate levels at the University of Delhi, was the opportunity I got to teach this paper from the outset, which further deepened my interest and inclination to undertake research in American Studies. This book on American history is not entirely original. It incorporates knowledge acquired from the works of generations of American historians who have researched various aspects of the United States' history and contributed to my understanding of the rise of the world's first modern nation.

Apart from academics, my interest in American History stems more from my childhood experiences, as I spent formative years of my life in the erstwhile Soviet Union, which left a deep imprint on my mind and helped me become cosmopolitan, with a global perspective, and with a deep interest in history as I got the opportunity to travel the length and breadth of Europe, which was still recovering from the aftermath of World War II. As I grew up, I wanted to expand my horizon and developed a deep interest in American Studies, especially in Indigenous societies and the history of African Americans. My empathy with both cultures and people probably stems from my own life, which has seen me face formidable hurdles, life-threatening situations, and circumstances that I have managed to navigate and circumvent through a balanced mindset, the application of knowledge acquired through in-depth studies, and lessons learnt from life, people, and historical studies.

At a crucial juncture of my career, when I was going full throttle on this book, illness struck and incapacitated me for years. During that time, I faced numerous problems, and the idea and time to work on the book receded into the remotest corner of my mind. Gradually, I gathered myself to work more sincerely on the book during the Covid-19 pandemic. However, just then, more dark clouds began to gather around me, threatening to halt the work completely. At this juncture, a phone call from Roopa Sharma of Orient BlackSwan gave me the impetus to complete this work and see it through to the end.

The generous support of various institutions, colleagues, friends, and family made the completion of this book possible. The entire manuscript was meticulously researched and written over a significant period, starting in 2005. The journey began with the collection of materials during visits to the Indo-American Centre for International Studies at Osmania University, Hyderabad.

The Canadian Studies Doctoral Research Fellowship (2001–2002) at the University of Victoria, B.C. Canada provided me with exposure to North America and, in particular, introduced me to many Indigenous scholars and professors, including Michael Asch, Leroy Little Bear, Taiaiake Alfred (Director of Indigenous Governance Programs, 2001), who became my 'Indian' brother, and Stephen Greymorning. My selection for the Fulbright fellowship (sponsored by the Department of State, Washington D.C.) on 'The Civilisation of the United States' at New York University, Steinhardt School of Education, Multinational Institute of American Studies (2002) assisted me in understanding and appreciating America's historical, political, and cultural aspects. The Fulbright fellowship not only provided me with the opportunity to travel throughout this fascinating nation and live in Pueblo, New Mexico, but also enabled me to visit libraries (Yale, Harvard, and Columbia Universities), historical sites, cities, families, and museums across the United States. The Director of this programme, Professor Phil Hosey, provided me with full assistance in collecting material and working on this project, along with the support of many other professors at the University. The University Grants Commission awarded me a Minor Research Fellowship, which enabled me to purchase books. The American Centre Library and its staff, along with the library at Jawaharlal Nehru University and the Prime Minister's Library at Teen Murti, have been used to source articles, books, and journals for this book. The administrative support of these institutions and individuals has played a significant role in the completion of this book.

The completion of the first draft during the challenging Covid-19 pandemic was a significant milestone. Subsequently, I received revisions and suggestions from the anonymous reviewers of Orient BlackSwan, who read my manuscript and provided valuable feedback. Their suggestions have been instrumental in the compilation and completion of this voluminous work, for which I am deeply grateful.

The list of people who have contributed to my journey of becoming an author begins with my two undergraduate teachers at Kamala Nehru College, Mridula Abrol who till this day has remained my constant support, and Anita Nahal who taught me the history of the USA in a manner that made it more interesting, interdisciplinary, and interactive. My postgraduate professors, in particular the late H. C. Verma, T. K. V. Subrahmanyam, the late B. P. Sahu, the late Sunil Kumar, Z. H. N. Jafari, Seema Bawa, Amar Farooqui, and Prabhu Mahapatra, all nurtured my interest in history. I am also indebted to my guide, Christopher Raj, as well as Abdul Nafey and K. P. Vijaylakshmi of Jawaharlal Nehru University.

I want to express my sincere gratitude to Kamala Nehru College, where I have been both a student and a faculty member, and particularly to Pavitra Bhardwaj, the principal, for granting me sabbatical leave, which provided me the necessary space, time, and flexibility to complete this work. My two former principals, Surinder J. Sharma, who believed in my academic abilities, and the late Minoti Chatterjee, who gave me her full support, have also been instrumental in my academic development. My friends in the college, Shubhra Sinha, Vinita Malik, Jayanti Bala Gupta, along with Geetish Nirban, Bharati Dave, Naresh Kumar and my colleagues in the department of History—their constant encouragement became an invisible source of energy. My two friends, the late Jayashree Deshpande of Lady Shri Ram College, who handed over all her books and articles to me, and Renu Maira of Gargi College, who also gifted me all her books on the history of the USA. These two friends believed that one day, I would succeed in finishing the book, and I want to thank them for believing in me. I would also like to thank the students of my undergraduate and postgraduate classes, from whom I learnt more than they did from me. I am indebted to all these people, as without their contributions, this book would not have been completed.

I am grateful to the team at Orient BlackSwan for their constant support, encouragement, and guidance throughout the completion of this book, from 2021 to its final publication. Roopa Sharma and Nilanjana Majumdar worked tirelessly to support me. I would also like to thank Sanna Jain for the editorial work and calm composure during my frantic calls and queries. Further, I would like to thank the rest of the publishing house staff who were engaged in this project.

I have had the constant support and encouragement of my lifelong friends, Anuradha and Albina Maria Michael, who have been my two pillars of support for more than five decades. Additionally, I have been supported by my friends, Anil Rai (Department of Hindi, University of Delhi), the late Vedwati Vaidik, Aparna Vaidik (Ashoka University), Vimlesh Yadav (Principal, Aurobindo College), Meena Bhargava (Indraprastha College), Sharmila Shrivastava (Hansraj College), Ashwini Shankar (Deshbandhu College), and Mushtak Mufti of Jamia Millia Islamia. My nephews, Sunil Trivedi, Shailesh Trivedi; nieces, Nandita Tiwari, Divya Tiwari, Abha Boddhisatva, and Richa Tripathi. My cousin brothers, especially Purn Dev Upadhyaya, along with scores of students who also joined academics, too numerous to mention here, have made immense contributions to my personal life and academic career, and I will be forever indebted to them.

This book is dedicated to my parents and my sister. My father, the late Shri Raj Vallabh Ojha, a Hindi journalist, introduced me to the world of books, poems, and adventure, inculcating in me the spirit of romanticism and a belief in the power of empathy and humanity. My late mother, Shrimati Shiv Mohini Ojha, believed in me and supported me till her last breath, helping me achieve what I had set out to do in my life. My sister, the late Girija Trivedi, whose rock-solid support till her last days is something I will cherish throughout my life. How I wish they were all there to see the publication of this book. My sincere gratitude to my lawyers, Rukhsana Chaudhary and F. K. Jha, who guided me at every crucial step of my life. My home assistant, Rawista, whom I taught and is now a teacher, showed me the power of courage and determination. My life's anchor, mentor, guide, and the person I argue with the most is my older brother, Rajiv Ojha, who has stood by me through all the turbulences of my life with complete faith and belief in my abilities. Without his constant encouragement, this volume would not have seen the light of day.

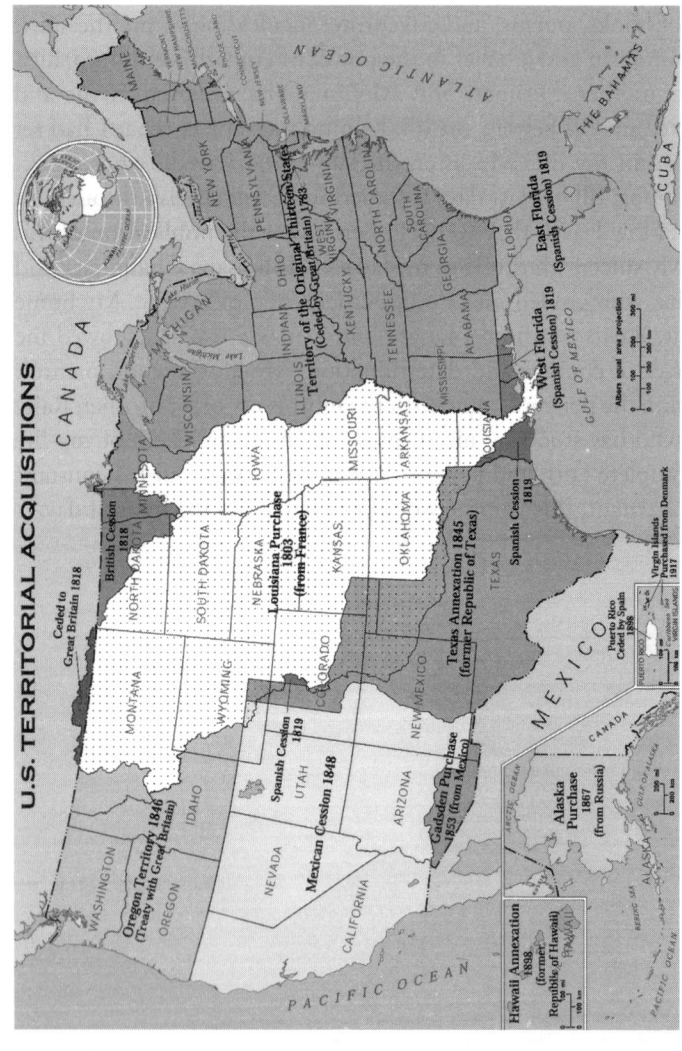

Map 1: Territorial Acquisitions of the USA

Source: US Geological Survey; Wikimedia Commons.

Introduction

Writing the history of the United States is a daunting task for a historian who has studied and taught American history for nearly four decades in India—in these decades, the study of American history has undergone a profound transformation, drawing extensively from other disciplines, particularly from sociology, anthropology, and economics. This interdisciplinary approach delves into aspects previously unaddressed in formalised historical narratives, with the aim not only to broaden the understanding of American history but also to bring in the approach of new schools of history that have made use of new primary sources and methods, including the history of communities, groups, and cultures neglected in earlier periods of research. The history of the United States is complex due to the vast geographical spread of this continental nation.

Geographically, the United States is almost the size of the entire continent of Europe. It varies significantly based on climatic and environmental conditions, which are highly diverse, ranging from mountains, plateaus, canyons, deserts, to plains, forests, and long coastlines, including the Appalachians and Rocky Mountains, the Great Desert, the Mississippi Basin, the Great Lakes, the Pacific and Atlantic coasts, and frozen Alaska. These geographical conditions fostered a spirit of adventurism and romanticism among the settler immigrants, and contributed to the emergence of political ideologies and institutions reflective of relative freedom from class, orthodox religiosity, and bureaucratic control. This uniqueness stems from the period of colonisation of the 'New World', as the Americas were termed by Europeans, when settler immigrants developed their self-governed institutional systems before the superimposition of the British imperial governance structures. The independent-spirited settlers rose in revolution against imperialist control, culminating in the emergence of a new, modern nation that, in 1776 and even now, boasts of great diversity in its people and regions.

The geographical vastness raised the problem of economic unification for political stability, forcing the nation to develop internal communication systems and transportation through technological innovation. This progression began with canoes (adopted from the Indigenous peoples), ships, and wagons in the seventeenth century. From the eighteenth century onwards, this evolved into steamboats, trains, and automobiles, culminating in the development of all-weather roads and highways. Simultaneously, this period saw the growth of flexible political institutions and judicial activism, which were among the most outstanding features of the progression of modern American history. And yet, this uniqueness also led to the beginning of secessionist impulses, eventually building up to the Civil War (1861–1865), which nearly pushed the young nation toward complete collapse and division, based on the prevalent political perception at the time that the union of states need not be essentially a unified whole.

To cover the entire spectrum of American history up to World War II, the book has been divided into two volumes. Volume I covers the period from the colonisation of the North American continent up to the Civil War. Volume II concentrates on the period from 1865, the Reconstruction era, up to World War II.

In Volume I, we shall explore the process of colonisation and settlement by the colonial European powers. Equally, we also focus on understanding the growth and development of chattel slavery and the transatlantic slave trade, especially within the context of a nation whose constitution emphasises 'social justice' and 'liberty' in creating the perfect union. This also includes studying the lives of enslaved people, and their socio-cultural world. The volume also reflects on the struggles and resistance of the Indigenous peoples, who suffered extreme forms of exploitation, population decimation, and marginalisation which, paradoxically, assisted the White settler immigrant populace in developing the 'American' brand of nationalism, liberalism, and democracy.

European Colonisation of North America: A Brief Outline

Colonies began to emerge and expand territorially in North America even before the development of governance structures for them. In the 1490s, European sailors began to explore the newly discovered lands in the Western Hemisphere, including the Caribbean. Italian explorer Amerigo Vespucci is credited with correcting the belief that Christopher Columbus (who arrived in the Americas in 1492) and other European explorers had discovered a sea route to Asia. He called the newly discovered continent the 'New World', and the name 'America' is derived from his name. The Western world asserted the right of 'Discovery' of the New World, which eventually led to the establishment of New Spain, New France, New Netherland, New England, and New Sweden. All of them were looking to discover new sources of precious metals and new wealth when they encountered the 'Indians' (Indigenous peoples), the original communities of North America, with archaeological evidence pointing to long-term inhabitation dating back centuries, for example ancient mound sites like the Moundsville Complex in West Virginia and the Serpent Mound in Ohio, and findings related to the Hopewell cultures in the Mississippi region.

Spanish Expansion into the West of North America

Historically, it was the Spanish conquistadors who began to expand into North America, landing in Florida in 1513. It was only in 1528 that the first Spanish expedition, led by Alvar Nunez Cabeza de Vaca, took place, followed by another Spanish expedition by Francisco Vazquez de Coronado in 1540, when Coronado explored what later became the southwestern states of the United States and discovered the Grand Canyon in Arizona. By this time, Pope Alexander VI had earmarked the newly acquired territories as an integral part of the Spanish dominion. Over time, Spanish explorers became familiar with the natural landscape, including unfamiliar species like the buffalo; they also became aware of Indigenous cultures in the southeastern United States, which extended to present-day Georgia; and they explored Appalachia[1] up to the Mississippi River.[2]

The first Spanish settlement was established in 1565 at St. Augustine, Florida. By 1603, the Spanish had reached Alaska, and by 1610, they had established a settlement at Santa Fe in New Mexico. Over time, they consolidated their position in the modern-day states of Texas, California, and New Mexico. Despite stiff resistance from Indigenous nations against their expansion, by the end of the eighteenth century Spain had successfully established mission stations to proselytise in the regions of Texas and California. Spanish settlers forced the defeated and converted Indigenous people to work as agricultural labourers and herders. Between 1760 and 1801, Spain began to fear the expansion of British and Russian colonial influence in the region and brought under its sovereign control a region that would later become Louisiana.

The Spanish influence over the western region of the United States is still visible in the form of the names of the earlier Spanish settlements and villages, and the names given in Spanish to specific regions due to their geographical importance. This included Albuquerque in New Mexico, Tucson in Arizona, San Antonio and El Paso in Texas, Los Angeles in California, the land of mountains that is Montana, Nevada, named after the mountainous 'land of snow' in Spain, and the land of coloured rivers, Colorado. It is in these Spanish-controlled regions that the 'Wild West' aspect of American culture later developed.

The French Expansion

It was the French, under the leadership of Jacques Cartier, who began exploring the St. Lawrence River by 1535, ultimately leading to the establishment of the French trading post of Quebec in 1608. In 1663, New France emerged as a crown colony under

Louis XIV. The French monarch sponsored Jesuit expeditions, whose aim was not only to establish more trading posts but also to spread Christianity in the region of modern-day Ontario, which led to significant conflict with the Indigenous nations. Despite several reversals, by 1675, the French had established control over the whole of French North America.[3] Just before that, in 1673, the French expedition led by Louis Jolliet and Jacques Marquette had discovered that the Mississippi River flowed into the Gulf of Mexico, which significantly aided the expansion of French settlement in the region. The region was subsequently named Louisiana by the French. More French explorations led to the settlement of Minnesota and the establishment of more French settlements at Biloxi in Mississippi, Cahokia in Illinois, Detroit in Michigan, and Mobile in Alabama, along with New Orleans in 1718. To prevent British expansion, the French explored and mapped the Ohio Valley region in 1749.

The Dutch Expansion

Another European power was emerging on the East Coast, as by 1624, the Dutch established a trading centre on Manhattan Island, the site of New Amsterdam. The Dutch colony expanded along the Hudson Valley, and by 1655, it had annexed the Swedish settlement along the Delaware, which later became part of the US states of Delaware and Pennsylvania.

The English Expansion

Italian explorer John Cabot claimed Newfoundland (in present-day Canada) for his sponsor, the English king Henry VII, in 1497. After a long period of neglect, Britain revived its interest in North America in 1585, when it began to focus on Roanoke, located in what is now North Carolina. However, this settlement did not last long. In 1603, under King James I, the process of colonisation was renewed, and in 1606 the London and Plymouth Companies in Virginia were established by the British Parliament. This led to the settlement of

Jamestown in 1607 (now in southern Virginia). The settlement faced disease, hunger, and war with the Indigenous nations. It was only around the 1630s that Virginia began to be well populated, especially with the introduction of tobacco as a crop, since the commodity had become a fashion in England and throughout Western Europe.

The Plymouth Colony (named after the River Plym) was established in 1620 by a group of Protestant English settlers called Pilgrims (they were also called Separatists as they had broken away from the Church of England). Faced with persecution in Britain, they left for the Netherlands, and eventually decided to travel to North America. They sailed on the *Mayflower*[4] and settled in Plymouth. With the assistance of the Wampanoag people, who provided them with knowledge of the land's food and resources, this early Pilgrim group survived against all odds. The miracle of their survival is celebrated as Thanksgiving Day.

When the Massachusetts Bay Company received its charter in 1629, they established the colony of Massachusetts in 1630. This was a Puritan[5] colony with strict adherence to orthodox Calvinist traditions; the Puritans were in constant conflict with other Christian sects, particularly the Quakers. This was followed by Connecticut (1636) and then Rhode Island (1647). The latter of the two was established by Roger Williams, a former Puritan who became opposed to them, as he believed in religious toleration and wanted land to be acquired from the Indigenous nations based on an equitable system of payment. Rhode Island thus represented a liberal colony during the era of intense conflict between various Christian denominations. By 1640, it had become the centre of the American Baptist Movement and also the home of America's first public synagogue. New Hampshire was established in 1679, with Boston becoming the capital of this region due to the commercial importance of its harbour.

It was tobacco that also assisted in the rise of Maryland in 1632 as a proprietary colony of Cecilius Calvert, who wanted the colony to become a refuge of persecuted English Catholics and attempted to develop it as a colony based on religious toleration, yet became involved in a protracted conflict between the Puritans and the Catholics that led to defeat of the Catholics. Tobacco became the primary item of trade, contributing to the rising population and prosperity of both Virginia and Maryland.

The Quakers[6] were the most radical of the Christian groups, challenging fundamental Christian beliefs and values, including those of the clergy. They began to establish separate settlements, first in New Jersey and then in Pennsylvania, under the leadership of William Penn. Over time, the Germans, English, Irish, and Welsh began to settle here, making it a multi-ethnic colony. Religious tolerance assisted in the growth and development of trade and agriculture, which in turn made Philadelphia a leading British colony in North America, having surpassed Boston by 1770. It competed with Dublin, then the British empire's second-largest city (after London), and by the nineteenth century had surpassed Dublin in terms of population.

In another significant step, the English took control of the Dutch colonies in New Amsterdam, in order to remove any threat to New England and the Chesapeake colonies, and renamed them New York. British colonisation also spread into the Carolinas: North Carolina was settled in the 1650s and South Carolina was settled in 1670.

By about 1675, the English settlers had established their claim over the eastern seaboard, and their settlements stretched from Spanish Florida in the south to the present-day states of Maine and Vermont in the north. The settlers were now looking to cross into the Appalachians and the mountain valleys that extended from the Carolinas and Virginia into New York. The period from 1675 to 1692 saw war between New England colonists and the Wampanoag nation, led by Metacom, also known by his English name, 'King Philip', in 1675. The result was so devastating that the settlers demanded more powers to face Indigenous opposition to their continuous expansion. In Virginia, conflict erupted between the settlers and the British governor, who refused to permit expansion into Indigenous lands, resulting in an open rebellion led by Nathaniel Bacon.[7] Attempts to bring colonies under direct control of the British monarch with the establishment of a Dominion of New England that extended from the Delaware River to the St Lawrence and New York. By 1689, most colonies had experienced conflict. Despite opposition, they were all proclaimed as royal colonies to establish a united British American imperial colony under the direct governance of the British monarch. By the middle of the eighteenth century, there were six major regions under Britain's control, three in the North and three in the South. In the North, New England lacked fertile soil. Still, it possessed extensive timberlands, as well as rich fishing and whaling resources. Further, the development of commercial shipping contributed to the rise of Boston as an important urban centre. Later, economic growth stemming from these factors also enabled the expansion and rise of Maine and New Hampshire.

The southern parts of New England were merged with New York, which had fertile soil and had developed trade along the Hudson River, spreading into Long Island. This development later brought immense prosperity to New York City. Newport, Rhode Island, and the port at the Delaware River region also saw tremendous growth and were rapidly urbanised.

The Chesapeake region continued to dominate based on its tobacco economy, and the rise of river trade facilitated the expansion of agriculture into the hinterlands, particularly in the production of wheat and corn in the Piedmont regions of Maryland, Virginia, and North Carolina, which were shipped through the Baltimore port.

In the extreme south were the British colonies of North and South Carolina. North Carolina, while still dependent on tobacco, had also diversified into timber and naval stores. In 1733, with the emergence of Georgia, rice and indigo plantations supported by enslaved labour led to the development of Charleston and Savannah.

The rise of new cities led to the introduction of new technologies and cultures. The publication in 1704 of *The Boston News-Letter* marked the emergence of a new print culture. By 1770, virtually every colony, except Delaware and New Jersey, had at least one newspaper. Most towns had a network of clubs, societies, and discussion groups, and the colonies were united by a postal system by 1710. Medical schools came up in Philadelphia in 1765; increased prosperity facilitated a burgeoning theatre culture. Slowly, colonies developed their own distinctive culture and social patterns. By 1775, out of the 13 colonies, eight were under the royal charter; Pennsylvania, Maryland, and Delaware remained proprietary colonies, while

Table I.1: Timeline for the Establishment of the Thirteen Colonies

	British colonies	Approximate date of settlement
	Northern Colonies	
1.	Connecticut	1636
2.	Massachusetts	1620
3.	New Hampshire	1623
4.	Rhode Island	1636
	Mid-Atlantic colonies	
5.	New Jersey	1664
6.	New York	1664
7.	Pennsylvania	1682
	South Atlantic colonies	
8.	Delaware	1638
9.	Georgia	1732
10.	Maryland	1634
11.	North Carolina	1663
12.	South Carolina	1663
13.	Virginia	1607

Source: Author.

Connecticut and Rhode Island were corporate colonies based on the charters obtained by the colonists themselves upon their arrival (see Chapter 2). By this time, all colonies had a governor appointed either by the king or the proprietor, and a legislature with two houses. The laws passed by these assemblies required approval from the British monarch. In all the colonies, British criminal laws were applied, thereby bringing the colonies under the political, economic, and judicial control of the British monarch. The American colonies were also integrated into the British empire's Atlantic trade routes. All the colonies, in terms of their societal formation, were highly fragmented, and tensions existed between the elites and the masses of colonists, as well as frontier settlers. Rapid urbanisation frequently led to religious and ethnic clashes.

The rapid colonisation and settlement of the British American colonies was made possible with the introduction, around 1700, of the indentured servant system to overcome a labour shortage. It quickly became a crucial mechanism for the survival and success of the thirteen colonies. This system was based on a contract labour arrangement, where the immigrant servant labour could work for their master until they had paid the cost of the continental voyage. In reality, the conditions of transportation, sale, labour, and exploitation meant that the system was only marginally better than the institution of slavery. Over time, fewer Europeans were persuaded to come to America as indentured servants; in 1717, the British government transported all those who had committed crimes that would have invited the death penalty to the New World. Despite this measure, British colonies continued to face a labour shortage, and this led to the introduction of enslaved Africans. During the process of colonisation and settlement, European explorers and later settlers discovered new types of crops, including corn, tobacco, and sweet potato. However, it was the discovery of pre-existing cotton cultivation, grown by Indigenous nations for thousands of years, that truly transformed the colonies and significantly increased the demand for bonded slave labour.

An Outline of the Book

In Chapter 1, 'The American Revolution: The Rise of a Nation', the study of the American Revolution is examined, with a particular emphasis on the political culture of the masses of colonists who later led the revolution. Another significant point made in the chapter is that the American Revolution would not have occurred without Indigenous resistance and their alliance with Britain. The American Revolution must be understood within the parameters of a settler society caught in the vortex of later stages of commercial revolution and the early stages of industrialisation: the gradual growth of a modern society that was committed to first an indentured labour system and later enslavement, based on differential patterns of relations between the races but also developing a radically new political system, new modes of communication, and societal relationships. Interestingly, Americans were the least taxed people among the British colonies, but still protested the imposition of imperial taxes, as it reflected their subordinate position as colonised settler people who, in turn, occupied the lands of original Indigenous people and exploited the labour of Black Africans. The chapter will examine not only the factors that pushed the colonies to rise in rebellion and ultimately dissociate themselves from the mother colony, but also the historiography of the event. The year 1775 marked the beginning of a revolutionary era when the independent nations established the Articles of Confederation and later, the American Constitution, the world's first modern, written constitution where the people are given sovereign powers. The latter point is discussed in Chapter 2, 'The Formulation of the American Constitution', that moves from socio-economic and political dynamics to the politics of constitutionalism.

This book attempts to move beyond the conventional writing of America's political, economic, constitutional, and intellectual history that was based on the perspective of presidential elections and their respective policies, to the study of the broad political culture of the period or even the 'public life' of a specific period, based on how some historians have attempted to emphasise the state's role and of various groups that tried to use it for their purposes. Chapter 3, 'Thomas Jefferson and Jeffersonian Democracy', without delving into the presidential eras of George Washington and John Adams, will move towards the rudimentary beginnings of the American party system due to differences between the Federalists and the Democratic-Republicans led by Thomas Jefferson. The election of 1800 represented the growing rift between these two political groups. The opponents of Jefferson, namely the Federalists, saw him as a dictatorial figure who surpassed the French emperor Napoleon Bonaparte. The election of Jefferson in 1800 marked the emergence of the Jeffersonian era that introduced a limited form of government and emphasised state rights. This era also saw the purchase of the territory of Louisiana from France in 1803, thereby doubling the territory of the United States. To maintain both political and economic unity of the ever-expanding nation, the Jeffersonian administration established a national system of canals and roads to unite East and West, and for the first time, the national government began to use its powers to promote the development of the newly acquired territories.

The presidency of Andrew Jackson (1829–1837), which ushered in the Jacksonian era, introduced a series of policies and new types of political rhetoric that sparked new forms of party conflict. This is discussed in Chapter 4, 'Andrew Jackson and the Emergence of a New Political Ethos'. Jackson won the election by mobilising social groups and regions that felt left out by the political establishment and the elites in American society. The West against the East, urban labourers against industrialists, farmers against the financiers. It marked the rise of populism in American politics, as more white men, particularly those of free status, gained the right to vote. Jackson also introduced the Spoils System, in which the ruling party gave government offices to its supporters. Jacksonian democracy brought politics into everyday life, as seen in the promotion of 'pet' banks and regional financial concerns over national ones. Jackson's party became so well entrenched that it won all presidential elections but two between 1828 and 1856. (To oppose the Democrats, the Whig party emerged and won the presidency in 1840 and 1848.) Jackson had completely transformed the American political discourse, and it was now based on the ethos of the ever-shifting 'frontier'. The book will emphasise how, before 1840, American politicians successfully managed to keep slavery out of national politics, constantly playing the 'compromise' card when faced with the threat of secession or force (the Nullification Crisis) and Congressional repression (imposition of gag rule in 1836). Jackson's administration opened up vast stretches of land in the western territories, facilitating the expansion of both agricultural and industrial economies, and to connect the two, he undertook massive investment in transportation networks, building canals, and expanding steamboat use. Voting rights were granted to White men regardless of property qualifications, which also contributed to the growth of the market economy, as it provided more opportunities for business innovation and calculated economic risks. The market revolution created the Democratic Party politics and further widened social differences between free labour and the enslaved person in the South, bringing slavery to the centre of national politics.

Chapter 5, 'Removal of Indigenous Peoples and Westward Expansion', revisits the early phases of settler colonialism to understand relations between European settlers and Indigenous communities in American history. The colonisation and settlement of European colonies led to the beginning of the Columbian Exchange; this encounter proved extremely detrimental to the Indigenous population, as European diseases nearly wiped out several communities. The rapid spread of commercial agriculture led to the destruction of the habitats inhabited by these societies for centuries, and the introduction of alcohol, all combined with continuous conflicts and wars, resulted in the biological, environmental and political destruction of the original Indigenous communities, lands and resources. By the beginning of the nineteenth century, the American expansionist agenda to take over the Mississippi region faced a hurdle in the form of the presence of Indigenous nations. The era marked the beginning of a series of wars with the Indigenous nations who offered stiff resistance in varied forms, and that continued to plague the United States till the end of the nineteenth century. The chapter throws a light on the human toll resulting from the process of colonisation of the New World and how a hunger for 'virgin land' became the cause of the marginalisation and destruction of the Indigenous nations of Turtle Island.

The history of the Indigenous nations has been presented here through a new lens, with emphasis on their internal colonisation through the policies of Jeffersonian and Jacksonian democracies, which were destructive to the Indigenous nations and exploitative of Black people. The chapter also focuses on the history of the American West and how expansionism led to further marginalisation and destruction of Indigenous land rights, culture, and nationhood. The American West is represented by the Missouri River, acquired by the United States through the Louisiana Purchase in 1803 and later acquisitions that brought Texas, the Oregon Territory and the Mexican Cession in the 1840s, which eventually ended with the 1853 Gadsden Purchase of the lands between the Gila River and the present Mexican boundary. Long before European colonisers came to the West, Indigenous nations had developed their own cultures and used various techniques to control, tame, and utilise natural resources to their optimum levels. The American West was not—as many White settlers, including nineteenth-century historian Frederick Jackson Turner, claimed—a land of wilderness. It was inhabited and made suitable for human settlement by the people of the Indigenous nations. The myth of a 'savage' or 'pristine' wilderness was necessary to justify their displacement. This book focuses on ideological and political conflicts at the centre of this significant period in US history, where the marginalisation and exploitation of Indigenous peoples and Black labour went hand-in-hand with the gradual development of a market economy that necessitated the growth of new-age electoral politics, ultimately coalescing into the distinct American brand of capitalism, albeit here in its rudimentary stage.

A significant problem that emerged in the early nineteenth century was the conflict between the northeastern and the western states of the US. While the Northeast included the original Thirteen Colonies and had a more 'European' orientation, the West viewed Great Britain with bitterness, and these differences informed their opposing views on the War of 1812. Chapter 6, 'The War of 1812', reflects on the deep divide between the Federalists and Republicans in American politics during the presidencies of Thomas Jefferson and James Madison (1809–1817), which eventually led the nation into the War of 1812. The war was concluded with the reassertion of the national independence of the United States, which was now infused with a new sense of patriotism. The Democratic-Republicans gained control over the national government in the period from 1801 to 1825, at a crucial juncture when the nation was emerging from the aftermath of the American Revolution.

Another problem that confronted the young nation was the widening chasm between the northern and southern states over the existence and expansion of slavery, as well as the political implications of maintaining a balance between slave and free states, discussed in Chapter 7, 'American Exceptionalism:[8] Chattel Enslavement'. The problem had a long history, rooted in geographical differences, distinct climatic conditions, and divergent economic orientations, which inevitably pushed the two warring sections into the Civil War

Introduction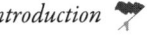

of 1861. The South developed an aristocratic social structure based on the slave-dependent rural economy. In contrast, the North, during the same period, developed a set of cultural and intellectual ideologies centred on the concepts of egalitarianism, free labour, urbanisation, and evangelical religious beliefs. The two sections began to break from each other by the late seventeenth century. This process sped up in the eighteenth century over the issue of African slavery and to what degree this labour system would be fundamental to the American economic order. The rise of regional politics in American history went hand in hand with the racial conflict that eventually shaped the political, economic, cultural, social, and, perhaps most importantly, the labour histories of the North, West, and South. The politics of race in the early stages of colonisation, built around an ideology of White supremacy, meant that both race and class were complex and extremely polarising factors in America.

Chapter 8, the last chapter in this volume, analyses the Civil War. The chapter deliberately moves beyond fundamental causes to explore the dynamics of race relations in both the North and the South. It emphasises how preserving the Union was more important to political groupings on either side than solving the problem of racism and exploitation of Black people. This approach helps initiate a new kind of debate regarding how Americans managed to sustain the Union for seven decades and the precise nature of the North-South conflict. Slavery proved to be the primary catalyst for the divide: The 'lifeline' of one region, as it were, became a symbol of all that had to be discarded in the other. The events from the 1850s, as we shall discuss, demonstrated that it was not possible to stem the expansion of slavery. There were only two alternatives before America: to let slavery spread across the entire nation or to abolish it altogether. With no solution in sight, the Union began to crumble. In other words, racial hostilities eventually led to racial polarisation in the South with its reliance on slave labour and plantation agriculture. In contrast, the North became a region of ethnic complexity as it moved towards industrial expansion and urbanisation. The availability of land and employment opportunities, combined with advances in ocean transportation, made the northern region a magnet for migrants. The South, on the other hand, was deeply rooted in the ethnic division between Black and White. It is important to note, however, that while the South indeed had a uniquely exploitative, racialised system, it may be problematic to characterise the North and West as ethnically diverse melting pots. While these regions did not have slave states, they were still built on a logic of White supremacy, denied equal rights (of voting, work, housing, and citizenship) to Black people, and participated in the decimation of Indigenous peoples.

In terms of sheer geographical size, as well as ethnic, racial, and religious diversity, the emergence of the United States reflects a unique trajectory. However, with European settlers quickly becoming the dominant social group in North America, the nation does share some standard political and economic features with Europe. It is essential to study this continental nation as a distinct entity, to understand the process of its emergence as a country that claims the status of the world's 'first modern nation'—a country that continues to attract immigrants and dominate global politics and the economy.

Notes

1. This is an important geographical region situated in the central and southern parts of the Appalachian Mountains, in the eastern part of North America.

2. The Mississippi River is a vital source of drinking water for millions of people, crucial for agricultural production, and ecologically sensitive, supporting a diverse array of fish, birds, and animals. This river played a vital role in the nineteenth-century US economy. It is a significant transportation route for carrying various types of goods from the Midwest to the Gulf of Mexico and beyond.

3. The French established their colonies in the Saint Lawrence River valley, particularly in Quebec, Montreal, and Trois-Rivieres. Other areas dominated by them were Nova Scotia, New Brunswick, and Prince Edward Island, which constitute the Maritime provinces of modern-day Canada. They also dominated Newfoundland, Île-Royale, now known as Cape Breton Island. The French gradually expanded into the Mississippi River basin, which now encompasses the modern-day states of Louisiana, Arkansas, Missouri, Illinois, and others. They came to control the region of the Great Lakes, which now constitutes Michigan, Wisconsin, and Indiana. They also expanded into the Ohio River Valley, which eventually led to the development of cities such as Detroit and Vincennes.

4. The *Mayflower* was a sailing ship that brought the Pilgrims from England to Holland and finally to Plymouth. This led to the settlement of the first European colony in North America.

5. They were English Protestants (sixteenth and seventeenth centuries) who attempted to 'purify' the Church of England from all forms of Roman Catholic Practices and practised simple worship with adherence to strict moral codes. They later migrated to North America to find land where they could practice religious freedom and establish a society based on their religious beliefs.

6. Another term used for them is the Religious Society of Friends, which originated in seventeenth-century England, with their firm belief in the concept of 'inner light' to achieve a direct personal experience of God and establish a society based on the principles of peace, equality, and social justice.

7. It is popularly known as Bacon's Rebellion, which took place in colonial Virginia from 1676 to 1677, with colonists clashing with the Indigenous community. However, Bacon later challenged the authority of the British governor, William Berkeley, a challenge that gradually led to the assertion of powers of self-government by the colonists.

8. This term refers to the fact that the United States was established on the foundations of republican ideals, which led to the Declaration of Independence and formulation of the American Constitution, both of which were 'divinely inspired' processes. All these make America an 'exceptional' power that is 'destined' to play a significant role in global affairs.

Chapter 1

The American Revolution
The Rise of a Nation

Introduction

The process of emigration to and colonisation of America was a testament to the resilience of individuals who, under the policy of mercantilism and later imperialism, spearheaded the division of North America among rival European colonial powers. The role of the government was only secondary. Britain eventually surged ahead, establishing 13 British American colonies wherein the colonising population, that is, White immigrant settlers, used the available natural resources and land according to their capacity, over time yielding material prosperity. During this process of colonisation, settlers formed colonial communities based on internal power structures that assisted in the development of a unique political culture. This culture was mainly shaped by modern Western education, and it encouraged the application of scientific ideas to bring about technological changes and maximise resource use in North America. It was this growing material and economic capacity that enabled the colonial population to rise up against the militarily superior European powers.

English immigrants had mainly arrived in the seventeenth century (till around 1680), and after the 1680s they were followed by immigrants from other European nations, many of whom had escaped political turmoil, poverty, and religious persecution.

This demographic shift impacted relations between the imperial masters and the colonial population, as the changing population profile meant that the other European immigrants had no loyalty or connection with Britain. American colonists in the **Thirteen Colonies** were driven to protect their political rights and economic freedom against British regulations. According to John Adams, for this reason, the **American Revolution** began in the 'hearts and minds' of the American people long before the first shot was fired.

To comprehend the complex chain of events that sparked the American Revolution, historians have generally categorised the historical events in two broad phases: the first phase before 1763, and the second after 1763 when settlers' sense of a distinct identity separate from their European identity began to crystallise. As historian Gregory Nobles has stated (1983), the roots of the American Revolution lay in two factors, based on shifts in British policy and transformations that had taken place in American society over time.[1]

Prelude to the American Revolution: The Old Colonial System

As noted in the introduction, before 1680, England was the primary source of immigration to North America. However, after 1680, a diverse group of Spaniards, Italians, Scots, Irish, Germans, and Portuguese began to settle on the continent, many fleeing war, oppression and absentee landlordism in Europe.[2] This shift changed the essential nature and character of settlements in American colonies, shifting from homogeneity to a fascinating heterogeneity. Each colony developed differently based on its demographic features, economic growth patterns, religion, and government. **Corporate colonies** like New England were ruled by officials based on the norms set in the charters; **proprietary colonies** like Pennsylvania were ruled by proprietors with regal powers. Virginia was a **royal colony**.

By the middle of the seventeenth century, the economic foundations of the colonies had begun to change. *First*, the southern colonies gradually gained prosperity due to surplus production of cash crops (indigo, sugarcane, tobacco, and rice in the colonies of Maryland, Carolina, and Virginia) based on enslaved labour. *Second*, handicraft industries began to develop in northern and mid-Atlantic colonies. *Third*, the shipbuilding industry led to the growth of rudimentary industries along with trade and commerce, and due to an extensive lumber business, by 1700 there were 15 shipyards participating in trade across the Atlantic Ocean and to the Mediterranean, the Caribbean region, and beyond. Britain, at this juncture, was in the grip of the commercial revolution and wanted to use America's growing commercial prosperity to bolster its own economy. To this end, and in line with its policy of mercantilism, Britain initiated a series of **Navigation Acts** that would maximise its natural resources and wealth and allow the British empire to become stronger and self-sufficient. The Navigation Acts were meant to reinforce a hierarchy between settlers and the 'mother country', redirecting the wealth that settlers generated to the mother country for its advancement. Britain overlooked the fact that the American colonies were developing unilaterally based on the entrepreneurial skills of their emerging capitalist classes, while the British aim was only to secure cheap raw materials. The aim was to manufacture goods from these raw materials and export them at high prices, in the process creating more markets along with deeper economic penetration to enable the growth of the British marine merchant system, increase its naval strength and pave the way for the expansion and establishment of more colonies within and outside America. American nationalist historian George Bancroft (2023) therefore concluded that the Navigation Acts were extremely oppressive and became a prelude to the beginning of the American Revolution.[3] However, this view is yet to be entirely accepted among historians, as George Bancroft made a generalisation in his analysis: he claimed that the regulation of Navigation Acts impacted all 13 colonies, but this was not the case.

The Navigation Acts: A Tool of Control

The British monarch, Charles II, passed the Navigation Acts, also known as the Acts of Trade and Navigation. The main aim of the Navigation Acts was to exert control over the colonies under the principles of the 'mercantilist system'. This was done through taxation and by enforcing a regime of economic domination. The provisions of the first Act (1651) stated that only ships built, owned and operated by the British or her colonies could be used for trade between England and her colonies. The second Act (1660) tightened the grip by stipulating that the import of European goods into the colonies was to pass through England and levied import duties. The third Act (1663) outlined specific articles that had to be first shipped to England, particularly tobacco, rice, furs, indigo and naval stores. Under the fourth Act (1696), Americans were forbidden to produce certain manufactured goods like hats, iron and wool.

These Acts aimed to subordinate American colonial trade in relation to the imperial core. There was a growing demand for tobacco, indigo, and naval stores, and this assisted in the rise and expansion of the New England shipbuilding industry, which was flourishing on the back of a '**triangular trade**' in which ships were taking lumber, fish, and meat to the West Indies, to be traded for sugar and salt, following which these two goods were taken to England and traded for British manufactured goods (textiles, hardware) and sold in American colonies. Another established trade circuit brought molasses from the West Indies back to New England, where it was used to produce rum, which was then taken to Africa, from where enslaved people were bought and then sold in the West Indies and American colonies. New England also traded with Spain and Portugal, where it supplied fish and bought wine and fruits; these were sold in Britain to buy British-manufactured goods. New England also carried the produce of the Carolinas and the Chesapeake Bay to Europe—this led to the development of a diversified economy and a distinct merchant community, and also paved the way for the first American iron foundry, Saugus Iron Works, in 1646. The foundry became a stepping stone for the increase of industrial enterprises. This trade assisted in the growing demand for American colonial goods, particularly tobacco, sugar, rice, indigo, naval stores, wheat, flour, ground vegetables, salted fish, meat, timber and livestock, bringing immense prosperity to southern American colonies. The fifth Act, also known as the **Molasses Act** (1733), imposed a heavy duty on foreign molasses and sugar imported into British colonies. In addition to the Navigation Acts, American colonies also faced issues with money supply as colonial governments issued paper money, which had to be redeemed within a specified period. In effect, this meant that New England had the maximum defaulters and suffered both financially and economically.

The American colonies' economic prosperity attracted the attention of the British monarchy, and the rest of the colonial settlements began to be handed over to British politicians who organised settlements and governance structures. By the 1670s, a rudimentary form of governance structure had begun to emerge in the British American colonies with the Crown-appointed governor and an advisory council that functioned as the legislature's upper house. These two powers appointed the judiciary. The settlers elected an assembly that closely coordinated with the council and governor in making laws. The British government thereby introduced a uniform system of administration that provoked sharp reactions from colonists and led to a series of colonial rebellions that were linked to the anti-Stuart revolution in England.

By the 1680s, American colonies had become economically self-sufficient, socially different from the parent country and politically self-governed units. France and Spain began to cast their imperialistic ambitions on these American colonies, and the two Stuart rulers, particularly Charles II (1674–85) and James II (1685–88), disliked the parliamentary government. Therefore, to prevent both France and Spain's expansionist designs and since they had no sympathy for American colonial assemblies, they initiated changes that would grant them more political and economic power. Charles II sought to bring the American colonies under his royal control by appointing high-ranking army men as Governors. By 1680, 60 per cent of American colonies had military governors.

One of the most influential American colonies, Massachusetts, was divided into two, carving out a separate colony, New Hampshire. This was deliberate: in 1661, the Massachusetts assembly had exempted its citizens from all laws and royal decrees from England except for the Declaration of War. They also ignored and sidestepped the Navigation Acts. In retaliation, the Massachusetts governor suppressed the legislative assembly, jailed citizens who had protested, tried to enforce the Anglican Church and impeded the growing popularity of Harvard College. By 1688, the Dominion of New England was formed as a single administrative unit that included Massachusetts, New Hampshire, Connecticut, Rhode Island, Plymouth, New York and New Jersey. In the meantime, both Charles II and James II converted to Catholicism and they took to persecuting Protestants, including followers of the Anglican Church, further complicating the picture in the British North American colonies.

Two events in Britain began to turn the tide. The heirs of James II—Mary and her husband William, who were still of the Anglican faith—led a coup in 1688 that came to be known as the **Glorious Revolution**. It led to a limited monarchy, a parliamentary government and respect for traditional civil liberties in England. These momentous events in Britain had a dramatic impact on the political culture of the colonies. All American colonies resumed their legislative assemblies, and the new British rulers dismantled the Dominion of New England. The colonies also began to accept the principles of the revolution, especially the primacy given to the notion of liberty, sanctity of private property, and opposition to the autocracy of the Pope. Simultaneously, significant internal changes took place in the American colonies: by the 1730s, with the development of the period of the '**Great Awakening**',[4] religious preachers began to reject established churches. Instead, they gave public sermons, eventually leading to the growth of various evangelical denominations based on the foundations of religious toleration.

The Beginnings of Separation from the Mother Country

By the end of the seventeenth century, North American colonies had developed their own political culture. They considered themselves to be 'commonwealth states' with only a loose association with the authorities in London. America was now a permanent homeland for the settler society, and over time they developed governance systems and structures based on political liberty, franchise, and a perceived immunity from British law. They adhered to the Magna Carta, which granted political and civil liberties based on the common law of precedent and tradition, and not statutory law as was practiced in Britain. Settlers considered themselves 'freemen' with the right to participate in their government. Over a period of time, they established systems of self-government (this precedent was set with the arrival of the *Mayflower*[5]). Another essential factor that began to create fissures of separation between Britain and its North American colonies was the vast ocean that separated the two, along with challenging environmental conditions that inculcated individualistic traits in the settlers.

It was at this juncture that Britain began to bring colonies under its mercantile control through the Navigation Acts to protect its commercial interests. This was around the 1680s, at the time when John Locke developed his revolutionary political ideology and theory of government, which he termed as a 'political contract' between the government and the governed, based on the logic that the people are endowed with natural rights of life, liberty, and property and therefore had the right to rebel when the government violated their rights. Influenced by this political ideology, American colonies began to assert their political 'rights' and individual 'liberties', especially regarding the right to tax and legislate on essential matters, since these frequently exposed the conflict of interests between the royal governors and legislative colonial assemblies.

In the meantime, armed conflict between France and England, in which they made Indigenous societies their pawn in the colonial game, became so intense that it threatened to wipe out the American colonies. It forced Britain to call for the **Albany Congress** in 1754. The agenda was to improve relations between the Indigenous peoples and American colonies in order to prevent French expansionist designs and secure the loyalty of American colonies to the British Crown. In Congress, Britain put forward a proposal known as the **Albany Plan of the Union** that required the political surrender of American rights to Britain; for this very reason, it was summarily rejected by the colonies. However, once Britain defeated France, its colonies came to dominate the East Coast of North America, with the exception of regions controlled by Spain. It now began to focus on proper and direct governance of its North American colonies, taking steps to organise colonial administration and make provisions to defend its American colonies by bringing all of them under a unified administrative system. The cost of maintaining imperial administration was now required to be paid by the colonies.

Lloyd deMause (1997) has used a psychohistorical perspective to argue that although the Navigation Acts had a significant impact on the elite colonial classes, the prolonged existence of British American colonies without being regulated or taxed was formative for their psyche.[6] Further, British colonial policy in North America had long been unstructured. This relative isolation and negligence provided space for independent politico-economic institutions and identities to develop, which took settlers further away from their mother country. Thus, while the Navigation Acts were framed within the overarching framework of mercantilism and to allow Britain to compete with rival European powers by amassing all the wealth generated by its colonies, this was at odds with the earlier lack of regulation. The problem was that before 1763, the British empire in America was governed by unregulated administrative machinery known as the **Privy Council** that appointed **Lords of Trade**, later known as the **Board of Trade and Plantations**, which supervised all the trade of Great Britain including all royal appointments in the colonies as well as laws enacted by the colonists (including the flow of information between the colonies and the mother country). However, the Board lacked the power of actual enforcement. So, realistically, Britain only controlled external trade and did not directly control the colonies. The colonists paid British officials and governors. Therefore, a dichotomy was created between the lower-level British officials, who easily catered to the interests of the colonial community, and the governors, who were hostile to local American interests.

Already grappling with these internal fissures, Britain was also involved in the **Seven Years War (1754–1763)** with France, known in America as the **French and Indian War** that ended in 1763, forcing France to cede its colonial regions east of the Mississippi River to Britain. However, this victory came at a high cost, and therefore the British government decided to impose a new set of taxes on its

Table 1.1: Important Events: The American Revolution

	Year	Events/Acts
1.	1764	Sugar Act
2.	1765	Stamp Act + Sons of Liberty + Stamp Act Congress
3.	1767	Townshend Acts
4.	1767–68	Letters From a Farmer in Pennsylvania
5.	1770	Boston Massacre
6.	1773	Tea Act + Boston Tea Party
7.	1774	Intolerable Acts + First Continental Congress
8.	1776	Thomas Paine's Common Sense + Declaration of Independence
9.	1783	Treaty of Paris

Source: Author.

American colonies. It was this decision that turned the tide towards the beginning of the American Revolution. Another crucial internal development in the colonies was the rise of a cosmopolitan culture that was reflected in colonial newspapers. This shift was first seen in 1704 with *The Boston News-Letter*, and by the 1750s, most colonies had multiple newspapers spreading ideas, news, events, and global happenings. Most northern colonies were also developing higher educational institutions, becoming modern societies, and producing professional classes that could easily rival the pace of the parent country. The southern colonies lagged behind, but they did develop a plantation economy dependent on an enslaved labour force.[7]

The Rise of Imperialism and the New Colonial System

This restructuring led to the decline of the old colonial system and the rise of imperialist control of Britain over its American colonies. The shift in British policy clashed directly with '**American Exceptionalism**'[8] prevalent in the colonies that emphasised an ideology of unrestrained individualism, natural rights and liberties, social mobility, and a liberal democratic spirit. Before 1763, all colonies had developed independently in one of three ways: they were either **royal**, **corporate**, or **proprietary colonies**. However, by the 1720s, the British Crown gradually began to control colonies by establishing bicameral legislation with a British governor as the top representative of the executive authority. This uniform governmental structure altered the political culture of the colonies, where Americans were long used to living in a relative 'oasis of freedom'. At the same time, Britain, under the aegis of tyrannical monarchial rule, was gradually extending its tentacles of imperialism over the colonies. This is evident from the imposition of the **Writ of Assistance Act of 1761**, which gave British custom officials the power of general warrant, allowing them to search for contraband or seize illegally imported goods. It was implemented to stop Americans from smuggling to overcome the Navigation Acts.

Scholars have discerned an ideological shift at this juncture that began to create distance between the American colonies and Britain. With increasing trade and the growing importance of American port cities up until 1763, which, as discussed earlier, fostered a cosmopolitan culture in almost all colonies, most Americans had lost their European roots and connectedness by the mid-eighteenth century. They now considered themselves 'native' to North America. This was a socially stratified society with elites like slave planters (with their large landholdings) and American merchants (who were engaged in commercial transactions with British merchants); both these classes were wealthy and politically powerful within colonial society. Even the long wars that settler Americans were involved in against Indigenous peoples enhanced their military knowledge and provided new modes of livelihood, for example, by becoming contractors to supply wartime supplies.

Significant cultural shifts occurred as well. The development of newspapers assisted in the rise of the American Revolution. The school and university education systems saw significant expansion, and simultaneously, the 'Great Awakening' became increasingly influential and birthed several evangelical churches.

Economic Changes after 1763

The new colonial system was imposed on the American colonies with the regulation of the **Sugar Act of 1764**, which meant that colonists could export sugar, lumber, iron, skins, hide, whalebone, logwood, wine, silk, calico, coffee, and other commodities to foreign countries only if the shipments first landed in Britain, else the items would be subject to increased custom duty. This decision must be seen in the context of a budget deficit that Britain faced at the end of the Anglo-French conflict, which had increased from 73 million pounds to 137 million pounds.[9] The administration of American colonies and inclusion of new territories due to **westward expansion** also increased the financial burden of maintenance and increasing garrison forces in the colonies (as 'protection' against Indigenous groups).[10] With the Sugar Act's imposition, Britain's first aim was to raise revenue from American colonies, thereby altering the relationship between Britain and America. The second aim was to strictly enforce the implementation of all the Navigation Acts by taxing Americans through customs duties and controlling its exports and imports: Since Americans now had to send their goods only to British ports or through British ships, they were forced to export raw materials to Britain, like tobacco, wheat, and furs, and then import the finished products from Britain. To implement the Act, Britain used its navy and established a Court of Admiralty which held trials against those found to be in violation of both the Navigation and Sugar Acts.[11]

The impact of the Sugar Act was felt most keenly in New England, especially in Massachusetts, Rhode Island, and Connecticut, as they all had rum distilleries dependent on molasses. However, this Act still impacted only the upper classes. Over time, Britain added more items to the enumerated list. It ensured strict enforcement of the Act, which began to affect internal American trade as there were no roads and most goods were transported through port systems. The very establishment of the Court of Admiralty was seen as a challenge to the colonial legal system and the tradition of common law that was in practice in American colonies[12] and led to the beginning of protests against the Sugar Act.

The first voices of protest were raised in the colonial assemblies, particularly in Boston, Connecticut, and New York (this is the colony that had first developed the system of stock and commodity exchange, insurance, and corporate governance that became the foundations of American capitalistic spirit) Virginia, Rhode Island, Pennsylvania (the largest city in British North America, second only to London, with their own merchant class and trade network), New Jersey, and South Carolina (which was based on plantation economy). James Otis wrote an article, 'The Right of the British Colonies Asserted and Proved' (1764), which sharpened colonial awareness about taxation: American colonies feared that the Sugar Act was a sign that taxes would soon be imposed on them by the British Parliament.[13] Therefore, these assemblies passed resolutions that asserted the right of colonial assemblies to levy internal taxes in their colonies. Their fears were soon proven right, as the Sugar Act was followed immediately by the **Currency Act of 1764**, which forbade the colonies from issuing paper money, thereby tightening financial imperial control over the colonies.

The middle of the eighteenth century was a period that brought about significant social, economic, and demographic changes in American society. The period witnessed the culmination of the commercial revolution and the rise of industrialisation, with a wage labour system appearing on the horizon along with the availability of a variety of consumer goods, the growth of literate classes, evangelical religious congregations, and non-English immigrants effecting a demographic transition (see Kenneth A. Lockridge,[14] Joyce Appleby[15] and Sean Wilentz[16]). The colonial economies now pursued self-interest to earn more capital profit and secure better opportunities to find new markets. It was the beginning of individualistic liberalism, which was termed 'the invisible hand' by Scottish economist and philosopher Adam Smith in his influential work, *The Wealth of Nations* (1776).

The Stamp Act

The **1765 Stamp Act**, which followed in the series of imposing sovereign control over the colonies, was a law that obliged Americans to purchase and use special stamped paper for newspapers, customs, documents, various licenses, college diplomas, legal forms, wills, land-buying and selling, playing cards, dice, and bonds. Funds secured through this Act were meant to station British forces in American colonies. It was also meant to show that the British Parliament had sovereign powers over American colonies and was the only power with the right to impose taxes and govern them.[17] Unlike the Sugar Act, the Stamp Act's impact was felt across social classes, and the reaction against it was swift. The colonies adopted three strategies:

(*i*) The first line of protest was political, and colonies used their colonial assemblies and political institutions to articulate their strong opposition to the Act.

(*ii*) The protest was amplified by exerting pressure through economic coercion to subvert British laws and by boycotting British goods directly and indirectly.

(*iii*) Finally, resistance was exerted through the application of public pressure in the form of crowd actions, open riots, and protest demonstrations against the Act.[18]

The colonies united in solidarity and convened the Stamp Act Congress, an inter-colonial meeting that put forward ideological and economic arguments against the Act. The Congress clarified that the British Parliament had no right to tax Americans and argued that taxation did not make economic sense for them either. However, this argument was contradictory as the Act brought Britain more revenue. The subsequent argument leveraged imperial logic: Since the colonies were loyal British subjects, they owed their allegiance to the King and Parliament. However, since Americans have no representation in Parliament, the King and Parliament could not tax Americans. This ideology became so strong that it led to the growth of an underground political movement led by artisans and shopkeepers who came to be known as 'Loyal Nine' and later this led to the rise of the semi-political organisation, the 'Sons of Liberty' whose primary focus was to generate opposition against British regulations.[19]

The fundamental issue in this ideological conflict was the assertion of the British Parliament's sovereignty over the American colonies and the rejection of this assertion by the colonies. The main lessons Americans learned from this is that they would have to fight united in defence of their liberties, and that they could not trust the British government. As one American politician commented, 'She (America) felt her Superiority...'. On the other hand, Britain characterised Americans as stubborn, wilful, lacking respect for and subordination to authority, and too selfish to contribute to their defence and maintenance.

THE DECLARATORY ACT

After intense opposition to the Stamp Act led to its repeal in 1765, Britain imposed the **Declaratory Act in 1766,** which asserted that the colonies were subordinate to the British Parliament and stated,

> [The] Parliament assembled, had, hath, and of right ought to have full power and authority to make laws and statutes of sufficient force and validity to bind the colonies and people of America, subjects of Crown of Great Britain, in all cases what so ever ... .

This meant that the British Parliament had the right to govern at will without the approval of the colonies. Americans interpreted the Declaratory Act differently. They understood it as a statement of Parliament's right to legislate for but not tax the colonies.[20] This contradiction or ambiguity became a source of confusion and conflict, and became an important factor contributing to the American Revolution.

THE TOWNSHEND ACTS

In 1767, British Prime Minister Townshend formulated his **'American Programme'** to raise revenue and impose stringent imperial control over the colonies. The programme consisted of four elements:

> (*i*) To use legislation and force the colonies to accept the provisions of the **Quartering Act** (1765), which required

colonies to make financial provisions to station the British army in American colonies.

(*ii*) Reforming the system of customs collection so that revenue collected was used to finance the appointment of customs officials, intelligence spies, coast guard ships, search warrants, writs of assistance, and the Board of Customs Commissioners in Boston.

(*iii*) Imposing direct revenue duties, payable at colonial ports, on items such as lead, glass, paper, silk, and tea.

(*iv*) Imposing a commercial duty on tea to help the British East India Company overcome its financial problems.

The greatest burden of the Quartering Act fell on New York as it was the headquarters of the British army in America. New York refused to accept the Act, and the result was that Britain passed the **New York Restraining Act**, which prohibited the New York Assembly from taking any legislative action until it complied with the Quartering Act. The implications of this Act were severe. Any colony that did not comply with the Quartering Act faced the end of their right to govern itself.[21] To strictly enforce the Townshend Act in 1767, the British government created an American Board of Customs Commissioners in Boston and subsequently established new Vice-Admiralty courts in 1768 in Boston, Philadelphia, and Charleston.

The Townshend duties aimed to give the British Parliament the right to collect revenue and govern colonies to uphold Parliament's sovereignty. In the long term, the aim was to expand the range of import duties Americans would be required to pay. In other words, the colonists were now to bear the cost of maintaining British American colonies.[22] For this reason, there was an immediate reaction against the Act, and the reaction was at the intellectual, political, and economic levels.

At the intellectual level, John Dickinson's article, 'Letters from a Farmer in Pennsylvania', published in the intervening period between 1767 and 1768, clearly outlined that while the British Parliament had the right to regulate the trade of the colonies, it did not have the right to tax them without the consent of the American people. It stated that the colonies and Britain were bound by beneficial trade relations and loyalty to the Crown, not by Parliament's authority. Political opposition came first from the Massachusetts assembly. Samuel Adams drafted a letter that urged other colonies to resist the Townshend Acts, resulting in the dissolution of many colonial assemblies that refused to recall these letters. Economic opposition came from Massachusetts and New York, where merchants adopted a non-importation agreement restricting trade with Britain until the Townshend Act was repealed. Two crucial consequences of this Act were that Americans began to stress the value of manufacturing goods themselves, and that it led to not only the revival of the Sons of Liberty but also provided impetus for people from the working classes, both White and Black, to join the movement, as well as women. The impact was extremely widespread; one encounter with British soldiers resulted in the infamous **Boston Massacre** on 5 March 1770, which eventually forced the British government to withdraw the Act in 1770. Still, it continued to collect taxes imposed on tea.[23]

The Tea Act

The **Tea Act in 1773** aimed to save the East India Company from complete bankruptcy. Duties paid by Americans on tea were meant to be given directly to the Company, and the Act also stipulated that tea had to be sold only by designated agents. Britain tried to argue that Americans were getting cheaper tea as a result. However, in reality, the aim was to reassert Parliament's right to impose direct revenue taxes on the colonies. The Americans understood the implications of this Act, which led to the beginning of colonial resistance and culminated in the **Boston Tea Party of 1773**, when 342 tea chests worth US $10,000 were thrown into the sea by Americans dressed as Indigenous tribesmen. A similar act of resistance was performed in New York in April 1774.

Impact of Opposition to the Tea Act: Series of 'Intolerable Acts'

The agitation against the Tea Act was rapid, and so was the severity of actions from the British government. It was followed by a series of acts in 1774 that Americans termed **Intolerable or Repressive Acts**.[24] The **Boston Port Act** called for the closure of the port of Boston until the colony paid for all the ruined tea. The **Massachusetts Government Act** altered the charters of the province, substituting an appointed council for an elected one, increasing the powers of the British governor and forbidding town meetings. The **Administration of Justice Act** applied the British colonial justice system in America to protect British officials charged with capital offences and allow them to stand for trial either in Britain or another colony. The Quartering Act was revived with more provisions, including more authority for military commanders. The Quebec Act provided religious freedom to Catholics within the former French colony, alarming American Protestants, especially those in New England. The Act also stated that the southern border of Quebec up to the Ohio River was demarcated as protected land for Indigenous peoples to provide them protection from the settlers, and the area was awarded to Quebec to establish French civil law and the Roman Catholic religion.[25]

The First Continental Congress

These Acts led to the beginning of the non-consumption of the British goods, which was the **American embargo**. Angry mobs of ordinary American people closed down all the military courts, and this growing popular resistance led to the 1774 meeting of 55 delegates at the **First Continental Congress** in Philadelphia. The objective of this Congress was threefold:

(*i*) To identify injustices meted out to America. The Congress argued that Parliament's authority was limited to governing colonies except in the case of trade legislation (that is, only commerce), and it had no right to raise revenue.

(*ii*) To define their constitutional connection with Britain, which was that Americans would govern themselves with the approval of the King (to be exercised through royal governors).

(*iii*) To develop a plan to remedy these injustices; they would form a Continental Association for the non-importation of goods from Britain.[26]

Among many pamphlets that were in circulation, Thomas Paine's 'Common Sense' (1776) was the most influential. It advocated for complete independence from Britain along the lines of the natural rights philosophy of John Locke and justified independence and revolution to secure natural rights. The intellectual guidance Paine provided ultimately resulted in the **Declaration of Independence**. Paine asserted that Americans' political linkages with England were not only artificial but would eventually retard America's growth; therefore, instead of reconciliation, Americans should strive towards complete independence from the mother country.[27]

The Second Continental Congress

The **Second Continental Congress** convened in 1776 and appointed Thomas Jefferson to draft the Declaration of Independence along with Benjamin Franklin and John Adams. Representatives of the Congress signed the draft on 4 July 1776, which made the new nation, the United States of America, independent of British rule and authority. In its introduction, the declaration states: 'We hold these truths to be self-evident that all men are created equal, that their creator endows them with certain unalienable rights that among these are life, liberty, and the pursuit of happiness' (borrowed from John Locke's *Second Treatise of Government* wherein he identifies 'life, liberty and property' as inalienable rights). The second part included a list of British regulations that had propelled the colonists to rise in resistance. The last part of the document was the statement of the Declaration of Independence, which stated the fundamental rights of individuals; it also justified the rebellion and establishment of democracy to achieve the principles of freedom, equality, and justice. The document articulates the philosophical basis of the American political system.

FIG. 1.1: Declaration of Independence, broadside, printed by John Dunlap in Philadelphia

Source: Wikimedia Commons.

Nature of the American Revolution

In the annals of American history, the American Revolution stands as a monumental event, a catalyst for epochal changes that continue to shape and nurture American life. It was the pivotal moment that freed America from British rule, bestowing upon it an independent identity. However, its influence extends far beyond the borders of the United States. The transformative effects of the American Revolution were so profound and intricate that they continue to be studied in new ways, and its global influence is a testament to its historical significance.

Analyses of the nature of the **War of Independence** have ignited a rich tapestry of interconnected debates. Two main perspectives have emerged, each offering a unique lens through which to view this complex event. The first perspective sees the event as a colonial rebellion, a struggle for limited independence from Britain. This viewpoint also encompasses the concepts of 'conservative revolution', 'civil war', and 'class conflict', offering a nuanced understanding of the event. The second perspective, in contrast, sees it as a 'true revolution', a transformative force permeating all aspects of life. Both perspectives draw on the Revolution's origins, impact, and social context, adding depth and complexity to the discussion.

First, let us delve into the terms 'rebellion' and 'revolution'. An uprising, in its essence, is an armed insurrection emerging out of dissatisfaction with the human conditions and demanding instant liberation from the existing situation.

In the context of North America, many scholars believed that the prolonged separation of the colonists from the metropolis led to the development of self-reliance, rather than dependence on English protection. Imbued with Enlightenment ideas, colonists overthrew the restraints of regulations imposed by Britain. The **Intellectual School** promoted this view, most prominently Bernard Bailyn,[28] Edmund S. Morgan and Mosses Taylor. They stressed ideas and principles as the prime mover of the American Revolution. In *The Ideological Origins of the American Revolution*, Bernard Bailyn attests to the importance of the democratic spirit, ideas of political liberty preached by the Enlightenment, and Thomas Paine's 'Common

Sense', which the revolutionaries expounded for the American Revolution. Pamphlets, newspapers, and magazines facilitated this. For Bailyn and other scholars belonging to the same school of thought, including Gordon Wood and J. G. A. Pocock, the Revolution was a radical intellectual movement based on the ideas of revolutionary leaders that resulted in the creation of America as a republican state.

In terms of the historical evaluation of the American Revolution, the interpretation of nationalist historian George Bancroft held sway for a long time. He represented an 'ultranationalist' viewpoint, wherein the onset of the Revolution was ordained by 'God' for all humanity to achieve greater human freedom, peace, and universal brotherhood.[29] America was a land of 'liberty' and 'progress' while Britain was associated with 'tyranny' and 'reaction'. Therefore, the character of the Revolution was radical. It represented a 'national struggle' of a people united by a shared belief in republican, democratic values, working to bring about 'peace' and an era of 'universal brotherhood'.[30]

The **Imperialist School** of historians presented a different perspective, based on a broader view that emphasised political and constitutional issues that had fundamentally altered the relationship between the British empire and its colonies in America. Steering the debate away from colonial policies being reactionary, George L. Beer opined that British imperial regulations were both 'liberal' and 'enlightened'. L. H. Gipson, in his book, *The British Empire before the American Revolution*, believed that the wealth and workforce invested by the British during the Anglo-French and Anglo-Indian wars justified the imposition of taxes on the American colonies.[31] On the other hand, Charles M. Andrews remarked in his book, *Colonial Period of American History*, that with the mother country's traditional and immutable nature (a popular stereotype of Britain), compared to the dynamic character of America, their separation was inevitable.[32] At that point, the colonies were developing into a dynamic, modern society with a strong economy and polity. They consisted of self-governing units that were held together by a shared sense of opposition to the Crown.

The British saw America as a set of dependent colonies to be brought under stringent imperial control and regulations. Eric Robson believed that 'conflicting political ideas', not tea and taxes, caused the secession. Thomas J. Wertenbaker, who also accorded greater weight to political factors, opined that the Americans rebelled despite their awareness of the economic situation. He saw the political desire for self-government as an important factor; this indicates the growing influence of the notion of democracy.³³ This logic is supported by Charles R. Ritcheson, who states in *British Policies and the American Revolution* that the lack of mutual understanding by leaders on either side produced the conflict.³⁴ Here, however, patriots are described as hypocrites pursuing their self-interest while playing up ideas about democracy and freedom for their own advantage. Max Savelle has evaluated the American Revolution as one of human history's greatest tragedies.³⁵

The Imperialist School's view, and their emphasis on the political dimensions of the Revolution, received a setback from the School of **Economic Determinists**, comprising Edward Channing, Louis Hacker, and Emory Johnson. Emery Johnson underlined the importance of financial freedom at the core of the Revolution.³⁶ Edward Channing, in his *History of the United States*, followed by Louis M. Hacker, opined that commercial interests had caused the conflict.³⁷ British mercantilism sowed the seeds of discontent. However, this argument was undercut by Lawrence A. Harper's contention that it was only after 1763 that merchants and farmers began to resent British economic measures.³⁸ Even then, this sentiment led to an agitation that was, in fact, not directed towards the Revolution. Nevertheless, in time, the Revolution followed from this discontent.

The **Progressive School** of historians emphasised social and economic causes. In social terms, the Revolution reflected a conflict between the upper and lower classes in colonial America, that is, an internal class conflict. At the same time, it represented economic competition and conflict between the colonies and the imperial core, and therefore had an external dimension. Carl L. Becker thus understood the American Revolution as two revolutions.³⁹ The first was responding to the question of home rule, sparking an external revolution with Britain due to a conflict in their economic interests. The other was the question of who should rule at home—this was the central question for the internal revolution between social classes. This view is supported by Charles H. Lincoln's survey, *Revolutionary Movement in Pennsylvania* (1901), which described the merging of inter-imperial and intra-colonial struggle, at least in the case of Pennsylvania, where people were eager to obtain independence within their colony. Charles Beard's commentary on the American Constitution supported historians' characterisation of the 1760s to 1780s as a period of relentless struggle between different social groups over competing economic interests.[40] Arthur M. Schlesinger, in *The Colonial Merchants and the American Revolution*, proposed that this conflict explains changing attitudes among different class groups.[41] The conservative elite initially played a dominant role in the Revolution as they had suffered economic losses due to the policy of imperial control. However, when even the lower classes joined the Revolution, they sought to limit the scope of the movement to prevent any challenge to their power. The actions of the elite class, therefore, later brought in a conservative counterrevolution that eventually culminated in the American Revolution. In this way, the undemocratic nature of American society produced class conflicts; therefore, the Revolution represented a movement by the masses to advance their economic life and take away greater political rights from the upper classes. J. F. Jameson also opined that the Revolution was a democratic upheaval against the privileges of the aristocratic class. Frederick B. Tollis and Merrill Jenson supported his view. Jenson considered it a democratic movement not in its origins but in its results, as it instituted limited adult enfranchisement (allowing all White, landed men to vote) and led to the abolition of primogeniture. In this way, the Progressive School of Historians emphasised the aspect of class conflict and disunity.[42]

To the **Neo-Conservative School** of historians, the Revolution was a conservative movement to preserve the American constitutional principles of liberty. It was a revolutionary era that broke with the colonial past, and the establishment of the American Constitution marked its culmination. These historians characterised colonial society as politically democratic and open, citing a high degree of social mobility. However, the Revolution was a conservative movement as it was begun to preserve the existing social order—one defined by the fundamental principles of self-government, which could only change through a consensus among the colonists. Contrary to this principle, Britain had attempted to bring about radical changes after the Anglo-French and Anglo-Indian Wars. In other words, these historians emphasised 'consensus and continuity' as core impulses of the Revolution. According to Robert E. Brown, the purpose of the Revolution was to preserve the existing democratic social order on the local level and resist any attempts to change it.[43] Daniel J. Boorstin concurred that it was a conservative movement on the imperial and local levels.[44] At the same time, in the words of Edmund S. Morgan, there are two themes – the consensus among Americans on the principles and the contiguity of ideas as Americans wanted to realise three principles: the protection of property and liberty, achievement of human equality and development of American nationalism based on the ideas of liberty and equality. In this way, this school stressed the concept of consensus based on the continuity between the British colonial past and the birth of a new nation.[45]

Three schools challenged the Neo-conservative approach, beginning with the **Neo-Progressive** historians. They considered the Revolution a democratic movement ushered in by increasing social inequalities to break down elite control over American political life.[46] The Revolution, from this perspective, was a social movement that manifested in the form of internal colonial struggles.

The **New Left** historians considered the Revolution a radical movement undertaken by particular social groups to fight the oppression of British rule. Marxist scholars, especially Herbert M. Morais, Wilhelm Z. Foster, and Barrington Moore, brought in new dimensions to the debate. Foster characterised the movement as a 'bourgeoisie Revolution' with strong democratic currents, which 'dealt a mighty blow to the feudal elements' and greatly stimulated democracy across the world. Barrington Moore, in keeping with Karl Marx's assessment, compared the American Revolution with the British Civil War of the sixteenth century and concluded that it brought the capitalist classes to the forefront.[47] Charles Beard has substantially supported this point. Another proponent of this theory was Jesse Lemirch, who additionally pointed out that the role of the 'inarticulate', poor masses—who could not write their own histories and were thus excluded from mainstream accounts—has not received adequate attention. According to Morais, the event had dual aspects, such as the colonial war of independence from Britain and the internal struggle among the American people for a better democratic order.

Historian Herbert Apetheker opined that the Revolution resulted from three currents. *First*, there was the conflict between colonial powers and colonies. *Second*, class stratification in the colonies resulted in a class struggle. *Third*, the developing sense of American nationality transcended class lines, rooted in the physical separation from England and varied origins of the colonial population. These three currents finally caused a revolt of the rising bourgeoisie in the colonies, pitted against a restraining bourgeoisie in Britain. He marks the removal of obstacles from the path of burgeoning capitalism as a fundamental achievement of independence. For Morais, the Revolution ushered in a modern era of revolutionary struggle and became the prototype for bourgeois democratic upheaval in Europe and elsewhere.[48]

For the **Loyalist School**, represented by William H. Nelson and Wallace Brown, the emphasis was on social history. They talk in terms of 'cultural minorities' who could not assimilate into American settler society, supported Tory politics, and looked towards Britain for protection against the growing aggression of the Whig majority, for example, Scots, British immigrants, Germans, Anglicans, and Quakers.[49]

The **Comparative School** included historians like Robert R. Palmer. In Palmer's view, the American and French revolutions were essentially part of a larger 'Age of Democratic Revolution' that spread across the trans-Atlantic world based on mutually evolving ideas, needs, and conflicts. However, the American Revolution was revolutionary and conservative, unlike the French example. According to Leslie Lipson in *European Responses to Revolution*, it inspired colonial struggles and registered a worldwide conceptual influence by prioritising individual rights. Max Silbuschividt describes the American Revolution as a pioneer of the anti-colonial movement in Asia, Africa, and Latin America. Henry Fairlie has provided the most emphatic analysis of its global impact in an article titled *The Shot Heard Around the World*. According to Fairlie, once the news of the fatal shot reached the courts of Europe, the monarchs were alert to the effect that the American events might have on the balance of power in Europe. Maria Theresa, the ruler of the Habsburg monarchy (1740–1780), was greatly alarmed about the consequences of the American Revolution for Europe. To the Psychological School of historians, the conflict was between British customs and American identity. Disputes over political issues were related to attitudes towards facets of private lives, including patriarchal norms, authority, and childrearing.

The fact remains that from 1660 onwards, Britain attempted to control colonial trade and use it to expand commerce and make London Europe's most powerful city. The scenario changed after 1763, when Britain tried to assert political and economic control by imposing structural political similarities on its American colonies by establishing bicameral legislative assemblies and a common-law judicial system. The aim was to alter the political culture in the North American colonies. However, Americans had by this time experienced an 'oasis of freedom' that allowed the ideas of liberty, property, and prosperity to flourish and become popular. In the period after 1763, American colonies began to develop a more cosmopolitan settler culture, fuelled by an increase in population and the development of mass media—including newspapers like *The Boston News-Letter*—that could quickly spread ideas and opinions. Simultaneously, the emergence of modern educational institutions stimulated the growth of professional classes in the North and the rise of enslavers in the South. Another significant factor was the American involvement on behalf of Britain in the Anglo-French conflict, which led to a massive loss of American lives but provided them with the valuable experience of fighting a war. It was also at this juncture that Indigenous peoples began to look with suspicion towards both British and American settlers, creating hurdles in the geographical expansion of the British American colonies.

Apart from understanding these internal changes, historians have also analysed the significant role played by the marginalised sections of the American colonies. In particular, they have studied the roles of the indentured servants, Black people, women, and impoverished classes. Theorists are increasingly placing the politics of the Revolution within a larger social context that was shaped by new forms of mass political participation, expansion of market relations, and changes in the economy and society. Jesse Lemisch has studied the American Revolution using a 'bottom-up' approach by narrating the experiences of poor and illiterate people who participated in the Revolution. A new wave of intellectual history has developed in America, whereby historians, through the analysis of pamphlets, sermons, books, and ideas of ordinary people, have brought to the forefront systems of thought in popular political culture that transformed the political mentality of the colonies.

According to Gregory Nobles, 'the roots of the revolution' lay not so much in the changes in British policy but in American society.[50] America was undergoing radical, social, economic, and demographic changes, along with the acceleration of a commercial revolution and industrialisation, the appearance of a wage labour system, consumerism, an increase in literacy, evangelical religious denominations, demographic shifts and the growth of relatively small families, and new social and economic relations based on a free market system. Economic life was based on self-interest, heightened profit expectations, and new market opportunities. At the other end of the spectrum, the American Revolution established an inegalitarian society as slavery persisted and in fact expanded, along with indentured White servitude, and poverty was widespread. The wealthy White groups continued to remain politically and economically powerful. Keeping these factors in mind, scholars began to re-analyse the American Revolution from the perspective of the ever-expanding American frontier that created a 'New World' settled by the 'New Man' whose identity was shaped by independent land ownership and whose ideology was characterised by individualism, democracy, and equality of opportunity.

This America was not a 'melting pot' as historians had earlier understood. Colonial American society consisted of different cultural groups that included Indigenous peoples, enslaved Africans, early Anglicans, and the Welsh, Germans, and Dutch, creating conflicting cultural confluence—while Indigenous societies had their own beliefs and practices, the rest brought along their own cultural traditions, which were voluntarily or involuntarily amalgamated with the American environment. This cultural convergence took place from 1700 onwards, especially between the 1730s and 1780s: Over this period the process of democratising and personalising religion gained ground; Indigenous peoples and enslaved Africans rapidly converted into Christian norms and religions; meanwhile the elite, wealthy merchants, planters, and professional classes continued to adhere to British aristocratic lifestyle. In the same period, colonies gradually began to develop vernacular popular cultures, wherein Indigenous communities inhabiting regions isolated from the settlers continued with their lifestyle; the immigrant Germans lived in rural communities of Pennsylvania; Quakers, Dutch, and Scots assembled in the Middle Colonies; Puritans dominated in New England; and enslaved people were made to toil in Chesapeake colonies and coastal South Carolina.

The period from the 1730s to 1780s also saw the spread of evangelicalism, in which preachers insisted upon the spiritual equality of all people. English became an ordinary person's language, thereby mitigating differences between ethnic groups (although these ideas remained circumscribed by race). The ideology of the yeoman—a category of ordinary White farmers—posed another hurdle to Britain as it moved to prevent the territorial expansion of Americans. (Britain sought to limit conflict between colonists and Indigenous groups.) These American farmers believed they had the right to secure and own land without governmental interference. In the meantime, American colonies had also developed economically by the beginning of the eighteenth century as northern colonies progressed from the fur trade and lumber export to playing an intermediary role in trading and manufacturing. After 1763, as we have seen, they were developing shipbuilding industries. The southern colonies were developing agricultural economies based on an enslaved labour force and producing commercial cash crops like tobacco, indigo, and rice. In political terms, American colonies harboured a deep hatred of monarchy and the imposition of taxes and the colonial assemblies believed in minimal interference in people's personal lives. For this reason, there was an instant reaction against the imposition of British regulations.

The Revolution brought cataclysmic changes, as attested by Dion Higginbotham.[51] According to him, the American Revolution was a revolution since ideas about democracy, the Constitution, and liberalism were translated into reality for the first time. In recent decades, a whole bunch of scholars', including Irving Kristol, Robert A. Nisbet, Gordon S. Wood and Caroline Robbins, have wholeheartedly supported the fact that the events that unfolded qualified as a real revolution: a social, moral, and institutional revolution that effected significant changes in the character of American society.

Robert A. Nisbet has highlighted the social implications of the Revolution as this momentous change was based on the participation of peasants, traders, merchants, farmers, lawyers, soldiers, and intellectuals.[52] This varied class participation cut across socio-economic boundaries. He also attaches importance to the concept of voluntary associations to the American Revolution and terms America as a 'nation of joiners'. In his lecture 'The Social Impact of the American Revolution', Nisbet argues that the Revolution effectively ended the feudal vestiges of primogeniture and entail. The confiscation of Tory estates and Crown lands followed it. The exodus of some 50,000 loyalists cleared the field for the 'levelling' ideas of unbridled democracy to swiftly travel across the land. The Revolution emphasised the relation of tolerance and stimulated the movement for complete religious freedom, thereby crystallising the concept of a secular state. The Virginia Statute for Relation of Freedom, which disestablished the Church of England and guaranteed freedom of religion, could be cited as a case in point. It led to the separation of church and state across the colonies, with the exception of New England.

The growth of trade organisations for artisans and labourers further stimulated social democracy. Egalitarian sentiments promoted by the movement likewise challenged the institution of slavery. Philadelphia Quakers, in 1775, founded the world's first anti-slavery society. The Continental Congress in 1774 called for a 'complete abolition of the slave trade'. Even women were not exempt from social transformation, and their conditions improved marginally. The origins of White American feminism, according to Linda K. Kerber, can be traced to the remarkable Abigail Adams, who had the support of her husband to pursue values and duties associated with private virtue for public good. Kerber has termed this 'Republican Motherhood'.

Economic changes begotten by the movement were equally conspicuous. The Revolution effectively scuttled British mercantilism. Production was enhanced, leading to a boom in the shipping industry and foreign trade. Though there was a phase of depression in 1784–85, the economy soon recovered. According to H. U. Faulkner, the policies of the emerging government encouraged the growth of rudimentary industries in the US, and to fight the Indigenous groups and increase firepower, the manufacture of arms and ammunition was encouraged.[53] Several companies were chartered for the construction of roads and bridges. The levering force of the Revolution also manifested in the agricultural sector. The production of tobacco, cotton and wool increased significantly.

In the political sphere, the Revolution marked the end of an era of imperialist domination and signalled the dawn of republican government. As Tocqueville has stated, the 'doctrine of the sovereignty of the people' took possession of the government. Though limited by property ownership, the enfranchisement of people is a legacy of the Revolution. Political leaders were no longer exclusively representatives of hegemonic aristocracy; there were now leaders of humble origin as well. The Articles of Confederation (1777) transferred power to the people, which ensured legislative sovereignty. This process of democratic churning initiated by the American Revolution culminated in the formation of the Constitution (1787), which also ensured parliamentary sovereignty.

In this way, the American Revolution was a testament to a successful revolution against the established order in the annals of modern history. It profoundly impacted America's social, political, and economic structure and dispelled the myth that the American War of Independence was only a rebellion. The 'War of Independence' was indeed a Revolution in a profound sense that, from some points of view, initiated the process of freedom worldwide.

Fig. 1.2: *Declaration of Independence*, by John Trumbull, oil on canvas (1819)
Source: Wikimedia Commons.

Conclusion

The causes of the American Revolution are varied and complex. Some participated to secure the right of self-rule and self-determination, others participated for economic reasons, some even fought for adventure, and then there were the loyalists who were aligned with the British Crown. The revolution did not end in 1776 with the Declaration of Independence, as all these events were followed by prolonged military conflict with Britain, which refused to grant independence to its British American colonies. This conflict finally culminated in the Treaty of Paris (1783), and subsequently Britain recognised the US as an independent nation, its borders extending from the Atlantic Ocean to the Mississippi River, and the southern border stretching up to just before the Spanish colony of Florida. The new nation was governed under the Articles of Confederation, which gave more powers to the state governments than the federal government. This later resulted in severe national crises that threatened the very existence and unity of the young nation, forcing leaders to evolve a new national government whose framework was drafted at the Constitutional Convention held in Philadelphia in 1787. This was ratified and approved, and has been in operation since 1789.

Notes

1. See Gregory H. Nobles, *Divisions Throughout the Whole: Politics and Society in Hampshire County, Massachusetts, 1740–1775* (Cambridge, 1983).
2. For a nuanced understanding of colonial American history, it is highly recommended that one read Bernard Bailyn's *Voyages to the West: A Passage in the Peopling of America on the Eve of Revolution* (New York, 1986).
3. George Bancroft, *History of Colonization of the United States*, vols 1–3 (New York, 2023).
4. The Great Awakening was a form of Protestant Revivalism that developed in eighteenth-century British America.
5. The *Mayflower* was a ship that took Pilgrims on an oceanic journey from England to northeast America. The ship has acquired historical significance as a symbol of early British settlers. At the end of their journey, the Pilgrims developed the first British colonial settlement, Plymouth, in 1620.
6. Lloyd deMause, 'The Psychogenic Theory of History', *Journal of Psychohistory* 25 (1): 112–183.
7. See Stanely N. Katz, John M. Murrin, and Douglas Greenberg, ed., *Colonial America: Essays in Politics and Social Development*, 4th ed. (New York, 1993).
8. This is an idea that the US is an exceptional nation in terms of its history, ideological underpinnings, and religious beliefs. The notion emphasised that the nation was established based on republican ideas and principles of good governance, as specified in the Declaration of Independence and the Constitution. Critics of the notion have argued that this notion tends to gloss over aspects of American history like slavery and the suffering of Indigenous peoples, since it projects an assumed superiority of the American way of life.
9. Francis D. Cogliano, *Revolutionary America 1763–1815: A Political History* (London and New York, 2000), p. 27.
10. Ibid.
11. Ibid., pp. 27–28.
12. Ibid., p. 29.
13. Ibid., p. 30.
14. Kenneth A. Lockridge, *Literacy in Colonial New England: An Enquiry into the Social Context of Literary in the Early Modern West* (New York, 1974).

15. Joyce O. Appleby, *Capitalism and a New Social Order: The Republican Vision of the 1790s* (New York, 1984).

16. Sean Wilentz, *Chants Democratic: New York City and the Rise of the American Working Class, 1788–1850* (New York, 1994).

17. Cogliano, *Revolutionary America 1763–1815*, pp. 31–33.

18. Ibid., p. 33.

19. Ibid., pp. 33–35.

20. Ibid., p. 37.

21. Ibid., pp. 38–39.

22. Ibid., p. 39.

23. Ibid., pp. 40–43.

24. Ibid., pp. 46–47.

25. Ibid., p. 47.

26. Ibid., p. 49.

27. Ibid., p. 50.

28. Bernard Bailyn, *Ideological Origins of the American Revolution* (Massachusetts, 1967).

29. Bancroft, *History of Colonization of the United States*, vols 1–3.

30. See Gerald N. Grob and George Athan Billias, ed., *Interpretations of American History: Patterns and Perspectives* (New York, 1978), pp. 105–106.

31. L. H. Gipson, *The British Empire Before the American Revolution*, vol. 8 (Caldwell, Idaho, 1936).

32. Charles M. Andrews, *Colonial Period of American History*, vol. 1 (Cambridge, 2018).

33. Thomas Jefferson Wertenbaker, *Tochbearer of the Revolution: The Story of Bacon's Rebellion and its Leaders* (Princeton, 1940).

34. Charles R. Ritcheson, *British Policies and the American Revolution* (Westport, 1981).

35. See Grob and Bilias, ed., *Interpretations of American History*, pp. 106–107.

36. Emory Richard Johnson, *History of Domestic and Foreign Commerce of the United States* (Washington, 1915).

37. Edward Channing, *History of the United States: The American Revolution, 1761–1789*, vol. 3 (New York, 1912).

38. Lawrence A. Harper, 'Mercantilism and the American Revolution', *Canadian Historical Review 23* (1).

39. Carl L. Becker, *The History of Political Parties in the Province of New York, 1770–1776* (Madison, 1909).

40. Charles A. Beard and Mary Beard, *The Rise of American Civilization* (New York, 1927).

41. Arthur M. Schlesinger, *The Colonial Merchants and the American Revolution, 1763–1776* (New York, 2013).

42. For more information on these perspectives, see Grob and Bilias, ed., *Interpretations of American History*, pp. 108–109.

43. Robert E. Brown, *Middle-Class Democracy and the Revolution in Massachusetts, 1691–1780* (Ithaca, 1955).

44. Daniel J. Boorstin, *The Genius of American Politics* (Chicago, 1953).
45. For a detailed account, see Grob and Bilias, ed., *Interpretations of American History*, pp. 110–113.
46. Ibid., p. 115.
47. Barrington Moore, Jr, *Social Origins of Dictatorship and Democracy: Lord and Peasant in the Making of the Modern World* (Boston, 1993).
48. Herbert Apetheker, *American Revolution, 1763–1783: A History of the American People: An Interpretation* (New York, 1960).
49. See Grob and Bilias, ed., *Interpretations of American History*, pp. 117–118.
50. Nobles, *Divisions Throughout the Whole*.
51. Dion Higginbotham, *The War of American Independence: Military Attitudes, Policies, and Practice, 1763–1789* (New York, 1983).
52. Robert A. Nisbet, *The Social Impact of Revolution* (Washington, 1973).
53. H. U. Faulkner, *American Economic History* (New York, 1960).

Chapter 2

The Formulation of the American Constitution

Any political institution evolves from historical and social practices. Thus, it follows that many American political concepts and institutions originated in the constitutional history of England. Early immigrant settlers brought with them ideas of popular sovereignty and legislative systems of representative government that eventually developed in almost all the North American colonies. The American Revolution did not produce immediate and drastic changes in the form of local governments; it only secured the political ties binding the 13 American colonies to the new nation. Despite their commonalities, distinct differences existed between the colonies and the mother country based on the accepted fact that the governments, like all human institutions, respond to environmental conditions and reflect in their organisation and operational systems historical experiences as well as cultural heritage. In 1789, America evolved a written constitution based on the federal system and judicial review that became examples of American innovation.

Evolution of Political Systems of British American Colonies

From the establishment of the first colony at Jamestown, Virginia, in 1607, to the point in 1733 when the last of the **Thirteen Colonies** was settled, each colony was established separately and had distinct characteristics. However, similar English influences and elements were present in all the colonies. Each colony had a bicameral legislature with a lower house elected by the people, a governor, and a system of courts.

Scholars have distinguished three principal types of colonies:

Royal colonies like Virginia, during its formative period, were financed by a joint stock company chartered by King James I in 1604. However, in 1624, it became a royal colony when the king appointed a governor as its chief executive, with substantial powers and exerting tremendous influence over the colony's affairs. He was assisted by a council body, whose members were also appointed by the king and formed the Upper House of the bicameral legislative assembly, the highest Court of appeal in the colony. The Lower House of the legislature was elected by the property owners, who qualified to vote and were responsible for passing taxes and managing their collections. During the American Revolution, this bicameral pattern of government was established in the colonies of Massachusetts, New Hampshire, New York, New Jersey, North and South Carolina and Georgia.

The second type was the **corporate colony**. New England, for example, had grown out of Massachusetts Bay, which in 1623 was just a fishing post but by 1629 became a corporation: The Company of Massachusetts Bay in New England received a charter from the King that granted to territory to them for a colony and vested in the stockholders, called 'freemen' authority to govern the settlers. At the meetings of the stockholders, called General Courts, laws and ordinances for the management of the company and government of the colony were to be passed, and officers were chosen, including the colonial governor and his assistants. The Puritans of New England joined the government of the corporation and the colony's government. Therefore, the General Court was the colony's legislature, which elected the governor and his assistants. With the admission of deputies chosen in each town, the General Court became somewhat representative.

The third type was the **proprietary colony**, for instance Pennsylvania, where the pattern of government was like that of the royal colony except that the governor was appointed by the proprietor instead of the king.

After the Glorious Revolution of 1688 in Britain, when the British Parliament gained supremacy over the king, Parliament began to take a more active interest in managing colonial affairs, especially trade, and handled these matters through the Privy Council, the Board of Trade, and other established agencies. Each colony was governed separately, as no capital city or central colonial office existed in America.

Two historical events would later play a significant role in American constitutional history. The first was the **New England Confederation**, established in 1634, which was formed to 'protect' White settlers from Indigenous groups and became the first cooperative agreement between the colonies. The second event was the **Albany Plan of 1754**, which aimed to unify all American colonies into a cohesive Union. For this purpose, the Board of Trade called the conference at Albany to work out the finer details. Benjamin Franklin proposed a union plan to the delegates (similar to the Articles of Confederation Constitution that were established later). However, it was not accepted by the Crown or the colonies.

Events Leading to the Revolution

The American colonies had evolved without any preconceived pattern, and the eighteenth century witnessed the rapid development of two opposing principles within this system. The American colonies, self-absorbed and pre-occupied with domestic problems, grew inwards towards self-government; Britain, faced with the complex issue of administering colonies and financing their defence, began to move towards imperialist control over the colonies, leaving behind the simple mercantilist control mechanisms applied in the first phase of the colonisation process. The subordination of the colonies to the home government was an accepted ideology within the political corridors of Britain. The period after the Paris Treaty, signed in 1763 (which had ended the French and Indian Wars), was accompanied by the reformulation of trade laws, better-coordinated administrative machinery, and a regime of taxes and regulations. As discussed in Chapter 1, the American colonies were brought under the sovereign control of the British Parliament through a sophisticated process, utilising the colonies to foster the Empire's economic prosperity. The imposition of the Sugar Act of 1764, followed by a series of laws that culminated in the 'Intolerable Acts' imposed on Americans in 1774, created an irreparable rift in a relationship that was already deeply fractured, prompting the formulation of the American Constitution which in turn marked the culmination of the American Revolution.

The First Continental Congress was called for in September 1774 in Philadelphia and was attended by delegates from every colony except Georgia. They adopted a resolution protesting the imperialist policies pursued by the British government. To put pressure on England, the Congress agreed to restrict all trade ties with Britain until it repealed all trade regulations and taxes imposed on the settlers.

Before the convening of the Second Continental Congress in Philadelphia in May 1775, a small armed battle between colonial immigrant settlers and the British army at Concord and Lexington propelled the thirteen colonies to send their representatives to initiate the movement towards complete freedom from British imperialistic control. The Second Continental Congress assembled in Philadelphia on 10 May 1775, representing all 13 colonies. John Hancock of Massachusetts was elected as the President of the Congress; Congress assumed the role of a provisional government on 14 June. Congress created a Continental Army with George Washington as its Commander-in-Chief. According to scholar Carl Becker, the critical question was—who should rule at home now that Britain had proved its inability to rule Americans? This was followed by the question of what type of government the 13 states should have, along with the structure of the new Union. The answer to these questions produced what some historians have termed the **Political Revolution**, which transformed America from 1776 to 1788. The general agreement on a framework for the new Union resolved:

(*i*) To have a republican form of government, instead of monarchy and aristocracy.

(*ii*) That the source of power and authority would be the American people, who will have sovereign power.
(*iii*) That the government would have a limited term.

Disagreements over the form of government led to the rise of two groups. The elites, that is, landowners, merchants, lawyers, and politicians with considerable political sway (the Founding Fathers of the US primarily came from this social strata) adopted the political tradition and ideology of the opposition in Britain—they wanted a republican government based on British constitutional traditions. They favoured **tripartite power sharing** between a **bicameral legislature**, an **executive**, and a **judiciary** appointed by the government. They felt the need for a solid national confederation in which franchises should be limited to property holders. Their leaders had national experience in terms of organising the Continental Congresses, the Army, and during the Revolutionary War. Their support base was in urban areas, commercial centres, and among big slave-owning planters.

Democrats were usually from less illustrious backgrounds and were the 'new men of revolution'. They wanted a more democratic government with decentralised powers and dispersed decision-making. They tried to establish **unicameral legislatures** with powers belonging to the national government, but a weak executive and broad electoral franchise, as well as elected judiciaries. They tried to hold frequent elections to prevent the government from becoming tyrannical. Their support base was small farmers who believed in the concept of liberty, self-governance, and the moral good of the people.

On 15 May 1776, the draft to declare the United Colonies as free and independent states was completed, and it was finally adopted on 4 July 1776. The Declaration of Independence, written by Thomas Jefferson, embodied the social contract philosophy conceptualised by John Locke. Based on the equality of man and the principle of natural rights, this philosophy emphasised that the government ruled by a social contract, which required the consent of the governed, and therefore, the governed had the right of Revolution whenever, in the minds of the people, a government ceased to rule justly. In form, the new state governments followed the patterns of colonial governments and were influenced by the political philosophy of John Locke and Montesquieu. Frequent references were made to popular sovereignty, the compact theory of government, natural rights, and the separation of powers. Because of the memories of autocratic royal governors, executive power was greatly circumscribed, and the preponderance of power was conferred on the legislative bodies, especially the lower houses, as being more representative of the people. Contradicting the liberal ideals championed in the Declaration of Independence, property qualifications for voting were imposed in all the state constitutions.

Articles of the Confederation Constitution

On 15 November 1777, Congress adopted the draft of a constitution prepared by a committee of its members headed by John Dickinson. The **Articles of the Confederation Constitution** were then submitted to the legislatures of all 13 states for approval and ratification. The Articles were completed and went into effect on 1 March 1781. The Articles of Confederation Constitution came into effect from 1781 to 1789, and its first notable feature was establishing a 'firm league of friendship' between the 13 states and the recognition of the states' complete and unchallenged sovereignty. The second noteworthy feature was the simplicity of the machinery used in the government setup, to which the Article provided a single organ, a Congress, composed of delegates appointed annually by the states in such a manner as directed by their legislature. Irrespective of population or wealth, each state was given one vote in Congress, and all-important measures required a vote of nine states (that is, a 2/3rd majority). Each year, Congress elected one member to preside as a moderator, the President of the Congress (not the President of the US). Committees managed executive and judicial matters, and Congress appointed and directed civil officers. A third feature of the Article was the rigid limitation it placed upon the powers of the national government. A list of the powers was specified: Power to determine peace and war; to send and receive ambassadors; to make treaties; to fix standards of weights and measures; to regulate the alloy and value of coins; to regulate trade and manage all affairs with the Indians (that is, Indigenous groups); to establish post offices; to borrow money; to build and equip a navy; to agree upon the number of land forces and make requisitions for the states' respective quotas.

Table 2.1: American Constitutional History

	Year	Event
1.	1777	Articles of Confederation
2.	1781	Articles of Confederation Ratified
3.	1783	Treaty of Paris
4.	1786–1787	Daniel Shay's Rebellion
5.	1787	Constitutional Convention
6.	1788	The Federalist + Constitution Ratified
7.	1791	Bill of Rights ratified

Source: Author.

The Articles of Confederation, therefore, established a loose bond between independent states, and the powers that did not belong to Congress were deemed to belong to the states. There was no leading executive power; committees and Congress were required to execute laws. States controlled commerce and trade, and Congress had no powers to force states to pay taxes. There were no courts above state courts; approval of a 2/3rd majority of states was required to pass laws; and Congress did not have powers to enforce laws over the people or states. In brief, the national government depended on the state governments for the exercise of power, since the Congress operated in the states in their corporate capacity. It was not a government but rather the 'central agency of an alliance' or 'diplomatic assembly', as described by John Adams.[1]

The Critical Period

John Fiske called the interval between the Revolutionary War's end and the Constitution's adoption 'the critical period of American history'.[2] The Articles of Confederation Constitution did not empower Congress to cope with political and economic problems related to foreign relations. It was becoming clear that the Articles were insufficient as they had established an inefficient system of government in a very awkward manner. Interestingly, it was also not ratified by all the states till 1781. Its impact was first felt during the uncoordinated Revolutionary War (1776–1783), where the Union lacked funds, men, and resources. As a result, the national leadership, alarmed at rising instances of popular revolt—such as the rebellion under Daniel Shays in Massachusetts (1786)—was to some extent willing to forgo the ideals of revolutionary liberation as expressed in the Declaration of Independence and to seek greater strength in the national government to ensure the economic, social, and national security of the young nation.

EVENTS LEADING TO THE CONSTITUTIONAL CONVENTION

In the Mount Vernon conference at Alexandria in 1785, delegates from Maryland and Virginia came together to discuss problems relating to the navigation of the Potomac River. At this conference, delegates recommended a general meeting that would include delegates from all the states since this was a shared concern. Representatives from New York, New Jersey, Pennsylvania, Delaware, and Virginia met at the Annapolis Convention in 1786. The delegates of these five states recommended the creation of a constitution that would enable a federal government structure helmed by a strong union government, which required revising the Articles of Confederation.

PHILADELPHIA CONVENTION OF 1787

Historians have analysed the social strata of the delegates who attended the Philadelphia Convention. The majority of the members were college graduates, and lawyers predominated, followed by plantation owners. Their main aim was the elimination of disunity and the establishment of national integrity. The conference was initially convened to amend the Articles and not create a new system of government; however, when the delegates realised that a weak national government had exposed the young nation to financial problems and the possibility of invasion by Britain, France, or Spain, all of which still controlled vast tracts of territory in North America, 12 states agreed to send delegates to the Constitutional Convention (the exception being Rhode Island). At this convention, two government plans were proposed.

Two Plans of Government

Two main Union plans were presented at the end of this federal convention. The **Virginia Plan** (written by James Madison) proposed a radical form of government in which the national government was made more powerful. If accepted, the states would transfer significant powers to the national government. Representation in the national legislature would be apportioned among the states according to the population of the states (that would give an advantage to big states like Virginia, Pennsylvania, and Massachusetts). The plan proposed a government with three branches: legislature, executive, and judiciary. A bicameral legislative assembly would be constituted: Members to the first branch of the legislature would be directly elected; in contrast, the second branch would consist of members selected by the first branch, based on nominations from the state assemblies. The national legislature would choose a national executive. The plan proposed a 'Supreme Court' as the apex body of the judiciary, whose judges were to be selected by the legislature. The Virginia Plan is also known as the **Large State Plan** or the **Randolph Plan**. It underscored governmental power derived from the unified American 'people', rather than the states.

New Jersey's plan proposed only a revision of the Articles, as it wanted a unicameral legislature with equal representation of the states (without considering state population). The executive branch would be a multi-person body chosen by the legislature. The judiciary would consist of 'a supreme tribunal' only. There would be no lower federal courts. The New Jersey plan is also known as the **Small State Plan** or the **Paterson Plan**. Its supporters, mainly delegates from the small states, were driven by a fear that their states would be outvoted and 'swallowed up' by the more populous states in a Union-based on the Virginia Plan. The New Jersey Plan was formulated on the assumption that the national government's power would be derived from the states and not a unified American people.

The Great Compromise or Connecticut Compromise

The document proposed seven Articles. The first three articles defined the branches of government. Article I outlined the power of Congress (power to enact laws); Article II related to the powers of the President (power to execute laws); Article III laid down the powers of the judiciary (the interpreter of the laws). This sequence was based on the understanding that the Congress (legislature) is the most powerful branch of government, in order to prevent the President from becoming tyrannical.

Establishment of a Bicameral Legislature

It was agreed that the Lower House, the House of Representatives, would be directly elected by the people and that representation would be based on the state population. Each state would have two representatives in the Upper House, also known as the Senate. In the initial phase, state legislatures were mandated to choose each state's Senators. That was, however, changed when the 17th Constitutional Amendment in 1913 which mandated the direct election of senators by the people. In the Lower House, members were to serve for a two-year term, and were required to have been US citizens for at least seven years. In the Senate, members served a six-year term, and only those who had been US citizens for at least nine years were eligible to be part of the House.

Establishment of the Executive Branch

Article II stipulated that the President had to be 35 years of age, a natural US citizen, and a resident of the country for at least 14 years. The President would serve for a four-year term of office, and terms were not specified in the Constitution; however, the first President, George Washington, set the precedent of not serving more than two terms. This is still being followed, with the sole exception of Franklin D. Roosevelt, who was elected for four terms due to the Great Depression and the beginning of World War II. In 1951, the 21st Constitutional Amendment was brought in, formally limiting the President to two terms in office. The President's election followed a unique format as the framers of the Constitution were part of the highly educated, affluent elite, and therefore reluctant to give too much power to ordinary people. In this format, the political parties were to choose a 'slate of electors' to vote for the President, called the Electoral College. Representation in the electoral college was calculated as the sum of the state's Representatives and Senators—thus, population played a role in representation. In all other states except for Maine and Nebraska, the Presidential candidate who scores the majority of the popular vote receives all of the state's electors.

To maintain a system of checks and balances and ensure a reasonable division of power, the framers of the Constitution included a provision for the impeachment of the President, that is, to remove them from office before the completion of their term. In the first part of this process, the House of Representatives must determine the grounds for impeachment and then put the Article of Impeachment to a vote, which requires only a simple majority for its passage. The Article then has to go to the Senate, where the Senators serve as the jury, and the Chief Justice of the Supreme Court oversees the entire proceedings. For the President to be impeached, he must be found guilty of 'High Crimes and Misdemeanors' and the motion must win with a two-thirds majority.

The Constitutional Convention established the judicial branch of government by setting up the framework for the Supreme Court. Although the number of judges was not specified at this point, later

The Formulation of the American Constitution

legislation would create provisions for nine members. Federal judges serve for life.

Article V of the Constitution articulates the process to amend the Constitution. The First Amendment brought in the **Bill of Rights** (1791). To the present day, there are two ways to propose an amendment: by a two-thirds vote in both houses of the US Congress, or at the request of two-thirds of the state legislatures. A three-quarters vote of all state legislators is required to ratify an amendment, or a special convention can be convened where three-quarters of all state legislators must vote in favour of the amendment.

The institution of slavery was referred to indirectly in in Article I, Section Two, Paragraph Three, which refers to the '**Three-Fifths Compromise**' that determined how enslaved people would be counted when determining the total population of a state. It stated that five enslaved people would be counted in the census as three White men. While the Constitutional Convention ultimately settled on this, the North did not want this compromise, arguing thatenslaved people were 'property', not 'persons', as they wanted to weaken the hold over national politics by states like Virginia. However, under pressure from the South, which wanted enslaved people to be counted in the population in order to boost their federal representation, this compromise was brought in. Otherwise, the ratification process could not have taken place to implement this Constitution.

Another significant compromise was over enumerated versus implied powers. The framers of the Constitution wanted it to be applicable under all circumstances, including those faced by future generations, and therefore it was ensured that it could be changed or modified. Article I, Section Eight, termed the Necessary and Proper Clause, permits expansion of the federal government's powers. However, this proved to be controversial and it was deemed necessary to limit the powers of the federal government while protecting the states' rights; this led to the 10th amendment, termed the Reserved Powers Clause, which states: 'The Powers not delegated to the United States by the Constitution, nor prohibited by it to the states, are reserved to the states respectively, or to the people.' This clause has generated controversy about whether the federal government has implied or enumerated powers. The confusion has led the US to the

Civil War and numerous conflicts between the states and between states and the federal government.³

The **Commerce and Enslaved Person Trade Compromise** was brought in, which gave Congress the power, by majority vote, and the right to regulate both external and internal commerce and with the Indigenous groups, except that the enslavement trade would not be prohibited (for twenty years) till 1808. There would not be any tax or duty levied on articles exported from any state.

During the ratification of the Constitution, supporters of the Constitution inserted a statement that ratification by nine states should be sufficient for establishing a constitution between the states so ratifying. In the Articles of Confederation constitution, the concurrence of all thirteen states for a constitutional amendment was required. Another significant fact was that the ratification process was conducted by elected conventions rather than by the legislature or popular vote to expedite the ratification process. Those favouring the Constitution's ratification were called **Federalists**, and those who opposed came to be known as the **Anti-Federalists**. As initially adopted, the Constitution consisted of a preamble and seven articles containing four thousand words.

The following were the **basic principles of the Constitution**:

(*i*) Popular sovereignty: Every state in the Union would have a republican form of government.⁴
(*ii*) Separation of powers: Legislative powers would remain with Congress, which would have two houses—the Senate and the House of Representatives. Executive powers were to be vested in the President of the USA, and judicial powers with the Supreme Court and other courts established by Congress.
(*iii*) Federalism: Powers vested with Congress were enumerated, and the powers not so delegated were reserved (residual) for the states.
(*iv*) Limited government: Sections 9 and 10 imposed specific limitations on national and state governments.
(v) Supremacy of national law: The Constitution and national government would be supreme within their delegated authority.

The new Constitution had strong ties of interdependence between states. Each state had two votes in the Upper House, as well as votes in the Lower House as per population. Congress now required a simple majority to pass any legislation, with the President having veto power. The new Constitution had the President appointed according to the constitutional provisions. Commerce and trade now came to be controlled by Congress, and it also had the power to pass and regulate taxes. A hierarchy of federal courts was established, with the Supreme Court at the top. The provision for a constitutional amendment is still rigorous but simplified, and more powers are now given to Congress than ever before.

Nature of the American Constitution

According to George Bancroft, a historian of the Nationalist School, the American Constitution symbolised the crowning success of the movement for a more popular government that had begun with the American Revolution. As we have discussed, John Fiske believed that the Articles of Confederation Constitution created a 'critical period' of conflicts between the centre and states, between states and states, along with economic depression and problems between the national government and foreign nations.

Progressive historians consider the American Constitution a 'reactionary' document written by the Conservatives to thwart the Radicals, who held more liberal views and had visions of completely reforming American society. Formulating the American Constitution represented class conflicts along economic lines. They went on to show how the Constitution was framed by elite men who wanted to protect their property rights. Therefore, it also represented a struggle between the upper and lower classes, and between 'real' property, public figures, and creditors versus debtors, commercial and agricultural classes. The first Progressive historian to critically analyse the American Constitution was Charles Beard, who, in *An Economic Interpretation of the Constitution of the United States*, examined the economic holdings of the framers of the Constitution.[5] He advanced a hypothesis that the events leading up to the Federal Convention of 1787 mirrored a long-standing split in American society that extended from the colonial period to the revolutionary era—a class conflict between the rich and poor, farmers and merchants, debtors and creditors, and owners of natural wealth and paper wealth. In short, Charles Beard viewed the period between the 1760s and 1780s as an 'internal class conflict'.

Charles Beard argued that the Constitution may be better interpreted in terms of the interests and attitudes of a specific economic group rather than political abstractions. After making a person-by-person study of the economic holdings of the Constitution's framers, Beard showed that most of these men owned more fluid forms of capital—money, public securities, or investments in manufacturing, shipping, and commerce—than most of the population, who instead held capital in the form of land or owned no property at all. Beard then advanced the hypothesis that the framers, bound together by a community of economic interests, sought to provide better protection for their specific property holdings through the Constitution.

Beard's thesis implied that the federal Constitution could be considered a 'counter-revolution', a claim that gained strength when he pointed out that the Convention had no mandate to draft a new Constitution. This interpretation received even more support when Charles and Mary Beard published the first volume of *The Rise of American Civilization* in 1927, a book in which they discussed both the Revolution and the Constitution. Beard presented the Revolution as a dual moment. On the one hand, it was a colonial rebellion against the British, caused mainly by a clash of economic interests between the growing colonies and the parent country. At the same time, it was an internal revolution to determine which of America's social classes would rule at home. According to Charles and Mary Beard, the Revolution resulted in a victory for the popular forces in American society, primarily comprised of rural interests. They wrote the democratic Articles of Confederation to preserve the political and economic rights they had sought throughout the colonial period. However, in the 1780s, the conservative elements in American society checked this tendency toward democracy by framing the federal Constitution to protect their specific property interests. The Constitution, in this view, represented a repudiation of the Revolution, and instead introduced points of 'conflict' and 'discontinuity' in American society.

The Constitution was, therefore, an 'economic document' drawn by men whose property interests were at stake. The framing of the American Constitution consisted of two fundamental parts—one positive and the other negative. The positive part comprised four great powers conferred on the new national government: taxation, war, commercial control, and disposition of western lands. This meant that the manufacturing class would benefit from the imposition of protective tariffs; trading and shipping groups would no longer face foreign competition, and for the money groups that gave money on loans, there was ample scope for making huge profits.

The negative part placed the burden of ratification on the states. According to Beard, only about a fourth of adult White men were eligible to vote, as the right to vote was based on property rights. Therefore, the group that voted for the ratification of the Constitution had an economic interest in manufacturing, mercantile, and public security. They represented the same strata of men who had attended the Philadelphia Convention earlier. The opposition to the Constitution came from agrarian classes and people in debt. In other words, Beard's interpretation of the American Constitution as an economic document is based on three propositions:

(*i*) The Philadelphia Convention consisted of Federalists, a consolidated economic group whose property interests were at stake. The members of this group were scattered throughout America, especially in regions where manufacturing, mercantile, and public securities were the focus of earning capital profits.

(*ii*) The Contest over Ratification (first proposition): The ultimate test of the validity of an economic interpretation of the Constitution would be based upon comparative analysis of the economic interests of all persons voting against ratification. He analysed the economic interests of some of the leaders in the movement for ratification. He concluded that ratification was reflective of conflict between property interests on the one hand and small farming and debtor interests on the other.

(*iii*) The Contest over Ratification (second proposition): Public securities were a dynamic element within the ratification process.

Charles Beard's '**economism**' highlighted the difference between aristocrats and democrats as an addition to 'internal class conflict'. Neo-Progressive historian Merrill Jenson continued with this tradition. In his two works, *The Articles of Confederation*[6] and *The New Nation*,[7] Jensen agreed with Beard that the Constitution was a counter-revolutionary document. He presented a progressive analysis of its role in the history of American democracy. The revolutionary period was a struggle between 'radicals' and 'conservatives'. The radicals under the Articles of Confederation established local self-government within the states; therefore, radicals were Democrats who supported state sovereignty. The conservatives were aristocrats and nationalists. The Declaration of Independence and Articles of Confederation represented radical ideals, while the conservatives framed the Constitution. Jensen's interpretation was challenged by Cecilia Kenyon, who stated that anti-Federalists 'were not latter-day democrats' and had no desire to establish 'majority' rule as the main factor for establishing government.[8]

Jackson Turner Main considered the struggle over the Constitution as a fight within each state between two cohesive 'parties' divided along socio-economic and geographical lines.[9] These parties were the commercial cosmopolitans on the one hand, and agrarian localists on the other. He, therefore, highlighted differences between political interests and political rhetoric. E. J. Ferguson emphasised the clash between mercantile capitalists and agrarian classes over the issue of public finance.[10] For Forrest McDonald, there were pluralistic political and economic interests at work rather than polarised interests at the local, state, and regional levels.[11]

Another progressive interpretation came from Gordon Wood in *Creation of the American Republic*, where he wrote that it was wrong to assume that the Constitution was a struggle between economic lines; it was a 'social conflict'.[12] The revolutionary era represented a popular challenge to the right of the elite to govern the ordinary people without their participation, which led to the Revolution. Therefore, according to Wood, the Constitution was an effort made by the elites to limit the power of the people, and the struggle over the ratification process was a struggle over democracy.

The problem with the progressive interpretation was that it focused disproportionately on the ideological differences between the Federalists and anti-Federalists. Wood's analysis highlighted the need to study political ideas, as the period between the Articles of Confederation and the Constitution represented shifts in political thought and classical political philosophy in America, from the Revolutionary period to the constitutional ratification period.

Neo-Conservative historians considered the Constitution to be evidence of a consensus among Americans. The revolutionary and constitutional periods represent a line of continuous growth. Benjamin F. Wright[13] considered the Constitution as a political document that was based on an existing consensus among the 'American people'. For Wright, the Constitution fulfilled the demands of revolutionary ideology as the same men who held public office in 1776 and led the Revolution continued in the same posts even in 1787. The political ideas of the Revolution were expressed in state constitutions, whose framers were the same men who had drafted the Declaration of Independence earlier. Robert E. Brown held that American society was democratic as the majority consisted of small farmers who owned enough land to qualify for the right to vote.[14] Therefore, the Constitution was a consensus document and represented the wishes of a democratically minded, broad middle class. Brown also studied the property-holdings of the Constitution framers and concluded that the framers had more capital invested in land and real estate than in securities. This evidence contradicts Beard's supposition that the framers had written the document to protect their personal property in securities from those who held land and real estate, and additionally challenged Beard's finding that a majority of Americans could not vote (and therefore could not participate in political processes). Henry Steel Commager considered the Constitution primarily a political document, focusing on the problem of federalism, and not an economic document. He characterised the constitutional period as a 'constructive' era.[15]

New Intellectual historians proposed an ideological interpretation of the American Constitution by placing the writing of the

Constitution within an Anglo-American framework. J. G. A. Pocock showed how the founders followed classical republicanism and believed that doing 'public good' was the exclusive purpose of republican government.[16] This process required the sacrifice of individual interests for the more significant needs of the whole. Therefore, the Constitution was not a conflict or an economic document, but was a by-product of 'republican synthesis'. According to Gary Schmitt and Robert Webking, all Americans were concerned with protecting their private property rights, and their differences were minor.[17] For both Joyce Appleby[18] and Isaac Kramnick,[19] the period was marked by efforts to teach individualism, pluralism, and competitive capitalism to be applied to introduce liberal ideals.

New Left historians were critical of Neo-Conservatives, New Intellectual and Neo-Progressive historians. According to W. A. Williams, the American Revolution represented the triumph of mercantilism, and therefore the Constitution represented a mercantilist outlook; it provided the foundation for a national system of economies and politics that called for a constantly expanding American empire, resulting in the expansion of the American frontier in the nineteenth-century through westward expansion. S. Lynd agreed with Beard that the Constitution represented a clash over economic issues between those who owned property and enslaved people and those who did not. The clash resulted in a second American Revolution, the Civil War, to settle the problem.[20] According to Max M. Edling, the anti-Federalist opposition to the Constitution was rooted in a distrust of central government, which they feared would lead America down the same path as the European nations.[21]

Merrill Jensen situates the question of whether the confederation constitution should be considered the 'critical period' in American history in terms of simultaneous processes of progress and backsliding in some areas.[22] Forrest McDonald has termed it a period of development. Michael Limisch suggests that Federalists created the 'critical period' myth to get the New Constitution ratified. According to Herbert Storing, even for anti-Federalists, the period was so precarious that they finally agreed to ratification.[23] Regarding the problem of **sectionalism**, a term used to denote conflicting

The Formulation of the American Constitution 71

regional aspirations in the US, Peter Onuf[24] traced two contradictory impulses: the expansion of centralised authority on the one hand, and reinforcement of state sovereignty on the other. Therefore, the issue of jurisdictional disputes emerged as a sectional crisis, later culminating in the beginning of the Civil War.

Notes

1. L. H. Butterfield, ed., *The Adams Papers: Diary and Autobiography of John Adams*, vol. 2, 1771–1781 (Cambridge, 1981).
2. John Fiske, *The Critical Period of American History, 1783–1789* (Cambridge, 1888).
3. M. Kammen, ed., *The Origins of the American Constitution: A Documentary History* (New York, 1986).
4. The United States is a constitutional republic, a representative democracy in which eligible voters (the electorate) choose their representatives, and the government is legitimised based on the Constitution that articulates the country's system of government, its laws, and the rights of its citizens.
5. Charles A. Beard, *An Economic Interpretation of the Constitution of the United States* (New York, 1914).
6. Merrill Jensen, *The Articles of Confederation: An Interpretation of the Social-Constitutional History of the American Revolution, 1774–1781* (Wisconsin, 1940).
7. Merrill Jensen, *The New Nation: A History of the United States during the Confederation, 1781–1789* (Boston, 1981).
8. Cecilia M. Kenyon, *The Antifederalists* (Boston, 1985).
9. Jackson Turner Main, *The Social Structure of Revolutionary America* (Princeton, 1965)
10. E. J. Ferguson, *The Power of the Purse: A History of American Public Finance (1776–1790)*, (North Carolina, 1968).
11. Forrest McDonald, *Novus Ordo Seculorum: The Intellectual Origins of the Constitution* (Lawrence, 1985).
12. Gordon Wood, *Creation of the American Republic 1776–1787* (Chapel Hill, 1969).
13. Benjamin F. Wright, *Consensus and Continuity, 1776–1787* (New York, 1967).
14. Robert E. Brown, *Charles Beard and the Constitution: A Critical Analysis of an Economic Interpretation of the Constitution* (New York, 2007).
15. Henry Steel Commager, ed., *Selections from The Federalist: A Commentary on the Constitution of the United States* (Illinois, 1985).
16. J. G. A. Pocock, *The Machiavellian Moment: Florentine Republican Thought and the Atlantic Republican Tradition* (Princeton, 1975).

17. Gary J. Schmitt and Robert H. Webking, 'Revolutionaries, Antifederalists, and Federalists: Comments on Godon Wood's Understanding of the American Founding, *The Political Science Reviewer 9* (Fall), (1979).

18. Joyce O. Appleby, *Capitalism and a New Social Order: The Republican Vision of the 1790s* (New York, 1984).

19. Isaac Kramnick, *Republicanism and Bourgeois Radicalism: Political Ideology in Late Eighteenth-Century England and America* (New York, 1990)

20. S. Lynd, ed., *Class Conflict, Slavery, and the United States Constitution* (Cambridge, 2009).

21. Max M. Edling, *A Revolution in Favor of Government: Origins of the US Constitution and the Making of the American State* (New York, 2008).

22. Merrill Jensen, *The Articles of Confederation*.

23. Herbert Storing, *What the Anti-Federalists Were For: The Political Thought of the Opponents of the Constitution* (Chicago, 2008). See also Bernard Bailyn and Gordon Wood, 'The Constitution: Conflict or Consensus?', in Grob, Gerald and Billias, ed., *Interpretations of American History: Patterns and Perspectives*, 3rd edition, vol. 1 (New York, 1978), pp. 145–167.

24. Peter S. Onuf, 'Reflections on the Founding: Constitutional Hustoriography in Bicentennial Perspective', *William and Mary Quarterly 46*, 3rd series (1989).

CHAPTER 3

Thomas Jefferson and Jeffersonian Democracy

In 1789, George Washington became the first President of the United States of America. His tenure as President reflected the dominance of the **Federalist Party** (formed by Alexander Hamilton), and in 1797 another Federalist, John Adams, won the election. From this period till 1801, Washington and Adams attempted to impose a federal taxation system to boost the economy's growth, aiming to leverage the potential for rapid industrialisation and urbanisation, at a time when an overwhelming majority of the nation's population lived in rural areas. It was in the 1800 election that Thomas Jefferson—an important political leader who had formed the **Democratic-Republicans** along with James Madison in the 1790s—became President of the United States. During the election, Jefferson pledged to establish an '**empire for liberty**' that would bring 'democratic ideology' into federal politics; his policies led to a temporary decline of banking and corporate institutions. The **1807 Embargo Act**, which aimed to protect the young republic from predatory and more established players in the world markets, was another step in this direction.[1]

From 1800 to 1820, the US doubled its land area and survived a scheme by former Vice President Aaron Burr to divide the Union.[2] The period also saw the Embargo and Non-Intercourse Acts, whereby the US stopped all its trade with Europe in order to avoid war with Britain and France. In 1812, it did in fact go to war with Britain and nearly lost; however, it managed to conclude with a peace treaty that was more favourable to it than to Britain. Soon after, the Union saw a near disintegration over the question of whether the practice of slavery would be allowed in the newly organised state of Missouri. The process of gradual territorial expansion began during this period and culminated in the continental expansion of the Union from the Atlantic to the Pacific Ocean.

The Washington and Adams Years

Federalists dominated in the first two Presidential elections, and their policies were markedly influenced by Adam Smith's philosophy of free trade and commerce. Therefore, the federal government began to formulate laws and policies to promote the growth and expansion of capitalism, which encouraged the development of a business acumen based on self-interest. Simultaneously, Britain's industrial revolution was underway, which now required a supply of cotton and agricultural products from America. Before 1800, only Philadelphia, Charleston, and the Chesapeake Bay regions catered to external markets. Most American farmers lived on a subsistence economy, as the cost of transporting staple crops to the coastal areas was very high. The shift came with the introduction of steam engines for both boats and railways, reducing transportation costs and assisting American farmers in moving towards single-crop production or monocropping. Moreover, the rise of liberal Republicans like Hamilton and the Federalists, who were promoting manufacturing and trade (by funding roads, bridges, and canals) and finance (by developing the National Bank), strengthened the federal government and forged a sense of American liberty. These economic transformations brought many political questions into the open.[3]

Jefferson opposed the federal government's interventions in the American economy, based on the political argument that the Constitution did not grant the federal government any powers to promote federal economic development. Therefore, he was also critical of the push towards earning capital and promoting materialism, which the Federalists sought to achieve by opening up internal and external markets and undertaking internal improvements to bring about economic integration. The Federalist-led economic policy also included heavy taxes on farmers, who would lean towards commercial or cash crop production, making them dependent on market forces.[4]

Jeffersonian Republicanism

American historians generally associate the **Jeffersonian era** with democracy, agrarianism, and supremacy of state rights. **Jeffersonian Republicans** were a political group that represented ordinary people, especially the small farmers; they were against a strong central government and the rise of corporate power; they favoured egalitarianism among settlers and were sympathetic to the spirit of the French Revolution. These factors have led some to call Jefferson's presidency the '**Revolution of 1800**'. The 'Jeffersonian Age' has been interpreted as a continuous struggle between the democratic aspirations of the ordinary people and the despotism of the upper classes. The Jeffersonian Republicans are popularly seen as forbearers of the democratic spirit, which later led to Jacksonian ideology, Populism, Progressivism, and the New Deal.

The first two presidents of this political group, Jefferson and James Madison, viewed politics on a grand scale—it was a process of transforming philosophical ideas into reality, rather than simply a pragmatic exercise to accommodate the needs of a diverse population. Moreover, this was the first time that political power was transferred between Federalists and Republicans, and therefore, every issue created friction between the two political parties. Both Jefferson and Madison had to strategise and gain widespread acceptance of specific baseline rules to run the new government.

In 1774, as a legislator in the state of Virginia, Jefferson had written 'A Summary View of the Rights of British America'. He had represented Virginia at the Continental Congress meeting in Philadelphia in 1775 and was the primary author of the Declaration of Independence in 1776. He served in Congress till 1782 and explored the questions of commercial navigation, land survey, and sale, which led to the Northwest Ordinance of 1785. Jefferson had also served as American ambassador to France in 1785 and was influenced by French ideas of justice and civility. Before becoming the President, Jefferson was Governor of Virginia, Secretary of State under George Washington, and Vice President of the US under John Adams.

According to Jefferson, the worst government was one that undermined popular liberty. He believed that the imposition of the whisky tax, creation of a standing army, and appointment of corrupt officials had made the federal government 'masters' and not 'servants' of the people. State governments, in his view, should retain authority in a vast republic marked by strong local attachments, as they were more responsive to the popular will than the federal government. Popular liberty required **popular virtue**, which meant placing the public good ahead of one's private interest and exercising vigilance to keep governments from growing out of control. Jefferson felt that educated farmers, who were accustomed to acting and thinking with independent mindsets, were the most virtuous, whereas cities were a menace to liberty as they were marked by mobs, poverty, and disparity.

Jefferson described his election as a 'revolution' and attempted to reverse an alleged drift towards despotism. For example, he was alarmed by the growth of the national debt by 10 million dollars under the Federalists. While Alexander Hamilton had argued that by giving creditors a financial stake in the federal government's health, the national debt would strengthen that government, Jefferson repealed whiskey and excise taxes (that is, internal taxes) and reduced the national debt immediately after his appointment, although he continued with tariff duties.

From the beginning, Jefferson had opposed Hamilton's financial plan to set up the **First Bank of the USA** and the policy to take on and consolidate the states' wartime debt at the federal level. Both Jefferson and Secretary of the Treasury Albert Gallatin articulated their views thus: To pay interests on debt, taxes would have to be imposed; these taxes would suck money from farmers, who were the backbone of the Republicans, and put it in the hands of wealthy creditors. The latter were parasites that lived off interest payments. The Federalist economic policy, he argued, created a new capitalist class, failed to compensate ordinary soldiers and small farmers (who were the original note-holders), and favoured financiers and manufacturers. They also feared that tax revenue would tempt the government to build another 'menace' to liberty—a strong standing army.

Overall, the policies encouraged a powerful federal government at the expense of state powers, and this, Jefferson contended, made George Washington and John Adams' governments more monarchical than republican. Instead of people's sovereignty, powers were concentrated in the hands of the rich. Jefferson also opposed the 'despotic' **Alien and Sedition Acts (1798)** passed by John Adams. It is worth noting that Jefferson, who had drafted the Declaration of Independence, and James Madison, authored key author of the Constitution, had declared at the time of the implementation of these Acts that the states had the right to treat any act of the National Congress as unconstitutional and non-operative if it went against their interests; this position was formalised in the **Kentucky and Virginia Resolutions of 1798** (South Carolina later used this rationale to secede from the Union).[5]

Policies of Thomas Jefferson

In his inaugural speech, Jefferson promised to provide equal justice and civil liberties to all Americans, irrespective of their political or religious affiliations. He believed in relying on the police rather than the military to maintain internal peace. As we have already discussed, Jefferson pursued a reduction in public expenditure and payment of debt. He encouraged agricultural economy and commerce, aiming to make the US an 'agrarian paradise'. According to Peter S. Onuf, Jefferson did not necessarily favour republicanism over 'federalism'; instead, he sought to establish a sound government that could guarantee individual citizens' liberty and natural rights.

Jefferson repealed internal taxes, but now the federal government was dependent on revenue from the tariff, which was inadequate to pay off national debt. Therefore, the second step was to cut federal expenditure, and for this purpose, American embassies in Madrid, Lisbon, and Hague were closed down. The strength of the standing army was reduced from 4,000 to 2,500, and he declared peace with the pirates of Tripoli, a piratical seafaring Barbary State on the north coast of Africa. The treaty with Tripoli pirates was meant to protect the nationalist and economic interests of America.

Judiciary

While in principle Jefferson supported non-partisan appointments to the judiciary, his policies were influenced by the fact that by 1800, there was no Republican judge on the federal Bench. Jefferson opposed the **Judiciary Act of 1801** as it would reduce the number of justices in the Supreme Court from six to five, which meant that Jefferson could not nominate a judge. The judiciary would therefore remain under the control of the Federalists. The Act also transferred many court cases from the states to the federal courts, strengthening the federal government, which went against Jeffersonian principles, as the federal courts were furthest removed from popular consent. The appointment of Federalist judges was also unacceptable since partisan appointments violated the principles of natural justice. Jefferson also opposed the timing of the selection of these judges by John Adams.

These arguments against the Judiciary Act raised important concerns. The Federalists dominated the Federal Court, which had passed the Alien and Sedition Acts. All of John Adams' '**midnight appointments**' were prominent Federalists; one was a loyalist during the Revolutionary War, and three were brothers or brothers-in-law of John Marshall, the Chief Justice, who was himself a Federalist. For Jefferson, an independent judiciary needed to be established by balancing appointments, which led Congressional Republicans to repeal the Judiciary Act of 1801 in his first term.

THE *MARBURY V. MADISON* CASE

This case arose out of the 'midnight appointment' of William Marbury by John Adams, just days before the end of his Presidential term. Jefferson refused to allow Secretary of State James Madison to issue Marbury an appointment letter, arguing that the appointment was void since the formalities had not been completed during Adams's term. When this matter went to the Supreme Court in 1803, Chief Justice John Marshall ruled that the Court could not compel Madison to deliver the commission. The Supreme Court did issue a writ of mandamus (which Marbury had sought), relying on its powers as per the Judiciary Act of 1789, and it ruled that withholding the appointment letter was unconstitutional. Therefore, in his judgment, John Marshall clarified that Madison's 'moral duty' was to deliver the commission to Marbury. However, the same Constitution had also not given powers to the Supreme Court to compel the government to issue the letter. Jefferson, in principle, agreed that the courts, like any other branch of government, have the right to judicial review over legislative or executive actions. However, he resented Marshall's assertion that Madison was morally obliged to issue the commission letter to Marbury. In American constitutional law, this is considered a landmark judgment as it led to the establishment of the process of judicial review, which gave the Supreme Court the authority to invalidate laws passed by Congress that it found to be unconstitutional. The case established the American judiciary as an equal branch of government and significantly impacted the American legal system.

In the next step, Jefferson attempted to remove John Pickering of the New Hampshire District Court, who was impeached on the grounds of alcoholism and announcing unlawful rulings in court.[6] However, this success was marred by the case of Samuel Chase in 1804–05, who was a staunch supporter of the Federalists and had jailed many Republicans by enforcing the Sedition Act of 1798. He was one of the midnight appointees of John Adams, but Jefferson could not get a two-thirds majority in the House of Representatives for his removal. In this way, Jefferson challenged Federalists' use of judicial powers for political goals. Jefferson tried to make the judiciary more responsive to the popular will by challenging a pair of judges whose behaviour had been outrageous. Despite these developments, the Federalists did not see a conflict between protecting the Constitution and advancing their party's cause.

Legislation Concering Land

In 1785, a minimum of 640 acres of land was given at US $1 per acre with no credit. The federal government attempted to secure revenue without providing any advantage to small farmers. In 1786, a minimum of 640 acres of land was given at US $2 per acre, and for the first time, a credit facility was introduced. In 1800, a minimum of 320 acres was given along with a credit facility for four years for the rapid settlement of westward territories and to provide an advantage to small farmers. In 1804, about 160 acres of land were given with better credit facilities. These liberal land acts stimulated more people to move towards the western region and resulted in the admission of Ohio as a new state in 1803.

Louisiana Purchase

The territory of Louisiana was situated near Lower Mississippi. A French colony was established here in 1718, and in 1723, New Orleans, named after Philippe Duc d'Orléans, became the capital of Louisiana controlled by the French. Americans controlled the eastern half of this area, including three new states: Kentucky, Tennessee, and Ohio. In 1803, it was purchased by the US federal government for US $15,000,000, but boundaries next to the Spanish colonies of Florida and Texas were not defined. Jefferson was committed to establishing an 'empire for liberty' covering the northern and southern states, not by conquest but by the 'inevitable' expansion of 'free' and 'virtuous' American people. The territorial expansion would allow for the growth of American farmers, who were the backbone of the Republicans and, in the eyes of Jefferson, the true guardians of liberty. Federalists opposed the Louisiana Purchase because it was felt that it would decrease the relative importance of their strongholds on the eastern seaboard. The federal government sent Lewis and Clark's expedition to survey the region under American control, stimulating the rapid westward expansion of US boundaries.

FIG. 3.1: *Hoisting American Colors, Louisiana Cession, 1803*, by Thure de Thulstrup, oil on canvas (1902)
Source: Wikimedia Commons.

The **Louisiana Purchase** reflected the gradual republicanisation of the lands beyond the Mississippi River. Jefferson was aware of the constitutional ambiguity in the move. He initially believed that a constitutional amendment should be enacted to include more territories within the US, instead of the federal government taking the decision unilaterally. However, ultimately he negotiated the purchase without any such legislation.

In acquiring this territory, Jefferson showed an eagerness to possess the land, rather than a principled will to apply republican concepts. His vision of westward expansion that could only apply to a population adopting eastern American values of republicanism, and therefore, Jeffersonian democracy had no place for the Indigenous people (the original peoples), who were a hindrance in his scheme of making the nation an 'empire for liberty'. The acquisition of Louisiana set the tone for developing the '**Manifest Destiny**' theory. Even though the Louisiana Purchase was between France and the USA, much of this land was at that point inhabited by Indigenous communities, who were systematically removed as White American settlers moved into the region. As we shall discuss in Chapter 5, the policy of expansion under Jefferson was part of the broader process of marginalisation and dispossession of Indigenous groups.

When the Presidential elections of 1804 were announced, Jefferson, who had doubled US territory and taken steps to pay off debts, had no political opponent. The country remained internally and externally at peace, guiding Jefferson to another electoral triumph.

Aaron Burr Conspiracy

The **12th Constitutional Amendment** provided separate and distinct ballots in the electoral colleges for President and Vice President. This amendment robbed Aaron Burr of the chance to be nominated for the post of President as he was convicted of two criminal acts—the first of these was the murder of Alexander Hamilton in a duel in 1804. The reason behind this murder was an alleged Federalist plot: they had planned to put up the candidature of Aaron Burr for Governorship of New York, who would then announce secession from the Union and join Canada by taking away New York and New England. It was Alexander Hamilton who exposed this plan, and this led to animosity, ultimately resulting in Hamilton's death. The second was after his electoral failure. Aaron Burr plotted to separate the western states from the Union by establishing a new government, and to achieve this goal, he even requested England and France for assistance. He was also accused of conspiring with James Wilkinson (the military governor of Louisiana) to separate the western states into an independent confederacy south of the Ohio River. This case was brought before Chief Justice John Marshall in 1807, who acquitted Burr due to lack of concrete evidence of treason. Aaron Burr's trial established an important precedent: For a conviction to take place, overt acts of treason must be proved.

Problems with Britain and France

From 1793 to 1815, Britain and France were embroiled first in the French Revolutionary Wars and then in the Napoleonic Wars. America took advantage of this war by supplying commodities that the two warring nations required, thereby making immense commercial gains. Americans devised a method based on re-export trade or '**broken voyage**'. Under this system, American ships brought goods from the French and Spanish West Indies to American ports, unloaded and passed them through customs, and reloaded and re-exported them to Europe as American produce. This procedure reduced the prices of British commodities, especially from the British West Indies. In 1805, however, Britain passed the **Essex Decision** that prevented American ships from supplying commodities from the French West Indies to France and stopped the system of broken voyage. Britain then began to seize ships violating its laws. This tension culminated in the *Chesapeake–Leopard* **Affair** on 22 June 1807. The *Chesapeake* was an American warship captured by the British warship, the *Leopard*, which led to further deterioration in the relations between the two nations. Britain also ordered the blockade of European port nations and forbade any neutral trade with France or her allies. On the other hand, France also issued the **Berlin Decrees in 1806**, which put in place a blockade of the British Isles. This was followed by the **Milan Decree in 1807**, whereby no neutral ships were allowed, and under which France confiscated many American ships.

When both European countries failed to respect American neutrality, Jefferson passed the **Non-Intercourse Act of 1809**, which stopped the importation of goods from England that could be bought elsewhere. This act was meant to put US pressure on Britain to accept American neutrality, but brought no concessions. Jefferson passed the **Embargo Act of 1807** after the *Chesapeake–Leopard* Affair. The Act prohibited ships from leaving American ports for foreign ports, resulting in many American seamen being out of work, merchants going bankrupt as exports were banned, and pushing many farmers into debt. The New England and Massachusetts shipping industries were particularly severely affected. Jefferson's foreign policy aimed to make the world accept the US trade policy of 'free commerce with all nations; political connections with none'. He firmly believed in 'commercial equality among nations', and this held true for him regardless of whether the US was equal to the European powers in military, political, and economic terms.[7]

Assessments of the Jeffersonian Age

It is due to these broad patterns that many nineteenth-century American historians wrote with an anti-Jefferson slant. Jefferson was seen to be primarily responsible for rising tensions on the issue of slavery, and therefore for precipitating the **American Civil War of 1861**. However, new perspectives emerged in the twentieth century, when historians from the Progressive School, including Charles A. Beard, Claude G. Brown, and V. L. Parrington, presented three new interpretations of the Jeffersonian period:

(*i*) Jeffersonian democracy was marked by the transfer of power from the capitalist classes to the agricultural masses.
(*ii*) It signalled the rise of popular forces against class-based despotism.
(*iii*) Jefferson represented a liberal and idealistic tradition against the conservative and materialistic forces of the Federalist era.

According to **Consensus historian** Richard Hofstadter, there was an essential agreement between Jefferson and the Federalists on the rights of property, the philosophy of economic individualism, the value of competition, and the economic virtues of capitalist culture.

The Federalists and Anti-Federalists adopted a middle-of-the-road approach that served the American nation. There was no 'Revolution of 1800', and Jefferson's electoral triumph represented only a change of leadership. Intellectual historians (who, as we have seen, focused on the role of ideas in influencing significant historical developments in the US) believed that Jefferson borrowed many ideas from the French Revolution and the English Enlightenment, and that these became the basis of his political policies.

According to New Political historians, 'the 1800s' represented a struggle between Federalists and Anti-Federalists. The early nineteenth century was an age of social conflict between different American groups—aristocrats versus democrats, rich versus poor—and, therefore, it was an age of political development in which the 'old school' was represented by Alexander Hamilton and George Washington, who had participated in the American Revolution and then 'stood for' office. The 'new school' was defined by Jefferson, who 'ran' for office and wanted the support of the common masses to win the election.

According to New Intellectual historians like J. G. A. Pocock, the '1800 Revolution' was not a forward-looking event that ushered America into a brave new liberal, capitalistic world. Instead, the revolution was a backwards-looking movement as Jefferson feared modernity and wished to bring back the medieval age. On the other hand, according to Joyce Appleby, Jefferson was a champion of capitalism and commercialism, which helped to bring about a new social order during this period. Richard Buel believes that different attitudes towards the role of public opinion in formulating government policy separated Jefferson from the former Federalists. Jefferson believed in accepting public opinion in the government's decision-making process.

Comparative historians like William N. Chambers opined that Jefferson's election brought about the rise of two-party system in American politics. America was touted as the first nation to invent the modern political party in world history. According to Robert R. Palmer, America was developing its two-party system at a time when monarchs ruled the Western world. For this reason, Jefferson also supported the French Revolution.

Conclusion

Jeffersonian democracy invokes America's idealised self-image as a land of human liberty and a manifestation of the specific political philosophy reflected in representative democracy. Nonetheless, Jeffersonian political philosophy stands in contrast with Jefferson's moderate actions in office. He faced several internal and external crises, and overcoming them took specific, sometimes controversial, steps, ultimately establishing a set of precedents. His showdown with the courts over political appointments tested his partisan resolve and adherence to the Constitution. The kidnapping of American seamen by Tripoli pirates and the seizure of American ships by Britain reflected America's lack of military readiness and challenged the Jeffersonian doctrine of peace and principled diplomacy. As a philosopher, Jefferson advocated personal humility, reserve, and belief in small government. However, these did not necessarily align with his actions in office.

The Jeffersonian concept of democracy was based on a belief in the liberal democratic framework and John Locke's idea of individual freedom from government interference. Jefferson believed in liberty from the federal government's usurpation of local and democratic sovereignty. The emphasis was on a small-scale, participatory republic's ability to protect individual rights and liberties and not form a highly centralised government. Freedom and liberty, in this framework, meant the individual's involvement in creating the society of which the individual was a natural part. Moreover, Jefferson was an advocate of freedom of religion and freedom of the press. Where the former was essential to understanding religious truths, the latter assisted in enlightening the mind, granting freedom from arbitrary rule and freedom to shape one's social destiny. These were necessary to create a decent and intelligent American citizen who would, in turn, create a harmonious society and a just state.

Jefferson also evolved the concept of citizenship virtues to establish economically independent, educated, and active democratic citizens who he believed were 'virtuous' in both the practical and moral sense. He wished the US to be a land of 'virtuous' individuals who would come together to benefit the common good, and he believed in protecting individuals' natural rights and securing life, liberty, and property rights. He supported a constitutional amendment to the Bill of Rights to develop man's public nature and political life, which extends beyond one's private interests.

Jefferson's supporters were small farmers, artisans, and workers, and he was against aristocratic privileges. He was supported by both enslavers and non-enslavers, despite opposing his moral opposition to the institution of slavery. He advocated its eventual abolition, as it was against the natural rights of liberty and contradicted the principles of equality enshrined in the Declaration of Independence. However, he considered enslaved people to be inferior to White people in terms of 'endowments of both body and mind' and wanted to send them back to Africa; further, he remained an enslaver all his life. This dichotomy prevented him from including emancipation in his democratic political agenda; it was also the case that slavery had not as yet become a sectional issue in American politics. Jefferson made the role of the Presidency more democratic and less ceremonial than his Federalist predecessors. Jefferson pursued a policy of geographic and commercial expansionism to propagate the agrarian philosophy of the Democratic-Republican Party. He created an 'Empire of Liberty' and doubled the area of the USA as he believed that agrarian Republicans would keep the nation youthful, vigorous, and healthy. Jefferson aimed to establish an agrarian republic based on territorial expansion to bring in more agricultural lands and to prepare the ground for a market revolution to usher in commercial development. On this premise, he had imposed both the Embargo and Non-Importation Acts that would assist in commercial expansion. However, these actions did not yield the expected results and exposed Jefferson's major weakness.

On the other hand, American diplomacy during the Continental War revealed a different aspect. It demonstrated that American ships could trade with almost all parts of the world, a testament to the nation's newfound political independence from Britain. However, the lack of diplomatic and military strength to fully protect their commercial interests was also apparent. This era was not just a period of transformative changes. It was a time that set several significant political precedents, shaping the course of the nation's history. Yet, these changes also led to the expansion of the institution of slavery and the rise of sectional politics in the country.

Notes

1. See Gordon S. Wood, *Empire for Liberty: A History of Early Republic, 1789–1815* (New York, 2009), pp. 13–15.
2. See Roger G. Kennedy, *Burr, Hamilton and Jefferson: A Study in Character* (New York, 2000).
3. See Allen C. Guelzo, *Fateful Lightning: A New History of the Civil War and Reconstruction* (New York, 2012), pp. 13–15.
4. See Guelzo, *Fateful Lightning*, p. 15.
5. See Guelzo, *Fateful Lightning*, p. 8.
6. See Art II.S4.4.3, 'Jurisprudence on Impeachable Offenses (1789–1860)', available at https://constitution.congress.gov (accessed June 2025).
7. Melvin I. Urofsky, *The American Presidents* (New York and London, 2000).

CHAPTER 4

Andrew Jackson and the Emergence of a New Political Ethos

Andrew Jackson, the seventh President of the United States (1829–1837), was an immensely controversial figure whose term continues to be a subject of fierce academic debate. Variously characterised as a 'saviour' or a 'tyrant', the war hero 'Old Hickory' or the 'chief architect of genocide', he was driven by a unique interpretation of democracy. Jackson's preference for 'majoritarianism' over liberal democracy or democracy (that is, democratic republicanism) was evident in his inaugural address, a critical moment that set the tone for his presidency:

> The first principle of our system [is] that the majority is to govern.

Jackson was born on 15 March 1767 in South Carolina. Orphaned by age 14, he later studied law and lived in the western province of Tennessee. In 1791, he was appointed by President Washington as a district attorney. Here, he learned that popular will and the practical realities of 'squatter's rights' and frontier experiences were constantly at odds with the duly-constituted legal authority. After unsuccessfully trying to become a judge, planter, and merchant, Jackson found his calling in the military, where he quickly became a hero. In the **War of 1812**, Jackson was an important leader (see Chapter 6, this volume). On 27 March 1814, he led the United States forces to victory in the **Battle of Tohopeka** (also called Horseshoe Bend), located in present-day Alabama, effectively ending the **Creek War**. On 8 January 1815, his forces won the **Battle of New Orleans** and turned away the British from Mississippi. In 1818, he undertook a military raid into Florida without proper sanction (the US had not declared war on Spain, which controlled the territory), and brought the region under US control.

Jackson's military achievements earned him the nickname 'Old Hickory'. Gradually, he began to emerge as a political force at the national level. It was increasingly difficult for the federal government to ignore Jackson. Still, it did not want to give him a significant post due to his controversial militaristic adventures as well as his 'uncivil behaviour'. He was finally made Governor of Florida; later, he stood from Tennessee to become a senator and retired in 1825 to aggressively pursue the presidency in 1828.[1]

Jackson had earlier contested the presidential elections of 1824. That year, he had finished first in the popular vote with 99 electoral votes, but fell short of a majority of electoral votes as required by the Constitution. In other words, the House of Representatives restricted him to third place. With 37 electoral votes, Henry Clay supported John Quincy Adams, who had secured 84 votes, and became the sixth president of the US. In return, John Quincy Adams appointed Henry Clay as the Secretary of State—this was termed by Jackson's supporters a 'corrupt bargain' that went against the popular will.

There were three overarching reasons for Jackson's success in 1828, when he defeated Adams with a 178 to 83 margin:

(*i*) Increased popular participation as more states moved towards expanding suffrage for White men (by removing restrictions based on property ownership)—Jackson had mass appeal among ordinary voters.

(*ii*) Instead of elites controlling American politics and voting patterns, urban classes, small farmers, and frontiersmen became increasingly prominent. Furthermore, this was termed as democratising American politics.

(*iii*) Jackson was also the first president who did not belong to Massachusetts or Virginia but was the product of the western frontier, marking the westward movement of federal political power.

Jackson came to office with little political experience. His autocratic approach was visible from the start and eventually led critics to label him '**King Andrew the First**'. The Cabinet during his Presidency mainly comprised close advisors and friends, such as Martin Van Buren (who became Secretary of State), and was therefore characterised as a '**kitchen cabinet**'. This was an outcome of his distrust for political and financial elites. Thus, Jackson brought to the American federal office an unorthodox style of functioning, and he was fairly indifferent to legal considerations, especially about some of his more polarising decisions, such as the pursuit of westward expansion. Martin Van Buren had written that Jackson thought 'to labour for the good of the masses was a special mission assigned to him by his Creator'.[2]

Jackson was, therefore, the president of the ordinary White man, and he brought into American politics his own experiences. His decisions were based on his assessment of what policies may have yielded equal opportunities to all Americans—this included, for example, opposition to institutions like the **Second Bank of the United States** (that is, the National Bank), which in his opinion was meant for the rich and run by them. He wanted to develop the US as a liberal, capitalist state where federal policies would benefit the agricultural and labouring classes. Jackson wanted rapid expansion in the agricultural economy to help small, independent property owners. In other words, Jackson envisioned a centralised Union, but not at the cost of state rights—he believed in equitable power sharing and mainly in protecting the rights of labour classes.

Historians have frequently compared Jeffersonian and **Jacksonian democracy**.[3] While both Presidents were seen to favour agricultural classes, their backgrounds differed considerably. Thomas Jefferson belonged to an aristocratic, wealthy planter family, whereas Andrew Jackson hailed from a poorer region (though he later became a man of considerable personal wealth). Jefferson sought to create a stable agricultural economy and his land policy aimed to create a nation of small farmers; he was deeply suspicious of the urban proletariat. On the other hand, Jackson believed in the **liberal-reformist tradition**[4] and wanted to develop a uniform, stable and measured economy suitable for the urban and agricultural base, and his land policy aimed to assist both agricultural and urban classes. In principle, Jefferson prioritised the rights of state governments over the Union; Jackson, too, believed in minimal federal intervention, but acknowledged that states and the Union were complementary. Jackson was against promoting and giving concessions to business classes—while he was not against industrialisation, he felt that the monopolistic tendencies of capitalist classes had to be controlled.

The 1828 election result ended the one-party system in America. Jackson's supporters formed the Democratic Party, inaugurating the two-party system at the federal level.

As we have discussed, the Jacksonian 'kitchen cabinet' comprised his close friends and associates. He also introduced the system of 'rotating in office' by enforcing the **Tenure of Office Act, 1820**, which authorised the President to remove office holders and appoint new ones in every government office, barring the War and Navy departments. While he reasoned that this would help rid the federal office of corrupt, incompetent and politically allied bureaucrats, he was accused of making partisan appointments, favouring those with personal, political, or military connections. Thus, while Jackson successfully reduced bureaucratic ossification, he introduced an element of political patronage that came to be known as the '**spoils system**'. He deployed a new political device known as the '**pocket veto**', which was used to nullify a Bill at the end of a Congress session by refusing to sign or veto it.

The Indian Removal Act

Jackson's first term saw the evolution of a federal policy to displace Indigenous peoples. The **Indian Removal Act** was signed into law in May 1830; under this law, Indigenous communities were forcibly removed to the west of the Mississippi River. This included the Choctaw, Chickasaw, Creek, and Seminole and resulted in mass dispossession and loss of life (for a detailed discussion, see Chapter 5, this volume).

The strain between settlers and Indigenous societies had grown through the nineteenth century. In Jackson's era, the Cherokee took up farming, cattle-rearing, and evolved a written language; they developed their Constitution, and applied to be admitted as a state within Georgia. This matter went to the Supreme Court in the **Cherokee Nation v. Georgia case (1831)**. Chief Justice John Marshall supported the Cherokee claim. However, Jackson was against giving any such power to Native Americans and had already passed the Indian Removal Act of 1830. He blocked the implementation of the Court's verdict in the 1831 case.

The Land Policy

Jackson could not resolve the growing conflict between different regions about land policy. The western states opposed the **Land Policy of 1820**, seeking to lower land prices and prioritise landownership for the pioneers who had settled the region. The eastern states were against this proposal of the West. They feared that low land prices would lure their workers away. Therefore, they favoured distribution, and the proceeds from the land sales should go to the state governments for internal improvements. Another proposal, the **Foote Resolution**, suggested ending the land sale for the time being. The southern states also opposed the eastern proposal as it would increase land prices and drain the federal treasury, increasing tariff rates. Jackson failed to resolve this growing rift between the three regions.

The Bank War

Jackson waged a veritable 'war' against the Second Bank of the United States.[5] The Second Bank had been established in 1816 with a 20-year charter to execute the federal government's financial transactions, and was a unifying force in establishing a stable currency system. The idea of a national bank had been contentious earlier as well (see the discussion about the First Bank in Chapter 3). Jackson was opposed to the National Bank, especially in the light of rumours that the Bank's president, Nicholas Biddle, had interfered in the 1828 election to support Jackson's rival.

FIG. 4.1: General Jackson Slaying the Many-Headed Monster, cartoon (1836)
Source: Wikimedia Commons.

To save the Bank, Nicholas Biddle began to use bank funds to win over political friends by giving them loans, offering them directorship, and opening bank branches in the home districts of influential politicians, confirming Jackson's allegation that commercial elites were using the Bank to fulfil their selfish economic interests. Jacksonians characterised the bank as an elite institution that enabled the concentration of power in private hands; as behaving ruthlessly towards defaulters, mortgaging their property; and as an institution that sought to control state banks, and pressured them from giving paper money or loans. Jackson also believed that the bank encouraged speculation, which led to unlimited economic growth and brought on cycles of depression in the American economy. Another reason for Jackson's hatred for the bank was that he had once engaged in land and commercial speculations based on credit, which led to his bankruptcy. This personal experience made Jackson prefer farming to a get-rich-quick mentality.[6]

Thus, the Bank in Jackson's view was an aristocratic and repressive institution that served established elites in consolidating their power. He famously called banks a 'hydra of corruption'.[7] The Bank's supporters, like John Quincy Adams, Henry Clay and Nicholas Biddle, were almost all from the Republican Party. Henry Clay introduced the re-charter Bill in early 1832 in both Houses and it was passed by the legislature. However, the President vetoed the Bill. To Martin Van Buren, Jackson declared: 'The bank… is trying to kill me, but I shall kill it.' In the run-up to the presidential election (November 1832), Biddle began to support Henry Clay, who believed in preserving a strong National Bank.

Thus proceeded the bank war. Jackson appointed his man, Roger B. Taney, as Secretary of the Treasury. Federal deposits were withdrawn from the Second Bank in 1833, effectively dismantling it, and distributed to '**pet banks**' of different states. In 1836, under the **Distribution or Deposit Act**, the surplus federal money was distributed to the states in proportion to their population. The Act increased the number of deposit banks, loosened federal control, and created more speculation and inflation. It also enabled state banks to increase their lending capacity. State banks began financing western state governments to construct roads and canals, encouraging rapid westward expansion. However, these banks were poorly managed and run by inexperienced people, who created speculative tendencies, fuelling rapid inflation in America. Henry Clay accused Jackson of assuming extra-constitutional power and authority not conferred on him by the Constitution. In his private correspondence, the Supreme Court Chief Justice linked the President with authoritarian rule. There was such severe opposition against Jackson that a new Whig Party emerged in opposition. The term Whig is significant, since the Whigs in Britain had come up in opposition to the monarchy. In this case, they challenged Jacksonian policies openly and branded him 'King Andrew the First' to critique decisions that they felt were undemocratic.

FIG. 4.2: King Andrew the First, lithograph (1833)
Source: Wikimedia Commons.

Specie Circular

In 1836, Jackson introduced the **Specie Circular**, which aimed to prevent the speculative tendencies that had evolved in the western territories. The circular required that land be bought only in *specie*, that is gold and silver currency (generally coins), which meant that those who had earlier taken loans from the bank in the form of banknotes could no longer use them to buy land and pay the government. Jackson's aim was to curb the speculative tendencies by introducing specie rather than banknotes. The Specie Circular was formally introduced after Congress passed the **Distribution Act**, which allowed the distribution of government surplus to the states. This surplus was then transferred to state banks and used to make payments to state governments in specie. The result was a sudden restriction in the money supply in markets, which led to a decline in the prices of commodities and financial problems, culminating in an economic crisis and depression known as the **Panic of 1837**.

Nullification Crisis

Jackson faced another crisis: a **Nullification Crisis** over tariff issues. The economic differences between the North and the South came to the surface in 1832 as the southern states wanted to reduce the tariff rates instituted in 1824 and 1828 on the import of manufactured goods. This forced the South to buy manufactured goods from the Northeast rather than securing cheaper imports from England in return for the cotton they exported there. Rice, indigo, and cotton planters had long seen prosperity and political dominance but feared competition from new cotton lands in Alabama and Mississippi. Therefore, they opposed the rapid exploitation of the new western territories. Jackson supported a Bill to lower the tariff duties in 1832 to defuse the situation, but could not assuage either side. Dissatisfaction led to the rise of southern politician John C. Calhoun, a nationalist who gradually became a states-rights secessionist. In 1828, Calhoun authored the **South Carolina Exposition and Protest**. He opposed the tariff measure introduced by President John Quincy Adams, but since he was the Vice President at the time, the document remained anonymous. In this document, he pointed out that since the US Constitution was a compact among the states, each state had the power and authority to nullify any law or federal authority that it considered unconstitutional to prevent the abuse of federal power. He was re-elected as Vice President with President Jackson. When Congress failed to reduce the tariff rate even under the new government, Calhoun openly spoke about the Doctrine of Nullification. In 1832, when Congress reduced tariff revenues yet retained a 50 per cent rate on cotton and woollen clothing, South

Carolina, in a special convention, formulated the '**South Carolina Ordinance of Nullification**' that proclaimed the tariff 'null' and 'void' within the state. The Doctrine stipulated:

(*i*) The states have conferred certain powers on the Union through the Constitution.
(*ii*) Each state may decide for itself when Congress exceeds that delegated authority.
(*iii*) When a state finds that a law has exceeded the scope of the Union's powers, the law may be declared null and void within the limits of that state.

These politicians also attempted to establish an alliance with western states. Emerging New England leader Daniel Webster added to the discussion of the nature of the Union by asserting that Nullification was possible. Jackson termed Nullification an 'abominable doctrine' that would reduce the government to anarchy. This stance was a departure from his earlier policy, since he now sided with the majority rather than with the state interest of South Carolina.[8] Jackson firmly believed that nullifiers were 'unprincipled men who would rather rule in hell than be subordinate in heaven'. Jackson emphasised that the Constitution had established 'a single nation' and not a league of nations. Therefore, if a state could nullify a law of Congress, the Union could not exist. He said, '… if one drop of blood be shed there in defiance of the laws of the United States, I will hang the first man of them I can get my hands on to the first tree I can find.'[9] Congress gave the President the right through the '**Force Bill**' to enforce tariff collection in South Carolina by dispatching the federal army. In the meantime, Congress agreed to lower the tariff rates over 10 years to bring it down to 20 per cent. The situation was saved with a well-crafted compromise worked out by Henry Clay, whose call for a planned reduction in tariff rates was accepted, and the nullification ordinance passed by South Carolina was withdrawn.

Jackson warned that the time would come when the South would again attempt to secede.[10] This marked the beginning of division, with the eastern states protecting their economic interests that were diametrically opposed to the interests of agricultural states like South Carolina and Virginia. The emerging problem of sectionalism was only temporarily defused. Jackson has been accused of enhancing his powers unconstitutionally to overcome the Nullification Crisis. He also destroyed the delicate balance of power between the three branches of government by overriding judicial judgements and the balance between the federal and state governments. Except for South Carolina, all politicians opposed Nullification, which showed the rising dominance of Democratic nationalism against state rights. However, some historians believe that the 'radical resistance' of South Carolina and its politicians against 'federal tyranny' was a significant catalyst for the beginning of sectionalism in America.

The Indian Removal Act, the Bank War, and the decrease in tariff rates marked Jackson as a strong defender of state rights. At the same time, his handling of the Nullification Crisis established him as a staunch Unionist. State rights and Unionism were compatible doctrines for Jackson. While cherishing the Union, Jackson believed the states were far too diverse to accept strong, purposeful direction from the federal government. So, he allowed the states considerable freedom, seeking to sustain their desire to remain within the Union and reject dangerous doctrines like Nullification.

By claiming to be the people's representative, Jackson brought an imbalance to the political system of compromise and consensus. However, Jackson was only sometimes successful in carrying out his philosophical ideas for the Congress, which challenged him as it also claimed to represent the same people! Therefore, despite Jackson's efforts to make American democracy more people-friendly, other American policymakers were committed to the constitutional forms of the founding generation, and were not inclined to permit him the complete freedom of movement that he desired.

Jacksonian democracy had another element. During the Bank War, Jackson did not adhere to rationalised public policy instruments but rather his own commitment to popular democracy. Another criticism of Jackson is that he was against minority rights to safeguard majority interests, and this became evident during implementation of the Indian Act when the lands of five Indigenous communities were taken over under a cloud of deceit, betrayal, and corruption, evident in the Trail of Tears (see Chapter 5, this volume). Jackson also began to use postal laws to stop the circulation of abolitionist literature throughout America. His tenure saw a growing abolitionist movement and literature, and he stepped in to stem its tide. In this way, Jacksonian democracy was not a revolution but marked a significant change in American politics.

Social Conflicts with Irish Immigrants

The Jacksonian period, spanning from the 1830s to the 1850s, saw the onset of a phase of social disorder, driven by emerging social and political issues, manifesting in the form of frequent 'collective violence'. At this juncture, America experienced rapid urbanisation, demographic profile changes, technological changes, and transformations in its economic structure. Urban policing rose sharply, supported by the rationale that it was needed to tackle discontent and bring a semblance of law and order amid rapid social change. Historian Richard Maxwell Brown analysed 35 riots from 1830 to 1860 in Baltimore, Philadelphia, New York, and Boston. He found that from the 1830s, nativist and anti-abolitionist riots were unleashed by the dominant factions to maintain their position in society. Therefore, these were reflective of social conservatism and vigilantism.[11] According to John C. Schneider, about 75 per cent of American cities with a population of 20,000 or greater experienced social conflict. Even President Abraham Lincoln had stated that riots had become 'the everyday news of the times'.[12] Scholars investigated the causes of these riots and motives or incitements to violence, how competition for jobs contributed to it, and whether it shifted the dynamics of status, power, wealth, and political influence for specific groups.

According to Michael Feldberg, who analysed the **Philadelphia Nativist Riots** (also known as the Native American Riots) of 1844, the 'political collective violence' was anti-immigrant, religious, anti-abolitionist, and anti-Black.[13] The riots were due to the simmering racial and ethnic tensions between the recent Irish immigrants whom the 'native' or naturalised American settlers deeply resented. Political institutions were unable to effectively respond to this conflict.

It is important to understand the violence in 1844 in Kensington, north of Philadelphia. In the 1840s, reading the Protestant version of the Bible was mandatory in Philadelphia schools. The Catholic Bishop of Philadelphia, Reverend Francis Patrick Kenrick, opposed this. He wanted the Douay version of the Bible to be read by Catholic students. In America, most Protestants considered the Catholic religion to be alien and un-democratic as it was controlled by two institutional figureheads, the Pope and the priests. The differences became an issue, and a compromise was worked out by the School Controller, Hugh Clark, who permitted Catholic students to leave the classroom during the Protestant Bible reading sessions. Another solution was to suspend all Bible reading sessions till a solution could be worked out. However, the Protestants feared that Irish Catholics were using the tension to convert public schools into Catholic institutions. To prepare themselves, they formed the American Protestant Association, a coalition of Baptists, Methodists, and Presbyterians, in what became the Sabbatarian movement. This association aimed to increase attendance at Protestant churches and prevent people from indulging in gambling, consumption of alcohol, picnics, fairs, and sports—vices that the group accused Catholics of indulging in. Their organising led to the Colportage movement where copies of the Protestant Bible were distributed for free to those who promised to read it. At this juncture, the action was still led by religious groups, but to gain ground, it was merged with the **American Republican Party (ARP)** and became a political movement.

The ARP made three demands: (*i*) a three-year waiting period to become a naturalised American citizen; (*ii*) that eligibility for public office be restricted to those who were 'native-born'; and (*iii*) regulations to prevent 'foreigners' from interacting with social, political and religious institutions of the US. The ARP mainly included middle and professional classes, lawyers, doctors, members of the clergy, newspaper editors, shopkeepers, artisans, printers, barbers, dentists, and teachers. The Methodist, Baptist, and Presbyterian churches staunchly supported the party. ARP members considered themselves the 'real' Americans and they were hostile to Irish immigrants and their alleged allegiance to Ireland

and the Roman Catholic Church. As for Irish immigrants, they believed that their cause for a free Ireland was connected to the Irish Catholic Church.

The Irish immigrants lived in ghettos that contained their Catholic churches and political and nationalist institutions. Ghettos were controlled by the Irish-born Catholic clergy, who influenced the voters to cast their vote for the Democratic Party. So, apart from religious differences, support for the Democratic party antagonised the Republican party supporters, who considered the Irish a 'foreign tyranny'; they assiduously followed George Washington's mandate to keep 'eternal vigilance' and 'beware of foreign influence' that they believed could harm American republicanism.

The ARP was a key player in the **Temperance Movement**, which advocated moderate alcohol consumption due to its perceived association with poverty, unemployment, crime, health issues, and broken families. This movement was particularly critical of Irish communities, who were known for running taverns and Irish saloons that sold alcohol exclusively to Irish Catholics. The Protestants, on the other hand, saw this as an 'unholy alliance' between the Irish clergy and tavern politics aimed at securing votes through the provision of alcohol. According to Feldberg, the ARP aimed to safeguard American political freedom from Catholic-sponsored conspiracies. In contrast, the Irish Catholic community invoked the American Constitution, which guaranteed religious freedom and belief in political freedom, including freedom of choice and association.

Communal violence was sparked when Hugh Clark suggested suspending Bible reading in schools, a suggestion that Henry Moore, a Methodist minister, publicly opposed. Moore's line of action was followed by ARP and other Protestant clergy members, who began to organise rallies, including one in the third ward of Kingston, where Irish and working classes dominated. On 3 May 1844, ARP held a march, but due to a rather thin crowd, it decided to reconvene on 6 May. On that day, the party managed to bring together a group of about 3,000 people, but a sudden downpour forced the public to take shelter at the Nancy Goat Market. This market was the main shopping centre and meeting place for the Irish community and their social centre. In a sudden turn of events, George Schiffler, the first victim of the riot, was killed by gunshot. Conflict between the two communities persisted into the night, till armed forces were called in to end the violence. Despite reinforcements, the nativists converged on the scene once again on 7 May and violence broke out. This time, the houses and shops of Irish people were specifically targeted, looted and burnt down, including the home of Hugh Clark along with the Irish Churches of St. Augustine Roman Catholic Church, resulting in the death of six people; about 50 sustained severe injuries.

Feldberg analysed the pattern of this community violence and found that rioters had few guns and limited ammunition. The primary weapons used were rocks, bricks, clubs, knives, and stone-slings, which reduced casualties. Rioting was not spontaneous—rioters 'restrained' themselves by targeting specifically the houses and churches of prominent Irish people. Most rioters belonged to the working classes, guided by ethnic identity and political cause. According to Feldberg, they were not influenced by economic oppression or a sense of alienation, and the fact is that rioting marked a shift from conflict over cultural identity to political conflict and manifested in a physical confrontation. The whole process of rioting also showed the inability of the police to enforce law and order.

American scholars turned their attention to understanding the social fabric of American society in its historical context only from the 1960s, when the country was under the influence of the Civil Rights Movement. This trend continued into the 1970s which saw growing anti-war protests over Vietnam and the first wave of the feminist movement. These events forced historians to study how interest groups and classes in America competed for power, choosing to identify with their race and ethnic identity rather than the nation at large. To understand this ground reality, historians turned to studying 'ordinary people'. They came to realise that American society was highly fragmented in terms of ethnic groups, and this forced scholars to begin the study of people from lower income groups, Black communities, and those excluded from the mainstream culture. Historical analysis to comprehend how racial and ethnic ideas and behaviours were woven into the fabric of American society developed over time.

The crux of the issue with Jacksonian democracy is that his style of governance, while adhering to his democratic ideals, often clashed with the fundamental principles of American liberalism, republicanism, and constitutionalism, creating multiple internal problems that pushed the country towards the beginning of the Civil War.

Notes

1. Melvin L. Urofsky, ed., *The American Presidents* (New York, 2000).
2. See Russell L. Riley, *Andrew Jackson, 1829–1837* (New York, 2000).
3. See Gerald N. Grob and Geoge Athan Billias, *Interpretations of Amerian History: Patterns and Perspectives*, 3rd edition (New York, 1978), pp. 181–197 and pp. 221–234.
4. Right from the period when the American Constitution was ratified, Americans believed in individual property rights, a limited form of government, and majority rule as the foundation of American politics. Classical liberalism is concerned with the political theory of natural rights, propounded by John Locke, and the laissez-faire economic theory of Adam Smith. Early liberals emerged during the American Revolution, as opponents to the Constitution came to be known as anti-Federalists. See Jeff Taylor, *Where Did the Party Go? William Jennings Bryan, Hubert Humphrey, and the Jeffersonian Legacy* (Columbia and London, 2006).
5. See Robert V. Remini, *Andrew Jackson and the Course of American Democracy, 1833–1845* (New York, 1984).
6. Ibid., pp. 161–178.
7. Ibid., pp. 161–178.
8. Allen C. Guelzo, *Fateful Lightning: A New History of Civil War and Reconstruction* (New York, 2012), pp. 19–20.
9. Remini, *The Course of American Democracy, 1833–1845*, vol. 3, pp. 24–44.
10. Ibid., pp. 20–22.
11. See Richard Maxwell Brown, *Strains of Violence: Historical Studies of American Violence and Vigilantism* (New York, 1975).
12. Abraham Lincoln, 'Address to the Young Men's Lyceum of Springfield, Illinois', in *Abraham Lincoln: Speeches and Writings, 1832–1858* (New York, 1989), pp. 29, 31, 32.
13. Michael Feldberg, *The Turbulent Era: Riot and Disorder in Jacksonian America* (New York, 1980).

CHAPTER 5

Removal of Indigenous Peoples and Westward Expansion

Background

North America was never the empty 'space' imagined by European settlers—the continent was inhabited by a variety of Indigenous societies. Each Indigenous group has its own story and myth to explain the origin of all living beings in the 'sacred space' that later came to be known as North America. To them, this was **Turtle Island**. Indigenous people believe that they are 'the original peoples' of the land and not 'migrants' or 'settlers' as they are made out to be. For example, the creation stories of Pueblo people speak of their emergence from the earth at specific places in the landscape. In other tribes, there are several stories of how living beings dived to the bottom of a great sea in quest of soil from which the first land was formed.[1]

While the Indigenous claim of having the 'original' right over land is supported by the fact that they arrived in North America centuries before the Europeans, migration theories have also been proposed about them. Archaeologists have unearthed hearths, animal bones, and stone tools dating back almost 10,000 years that can be linked to these communities. These material remnants were left behind by hunters who had tracked mammoths and other large animals of the last Ice Age from Asia into America. It is believed that during the second-to-last Ice Age, about 260 million years ago, sea levels dropped enough for a land bridge known as Beringia to emerge between the region of Siberia (in Eurasia) and Alaska (in North America). 'Hunting bands' entered North America through this land bridge, and by circa 8000 BCE, they had established themselves across the continent. These groups of hunting peoples gradually expanded to the Northeast, the western plains, and southwest and northern Alaska. They hunted mammoths, mastodons, giant bison, and other animals and lived in temporary dwellings. This migration ceased as the climate warmed and the sea engulfed Beringia. Another theory posits that humans may have migrated into North America from South America, as recent excavations in Brazil have revealed human settlements dating as far back as 30,000 years.[2]

As the climate began to warm, glaciers and tundra retreated to the north of the continent, and grasslands and forests emerged. Material remains suggest that Indigenous communities invented the bow and arrow, and pottery fragments also date to this period. Where they found suitable soil, they began cultivating maize, beans, and other crops. With the advent of agriculture, especially around the Mississippi and Ohio rivers, new cultures such as those of the Adena, Hopewell, and Mississippian peoples started to develop. They began cultivating maize, beans, and other crops where they found suitable soil. They had adequate natural resources and developed techniques to build urban centres, monuments, and art; they evolved various religious beliefs and new strategies for hunting and gathering food. These communities had distinct cultures that had developed in different natural environments and contexts; they had their own economic systems, languages, political systems, and social structures.[3] Therefore, North America was not the 'virginal' land it was made out to be before the arrival of European settlers. It flourished with life, energy, and patterns of Indigenous systems.

Pre-Colonial Cultural Landscape

To understand the Indigenous groups of North America, one may study them based on the geographical location of different cultures.

The following passages describe only a few societies from the thousands that existed across the continent.

The Northeast consists of forests, lakes, rivers, the Great Lakes, the St. Lawrence river glaciers, warm and fertile plains along the Atlantic coast, and the Mississippi and Ohio valleys. This area was mainly inhabited by the Ojibwe, Abenaki, Iroquois, and Micmac, whose languages all belonged to the Algonquian language group. They led a nomadic life and used canoes made from birch bark, living in conical *tipi*s or tents made from bark or animal hide. Their main economic activity were hunting, fishing, and gathering, and staple foods included wild rice, blueberries, deer, moose, eel, maize, beans, and squash. The Iroquois were farmers who used slash-and-burn agricultural techniques, and their original homeland corresponds to the modern-day state of New York. In the fifteenth century, a five-nation confederacy emerged in the region, bringing together the Cayuga, Mohawk, Oneida, Onondaga, and Seneca. The Confederacy was called **Haudenosaunee**, which meant '**People of the Longhouse**'. In 1714, a sixth nation, Tuscarora, joined the Confederacy.[4]

The Southeast includes the Appalachian Mountains, which extend till Florida, the Gulf of Mexico, and the lower Mississippi. The inhabitants of this region were village dwellers who mainly cultivated corn, squash, pumpkins, gourds, and sunflowers; they also grew bananas, sweet potatoes, sugarcane, edible fruits, and wild nuts. Hunting and fishing were important activities as well, and they caught whales and seals. The Creek, Choctaw, and Chickasaw, who shared a language family (Muskogean), were prominent among the groups here.[5]

The plains region consists of vast plains and prairies that include Manitoba, Saskatchewan, Alberta, Texas, the Rocky Mountains, the Mississippi Valley, and Nebraska. Bison, bears, deer, and rabbits were found across this region of abundant grass. The Indigenous inhabitants grew beans, squash, and tobacco. Groups in this region included the Pawnee in Nebraska, who were introduced to horses by the Spaniards in the sixteenth century; other important communities were the Cheyenne and Arikara, who lived in tipis.[6]

The Great Basin comprises mountains and rocky deserts and is surrounded by small rivers. Owing to its harsh climate, survival was a challenge. The Shoshoni, Ute, and Paiute peoples lived here. Their huts were made of brush or reeds. They hunted small animals such as rabbits, squirrels, rats, and groundhogs.[7]

The Southwest is arid—an expanse of sand and stone—with mountains and several big rivers like the Rio-Grande, Colorado, and so on. The Mogollon lived in the mountains, in well-insulated pit houses, and they grew corn, beans, squash, tobacco, and cotton. The Anasazi built enormous dwellings known as Pueblos, and communities in this region include the Hopi, Apache, and Navajo.[8] California is a coastal area, and tribes like the Hupa, Yurok, and Chumash lived by hunting whales, seals, sea lions, dolphins, and sea otters.[9]

This region's northwest coast and plateau now form part of modern-day Canada, and groups like the Nootka, Makah, Haida, and Tlingit used red cedar to build their houses. They were known for their totem poles and lived by hunting salmon, trout, cod, halibut, and herring.[10]

The Beginning of Enslavement of Indigenous Peoples

The arrival of **Christopher Columbus** (1451–1506) set in motion the process of the entrapment of Indigenous people. He later institutionalised the ***encomienda* system**, a Spanish labour system that justified the forced labour of Indigenous peoples in the Spanish colonies of the New World. The French and the Dutch, on the other hand, initially sought out Indigenous people to act as guides, hunters, fishers, and trappers. Much later, they began to exploit them as slaves to be sold off in Spanish plantations.

When the English established the Jamestown colony of Virginia in 1607, they initially looked to Indigenous people, such as those from the **Powhatan Confederacy**, for support as they familiarised themselves with the region's geography and environment. But from 1610 to 1646, when the war broke out between the English and the Powhatan Confederacy, Indigenous people were captured and enslaved. The first mass enslavement occurred in the New England colonies when conflict erupted over land and trade rights between the two. This manifested in the **Pequot War (1636–1638)**, which culminated in mass enslavement.

With the gradual expansion of British American colonies, the Indigenous slave trade also expanded. The process significantly altered over time: the Westo, an Indigenous community, took to assisting the colonists in defeating and enslaving other Indigenous groups. The Westo were originally from the region around Lake Erie and gradually entered the areas that now constitute Georgia and Virginia. They raided and defeated other tribes. Later, the Shawnee sided with the colonists to destroy the Westo by 1680, leading to the enslavement of the latter. The Shawnee then continued the enslavement of other tribes. The Spanish, too, continued to enslave Pueblo Indians till 1680 (in present-day New Mexico) and the beginning of the Pueblo Revolt that led to Spanish defeat. Indigenous people destroyed all Spanish churches, killed missionaries, and declared Jesus Christ and the Virgin Mary to be dead. More wars continued, such as the **Tuscarora War (1711–1715)** in North Carolina and the **Yamasee War (1715–1717)** in South Carolina, which perpetuated the enslavement process.

Over a period of time, Indigenous peoples were removed from their traditional spaces through **westward expansion**. This was achieved through land surrender treaties, subjugation, and subordination, systemically carried out through wars and the spread of European diseases. It eroded a long history of connection between the Indigenous people and their lands and their sustainable systems of existence. An end to the right over their ancestral lands meant the annihilation of their right to self-determination and extinguished their political and economic freedom over lands that they considered sacred. This process of deliberate marginalisation assisted the federal government in alienating the surviving Indigenous peoples from their traditional way of life and livelihood. It transformed independent nations into domestic, dependent nations. It assisted the White settler society in becoming a dominant community and led to the introduction of internal colonisation policies.[11]

Beginning of External Colonisation

The White settlers' desire for land and natural resources led to an inward push, that is, a push from the East Coast into the continent. This marked the beginning of 'westward' or 'frontier' expansion that became increasingly aggressive from the nineteenth century, with President Thomas Jefferson envisioning the US as an 'empire of liberty' that must expand into 'empty lands'. From 1600 to the beginning of the 1700s, one may trace a history of contact with Indigenous peoples, generally established through mission trading posts. Over time, the White settlers trapped the Indigenous communities in a position of dependency, beginning with the federal government-sponsored expedition across the continent to the Pacific coast (undertaken by Meriwether Lewis and William Clarke in 1804–1806). The colonisers later created a web of inter-tribal warring techniques (like they did with the Westo and later, when, to eliminate the Westo, they aligned with the Shawnee) that weakened the Indigenous communities, converting them to enslaved people in the British American colonies as well as on the sugar plantations of the West Indies. In 1703, James Moore, with the assistance of three groups—the Creek, the Apalachicola, and the Yuchi—defeated the Apalachee, Timucua, and Calusa tribes from Spanish Florida and captured them as enslaved people. The Iroquoian League consisted of six nations' alliances with the Dutch and English, who defeated the Huron and pushed the Ojibwe into Sioux territory (the western region of the Great Lakes). The Ojibwe, in turn, displaced the Sioux into the plain areas. The Iroquois were finally defeated after the American War of Independence and fled to present-day Canada.[12]

Internal Colonisation

Westward expansion was initiated by the **Land Ordinance of 1785** passed by the US Congress, which led to the survey and sale of land to White settlers, even as the Ordinance declared that '[the Indian] land and property shall never be taken from them without their consent'. In spite of such claims, lands were taken and sold at one dollar per acre with a minimum of 640 acres. In 1787, the Northwest Ordinance led to the systematic transformation of western territories into states.[13] From 1787 to 1790, Indigenous groups were involved in a series of conflicts and defeated American forces in Ohio and Indiana with military assistance from Britain. George Washington was then appointed special general. Between 1793 and 1794, the Indigenous groups were defeated under his leadership. In 1795, Washington signed the **Treaty of Greenville**, forcing them to cede the region of Ohio and Indiana. From 1790 to 1793, the USA faced problems with the Creeks and finally signed a treaty with them. In 1796, the **Indian Intercourse Act** was passed, and the federal government promised to regulate relations between Indigenous peoples and American traders and settlers more effectively to prevent friction between the two groups. However, the Act was meant to assist White settler society as it gradually opened up a vast area for their settlement.

Land, labour, and market expansion led to the establishment of the 'empire of liberty' (the Jeffersonian era) following the 1803 Louisiana Purchase, which brought the whole of Mississippi under American control. Westward development facilitated the ownership and cultivation of land, thereby making America more independent economically. Before the War of 1812, the policy of forceful removal of Indigenous communities through war and disease was aggressively pursued. After the War, lands east of the Mississippi became available for White settlement. Further, technological advancements in transportation, industry, and agriculture enabled for extensive westward expansion.

Several inventions and discoveries contirbuted to rapid westward development. The most prominent was the invention of the cotton gin machine by Eli Whitney in 1793, which led to the rapid expansion of cotton cultivation and saw an accompanying rise in the enslavement of Black people. The westward expansion also led to advances in agricultural production, with the spread of cotton, sugarcane, tobacco, corn, and wheat cultivation, as well as livestock production. Applying the technical principle of interchangeable parts allowed for mass manufacture through assembly line production. In 1819, cast-iron ploughs and steel ploughs began to be driven by horses and mules instead of oxen. The development of the horse-drawn mechanical reaper and the automatic thrasher in 1840 was another factor in expanding the commercial agriculture and manufacturing sectors. The construction of turnpikes, also called toll roads, introduced a method of all-weather overland transportation. This led to the private financing, construction, and operation of highways that would later be integrated into the public transport system. Water transportation represented another means of conquering the continent—the first advancement in this direction was made by John Fitch in 1790 when he invented the steamboat, making it possible to navigate the Mississippi River. In 1817, work on the Erie Canal started and was completed in 1825. This engineering marvel became an example of canal development, bringing an inexpensive and fast-moving transportation system. The canal carried barges from New York City to Buffalo on Lake Erie. This led to an increase in the population of New York, making it more significant than Boston and Philadelphia. However, the invention and development of railroads was perhaps the most crucial step in 'conquering' the vast terrain of North America.

These transformations led to increased annual migration to the West after the War of 1812. The area also acted as a catalyst for urban and industrial development. By 1815, demographic pressure and shrinking land supply in the East had led to the beginning of out-migration. The East was also negatively impacted by rapid soil erosion due to excessive cultivation. Big planters forcibly bought out tenant farmers in the south. The tenant farmers, in turn, were forced to move out to the westward region, which offered them the chance of rapid upward mobility, material self-improvement, and land for economic independence. The western region became America's '**Manifest Destiny**', wherein Americans could preserve their economic freedom and political sovereignty by continuously moving westward to maintain their faith in the American ethos of 'equality' of opportunities for all, except enslaved people and Indigenous communities.[14] This led to the emergence of new states: Ohio (1803), Louisiana (1812), Indiana (1816), Mississippi (1817), Illinois (1818), Alabama (1819), Missouri (1821), Arkansas (1836), and Michigan (1837). The insatiable hunger for land, resources, and markets was marked by the annexation of Texas in 1845 and New Mexico in 1846 through the **Treaty of Guadalupe Hidalgo**. California followed in 1848, and Utah in 1850, as an outcome of war with Mexico. Oregon was acquired in 1846 through the **Oregon Treaty** with Britain. Westward expansion became rapid and aggressive, and the precursor to it was the **Indian Removal Act** passed during the presidency of Andrew Jackson.

The Indian Removal Act

In 1830, the Indian Removal Act was passed, which compelled Indigenous people to move west of the Mississippi, leaving the entire East to the White settlers. The Indian Removal Act was specifically implemented to relocate Indigenous peoples from a vast territory that later became the states of Kansas, Oklahoma, Nebraska, Colorado, and Wyoming. The Act gradually converted Indigenous ancestral territories into American states, placing the original people behind '**reserves**'. This was a method of internal colonisation ratified by federal policy, and it resulted in the beginning of several wars between the settlers and Indigenous groups. The reserve system began with the Navajo, who engaged in a protracted struggle with White settlers from the 1850s to 1864. The Navajo were defeated and placed in a reserve.

American historians viewed the removal of Indigenous communities from their ancestral lands in a dualistic way. They believed that displacing these communities and relocating them to reserves was the only means of protecting Indigenous peoples and their culture from the encroachment of White settlers. However, historian Ronald N. Satz critically analysed the goals, execution, and results of the Indigenous removal policy between the 1830s and 1840s, as applied in the Northwest region, and found that the stated rationale for this policy did not reflect the real motivations and effects on the ground.[15] Robert V. Remini has suggested that Jackson's era is mired in contradictions: He advocated liberty, individualism, and minimal governmental intervention, but did precisely the opposite when it came to the Indigenous population. Jackson unleashed a set of internal colonial policies to take over Indigenous lands and destroy their political systems, economic activities, and social setup. From being the original inhabitants of the continent, these people became landless 'noble savages', and the 'White Man's Burden'.

The problem with these two interpretations, and similar analyses by scholars like George Brown Tindall, David E. Shi, John Farragher, and Gary B. Nash, is that they all assume that the Indian Removal Act was implemented just as the Congress had envisioned when it passed the Act. In fact, the Congress had never authorised President Jackson to overlook Indian treaties nor permitted him to remove them from their ancestral lands. In this new line of interpretation, historian Alfred A. Cave argues that many Congressmen opposed the Act (it was passed with 102 in support and 97 against, with the strongest opposition coming from the northeastern states). President Jackson engineered consent for the removal process by using misleading language in the Act. The law described the relocation of Indigenous peoples as 'voluntary', playing on the image of the federal government as a benevolent institution. In reality, the Act provided enough elasticity to the state governments to carry out territorial expansion in whatever manner they deemed fit.[16]

The process of dispossession had begun long ago, when President George Washington and Thomas Jefferson's policies marginalised the Indigenous peoples and then attempted to assimilate them into the Western civilisational mode and the Christian religion. Jefferson was the first to suggest their removal. It is this idea that President Jackson and later Martin Van Buren picked up. In formulating this policy, they sought to prioritise the needs of White settlers; to justify the same, they asserted that the removal of Indigenous communities was the only way of protecting them from 'complete extinction'.[17]

According to Robert Berkhofer, Jr, the eagerness of successive presidents to remove Indigenous peoples from their ancestral territories was rooted in the American belief in private individual ownership of land. Private ownership was viewed as an economic imperative that would safeguard the American political and social system. Secondly, the American way of life was 'destined' to expand within the boundaries of the US and even beyond. The 'empire for liberty' had no place for 'aliens' like the Indigenous peoples, who could not be reconciled with American ideals and institutions and were racially 'Other'.[18]

According to Remini, Jackson's 'Indian Policy' developed from his frontier experiences, his expansionist dreams, his belief in states' rights and his concept of nationalism (wherein he regarded any 'foreign' element that could create problems for the American Union with suspicion; he categorised Indigenous peoples as one such element).[19] Robert Berkhofer studied the West in relation to two issues: the presence of Spanish and British colonies, and the Indigenous nations. The West presented diplomatic and military challenges for the US government.[20]

When Jackson introduced the Indian Removal Act in 1830, three federal departments—the White House, the War Department, and the Office of Indian Affairs (which included Indigenous agents)—asserted that the removal policy would bring four benefits to the Indigenous communities:

(*i*) It would provide fixed and permanent boundaries to the Indigenous groups where state governments and territories would have no jurisdictional powers.
(*ii*) It would protect Indigenous people from 'corrupt' White elements like gamblers, prostitutes, whiskey vendors, etc.
(*iii*) Indigenous groups would be governed by powers of self-government and not by state or territorial laws.
(*iv*) The federal government would assist in the assimilation of Indigenous societies through the 'civilising' process through religious conversion and conversion of sacred land into private property, along with acquainting them with the knowledge of agriculture and mechanical techniques of using machines.[21]

The Act of 1830 allowed President Jackson to exchange unauthorised public land in the trans-Mississippi West for Indigenous land in the East. The Indigenous groups would be given the title to their new land, compensation for their original land, the federal government would bear the cost of their removal, and they would be assisted for the first year after their removal.[22] The hidden agenda behind the Act was not 'protection' but the subjugation of independent Indigenous societies. White political leaders were influenced by the theory of Social Darwinism, a popular Western theory of human society that placed all societies on a continuum from the most to the least evolved, with the West representing the pinnacle of civilisation. This hierarchical view reflects the racist and colonialist thinking prevalent in this period.

In political terms, the federal government treated Indigenous peoples as 'nations' existing within the boundaries of the US and acknowledged the title to their respective lands till 1830; Indigenous nations were recognised as sovereign, independent entities, with the federal government having exclusive rights to deal with 'Indian Affairs'. When Jackson began the removal of the communities living east of the Mississippi to new lands west of the river, the Cherokee and other southern tribes resisted their displacement. Jackson granted the state of Georgia and other neighbouring states the right to extend their laws over the Indigenous nations. This singular decision created a series of crises among five communities—the Choctaw, Chickasaw, Creek, Seminole, and Cherokee. This matter went up to the Supreme Court in **Cherokee Nation v. Georgia** (1831; see Chapter 4, this volume) and **Worcester v. Georgia** (1832). The two verdicts passed by Chief Justice John Marshall ruled that:

(*i*) Indigenous societies were defined as 'domestic dependent nations' with no right to deal with foreign nations as they were under the 'protection' of the US; and

(*ii*) they were exempted from state laws and had the right to their internal powers.

Taken together, these two judgments created a paradox based on the combined application of a logic of wardship on the one hand, and sovereignty on the other. If the Cherokee and other tribes stayed in their ancestral homeland, they would have to relinquish their political rights to negotiate and trade beyond their borders; if they moved to a new land, they would have to abandon their hold over ancestral territory. This became the policy of 'Indian Removal', the cornerstone of federal Indian policy in the West.

This process of marginalisation, marked by injustice and tragedy, was recast by Jackson as necessary to the Indigenous peoples: by creating separate reserves, 'that ill-fated race had been at length placed beyond the reach of injury or oppression'. Jefferson's vision that 'we shall all be American' under Jackson became an explicitly racist policy, for he asserted that Indians had 'neither the intelligence, the industry, the moral habits, nor desire of improvement' to live among the Whites. The southern tribes became casualties of American expansionism and the penetration of American political culture. In 1832, Congress established the office of Commissioner of Indian Affairs; in 1834, it reorganised the Indian Department, which later became the Bureau of Indian Affairs. The Trade and Intercourse Act of 1834 regularised federal supervision for trade within the unceded lands of the West.

Over a period of time, with the American acquisition of Texas, California, and Oregon, all Indigenous territories fell to American expansionism. Indigenous territories began to be encroached on by land speculators, settlers, and timber thieves, effectively confining these groups to the reserves as a form of ethnic cleansing. American negotiators fabricated the signed treaties to enable the expansion of the White settlements. This led to a series of wars that can be categorised into three: the wars on the Great Plains, involving the Sioux, Lakota, and Comanche peoples; the wars in the Southwest, with the Navajo in the 1830s and with the Apache in the 1880s; and the wars in western Washington with much weaker Indigenous groups. After the Civil War in the 1860s, Americans began the process of Christianisation and 'civilisation' under the Reform Policy and ended the Treaty System. The Reform Policy was a series of processes or policies intended to forcibly assimilate Indigenous peoples into Western culture and religion after the failure to annihilate them. It meant the dissolution of their distinct identity, culture, and nations. This process continued into the 1960s.[23]

Theoretical Debates: Frontier Expansion of What?

Frederick Jackson Turner was the first historian to highlight the importance of the '**frontier**' in the rise of a distinct national character and termed the process as the 'colonization of the Great West'. The term 'frontier', here, is used to denote the ever-shifting border as settlers persisted with westward expansion. The frontier, he theorised, was the 'meeting point between savagery and civilization'. This phenomenon contributed to a distinct national character, provided the rationale to secure 'free land', and attracted migration, leading to a settlement process that eventually triggered institutional changes and constitutional amendments in the US. Each frontier was expanded by defeating Indigenous inhabitants from whom the settlers also borrowed the knowledge of taming the environment. In Turner's view, the first frontier was the Atlantic coast, which was settled based on European customs, traditions, and cultural elements. However, movement inside the frontier attracted traders, European immigrants, hunters, agriculturalists, miners, industrialists, and ranchers, all of whom combined their frontier insight to develop the process of **Americanisation**.[24]

Settlers had to surmount the mountains that separated the western states from the Atlantic seaboard in order to pursue settler expansion. It was initiated through the application of federal programmes that ushered in funds for internal improvement, sparking a transportation revolution in the form of all-weather roads, canals, bridges, and railroads, which subsequently ushered in an era of economic integration. The federal government imposed high tariffs to protect nascent American industries from European competition and secure internal markets for domestic manufactured goods.

By 1820, Americans began to settle in the region around the Great Lakes, which led to the displacement of Indigenous communities. This upheaval profoundly impacted their way of life and led to the beginning of military conflicts that became significant issues for American political and military leaders. At the same time, the pursuit of economic opportunity in California, Oregon, and Utah sparked the Gold Rush,[25] drawing many settlers to these new territories. The push towards the Rocky Mountains assisted in the discovery of mines in Colorado, Montana, and Idaho. Continuous frontier expansion changed the contours of the United States. In 1776, the states had come together to establish the federal government. By 1861, the federal government established states that joined the Union. Federal funds and lands were provided to develop the railroad system that would integrate this vast geographical space. The spatial vastness of the frontier was seen to promote democracy, individualism, and nationalism. At the frontiers, Americans encountered European colonisers as well. France and Britain had farming and trading frontiers in North America, and both used Indigenous 'allies' to maintain their colonial hold, which led to a series of wars involving European, Indigenous, and American armed forces. The federal government therefore had to spend significant funds on enlarging the army, formulating land policies, and establishing a powerful federal government.

According to Turner, frontier expansion resulted in the development of a composite nationality (in other words, Americanisation); the rise of new urban centres; the development of powers of the national government; rapid industrialisation; federal policies for the sale of public lands; a new tariff system to protect nascent American industries; internal improvements; and nationalisation along with the rise of Jeffersonian philosophy. It was also consonant with the **Monroe Doctrine** which, together with the idea of '**Manifest Destiny**' fundamental to frontier logic, brought the Western hemisphere under the control of the US. The 'mandate from Heaven' led to continental expansion of the nation. Frontier expansion later contributed to the rise of Jacksonianism and the promotion of new religious groups, along with the emergence of new religious organisations, as well as the growth of new intellectual movements based on materialism.

Turner portrayed the American West as a creative frontier with 'free land' where Americans developed ideas of democracy, equality, and individualism, transforming immigrants and initiating the process of Americanisation. This assisted in the capitalistic growth of the American economy and labour, marked by America's political and commercial expansion between the two oceans, which led to American entry into world politics and the emergence of new political ideas including socialism, populism, and progressivism.

CRITICISM OF FRONTIER THEORY

Charles Beard contended that Turner had overlooked the forces of industrialisation and class struggle, and that his theory was limited to agrarian history. Marxist historians termed the period of westward expansion as representative of the growth and expansion of industries and the emergence of capitalist logic, creating the conditions for class struggle, all of which Turner neglected. According to liberal historians, Turner placed more emphasis on individualism than collective action. Internationalist historians asserted that Turner's theory is too simplistic, as it is explained based on external, physical, and material conditions of life rather than focusing on creative and causative factors in history. Even as Turner overemphasised geographical influence, he neglected factors like immigration, urbanisation, industrialisation, and the impact of Europe on America. To many historians, the term 'frontier' is problematic as it does not significantly contribute to our understanding of westward movement.

Turner assumed that settlers living on the margins of the western region provided new intellectual stimulus to the political and social fabric of the nation. However, according to Louis M. Hacker, westward movement was inward-looking and had no 'transforming influence' on the country. Agricultural growth enabled further expansion and entrenchment of the institution of slavery. With the advent of industrialisation, the agricultural economy began to be neglected. Turner was wrong to assume that labour unions emerged due to frontier expansion. They appeared only after 1890, when westward expansion had already been completed. The expansion of slavery, marginalisation and decimation of Indigenous peoples were also the byproducts of the 'frontier' expansion. Three groups never became 'free' on 'free land': the Black people, the Indigenous people, and women. Therefore, Turner's definition of 'freedom' reflected several hidden biases.

According to Benjamin F. Wright in *Political Institutions and the Frontier*, Turner wrongly assumed that settlers brought about changes in the political institutions of America. The settlers only transplanted the same institutions already developed and practised in the ancient Greco-Roman world, adapted by European nations over time and brought to America with the European immigrant settlers. The region's peculiarities were its settlement patterns based on its environmental conditions. Industrialisation initiated by frontier expansion brought about class conflict, monopolistic capitalism, and imperialism. As America pursued imperialism and became deeply involved in global politics, it began to resemble Europe.

George Wilson Pierson's *The Frontier and American Institutions: A Criticism of the Turner Theory* finds Turner's theory to be contradictory as it fails to analyse how nationalism gave rise to sectionalism, leading to the Civil War of 1861. Historically, all technological innovations and discoveries were made in the Atlantic seaboard states. The march of Western civilisation was achieved at the cost of displacement and the eventual extinguishment of Indigenous nations. Therefore, 'barbarity' was introduced before Western notions of civilisation were superimposed. The American ideal of material comforts was achieved through the relentless exploitation of natural resources. Turner was unable to establish interconnectedness between westward expansion and the beginning of industrial, commercial, and agricultural revolutions in America. He also failed to draw parallels between the frontier experience and other world experiences in a comparative sense.

According to Carlton J. H. Hayes, in *The American Frontier: Frontier of What?*, the foundations of Western culture were based on the Greco-Roman tradition, language, philosophy, architecture, art, law, and political concepts. Its cultural practices, ethics, and societal structures were based on Judeo-Christian rules of individualism, which were also a European construct. Even the exploration of 'virgin' lands came from the Christian tradition, as evident in missionary activities and the crusading zeal seen during the early phases of the colonisation of America. Therefore, Turner's 'frontier' was a European construct and not an American trait.

Defenders of Turner's Theory

Historian Avery Craven defended Turner's theory. Craven argued that Turner brought attention to neglected factors of American history, as he outlined the occupation from the Atlantic to the Pacific Ocean. Turner's frontier was an environment that represented democracy and nationalism, creating new currents of intellectual freedom and individualism. For Turner, American history represented the process of colonisation of diverse geographical areas, whose settlers distanced themselves from their European ancestry to constitute distinctly American individuals. The frontier was a continuation of the social process that promoted American nationalism: Americanisation through the erosion of European values and increasing claims on 'free' land led to the growth of the market economy. An influential national government assisted in the nation's economic and social development. The frontier encouraged democratic individualism, offering freedom from political oppression and sectionalism and became a site of minimal government interference. It strongly encouraged individual growth. Nevertheless, the frontier could not prevent the spread of slavery as it inherited many of the contradictions of the Atlantic seaboard region. According to Craven, Turner's analysis was guided by the 'spirit of inquiry' rather than plain historical facts.

According to Walter Prescott Webb's *The Frontier and the Four Hundred Years Boom*, the frontier assisted in democratising government and political institutions, fostered an agricultural economy, increased population mobility, and established a new social ethos and conduct. The frontier provided 'free' land, capital resources, especially gold and silver and economic mobility, and all these factors combined to increase the population. Economic prosperity sparked new intellectual ideas and political institutions rooted in Protestantism, capitalism, and democracy.

Arthur E. Bestor Jr. argued that four sets of ideas developed in conjunction with westward movement and during the post-frontier phase.[26] These ideas, rooted in the concept of rapid population growth based on economic potentialities, instilled a sense of greatness (through increased political and economic power) and provided opportunities for experimentation in governance structures. They also opened up new avenues for people to make a better life, leading to an increasingly complex society. At this point, the American West began to exert a significant influence on the American way of life, underscoring the historical significance of the westward movement in shaping the nation.

Taking the same line of argument further, Tiziano Bonazzi has argued that Turner's frontier theory was a new way of writing the history of the development of American society.[27] The conquest of the frontier, availability of free land, and advancement of American settlements led to the transformation of American institutions, constitution, and cultural norms. The frontier, therefore, came to stand for a process of social evolution that led to economic and technological complexity in American society. This new process of Americanisation was divorced from European culture (which was based on a 'forest philosophy'), and as we have discussed, led to the development of a 'free individual' who possessed a 'free mind'.[28] With the vestiges of European culture thus abandoned, American settlers were made into 'moral agents' who were free to develop a new society based on new elements of 'natural civilisation', through the rebirth and regeneration of genuinely human qualities. The frontier led to the development of new political ideals of individualism and democracy, including the growth and development of an industrialised society. Bonazzi said the frontier established a more progressive and complex 'free' land environment to develop an industrial organisation.

This society, for both Turner and Bonazzi, became a 'frontierless' social and industrial society that was no longer 'natural', but now dependent on 'fields' of human knowledge based on scientific discoveries. Thus, in the first stage, there was free land that enabled pioneers to undertake westward expansion. In contrast, in the second stage, the modern-day new frontier was a science that opened up new 'spaces' (not lands) to American society. In this way, American history has seen two kinds of frontier movement: *First*, there was a horizontal movement that marked the beginning of frontier expansion, characterised by the pursuit of natural resources and free lands. *Second*, there was a vertical frontier based on the rapid spread of public education, science, and industrialisation. This has permitted the birth of a non-authoritarian government and the growth of a rational society and democracy. According to Bonazzi, this makes Turner a historian of American continuity whose objective was to bring self-consciousness to the present.²⁹

New Ways of Looking at the Westward Expansion

Turner's theory has since been rejected. Historians now study this region from the perspective of race, class, gender, environment, settlements, and community formation history. They also critically evaluate the history of federal government policies in the region and the history of Indigenous peoples that earlier historians, particularly Turner, should have addressed.

Regionalist scholars and **Neo-Turnerians** were the leading voices in the New History of the West engaged in intellectual debate. The crux of their disagreement lies in differing interpretations of the West: while one views the West as a process of frontier expansion, the other views the it as a distinct region.

Neo-Turnerians, in particular, view the region as a process of settlement involving Indigenous communities, immigrants, women, and other non-White people who were overlooked in Turner's thesis. In their evaluation of the West, they emphasise the role of the market economy. Southern enslavers sought new fertile lands and the northerners were looking for discovery of new types of natural resources, free land, and expansion of new markets for their industrial goods, along with economic and employment opportunities. Settlement in the West was fueled by assistance from both the federal and state governments, as well as internal factors (the movement of White settlers, squatters, speculators, enslaved people, free wage labourers, and adventurers), and external factors (immigration from Europe due to political turmoil and high demand for American cotton in Europe). Two Neo-Turnerian scholars, in particular, John Mack Faragher (*Women and Men on the Oregon Trail and Sugar Creek*) and William Cronon (*Nature Metropolis*) sought to establish strong linkages between continuous waves of American settlers and immigrants who were going to the West, and the availability of inexpensive 'virgin' lands that were made vacant due to displacement

Removal of Indigenous Peoples and Westward Expansion 125

of Indigenous communities. Faragher focused on social histories to establish interconnectedness between the frontier communities of the Midwest and the newly established communities of the West. Kinship relations and structures of the gendered division of labour were in flux during the migration period, sparking transformations in families and communities. Cronon has studied the impact of external markets and environmental conditions on the development of Chicago, ultimately leading to the growth of both the rural Midwest and the West.

On the other side of the spectrum, regionalist historians emphasised the study of space in the West where people encountered different geographical conditions that shaped their culture, social structures, economic activities, and political development. Donald Worster focused on aridity and linked the environment with history. Patricia Limerick argues that the West had one peculiarity: both Indigenous societies and Mexican Americans were conquered but remained in their territories, which eventually led to intermixing. Willam Robbins understands that the West is closely associated with the capitalist East. Therefore, capitalism played a significant role in its growth and expansion.

According to Carl Abbott, a major factor in the urbanisation of the American West was the automobile, as it provided connectivity and thus assisted in the growth of Los Angeles, Orange County, Phoenix, and Seattle. He terms this urban development process as the 'metropolitanisation' of the West. John Findlay argues that after World War II (1939–1945), the urban metropolitan areas of the West developed 'magic lands' like Disneyland, the Stanford Industrial Park, and the Sun City, reflecting different growth patterns compared to the East.

According to Richard White, who disagrees with the regionalists, the West was a product of changing relations with other regions, including the East and South, Europe, and Mexico, some of which were long-term while others remained transitory. White argues that at the time of Missouri's formation, the federal government was powerful. The West had non-agricultural lands, and settlers migrated to it from the South and the East. With the emergence of Missouri, migrants from the North moved into the Midwest while the planters and enslaved people moved from the South to Ohio and the Gulf of Mexico. The North and the South then moved across the Mississippi, and this internal expansion resulted in the emergence of the Old Northwest and Old Southwest. The only way the two regions could be distinguished from each other was through the institution of slavery. The Civil War later marked the end of slavery, the rise of a more powerful federal government, and the rapid geographical expansion of the USA. Unlike the experience of the East, the nineteenth-century American West did not require a powerful national army. The peculiarity of the West also led to the development of specialised governance structures like the Bureau of Indian Affairs, the Geographical Survey, the Bureau of Reclamation, the Forest Service, the National Park Service, and the Bureau of Land Management. White claimed that these structures developed due to distinct environmental conditions that necessitated a '**managerial state**' to maintain federal control over large tracts of land. The West was, therefore, not a homogenous entity but a heterogeneous space where urban areas were juxtaposed with rural communities. Both depended on the federal government, with an economy based on the extraction of natural resources and a service-based economy dependent on each other. The West developed a dual labour system that was dependent on race, minority groups, and those coming from the East and the South.

Historian Alfred Crosby, in particular, has discussed the impact of the **Columbian Exchange** on Indigenous communities. The term 'Columbian Exchange' refers to the broad transfer of people, plants, animals, and diseases between the Old World (Africa and Eurasia) and the New World (the Americas) from the late fifteenth century onward. The Indigenous peoples had to contend with White settlers and new diseases brought by them from Europe. These caused what Crosby termed 'virgin-soil epidemics'—since the Indigenous population had never been exposed to these diseases, they had no natural immunity from them and were vulnerable to devastating outbreaks. The settlement of the West brought slavery, wars, the decline of hunting game, and the loss of Indigenous peoples' sacred spaces. The encounter transformed the political organisation and social and cultural identities of Indigenous societies, leading to the development of new economic systems; the Navajo, for instance, began sheep herding, and the peoples of the Great Plains adopted pastoralism. According to Dan Flores and Elliot West, epizootic disease reduced bison populations to near-extinction. Another factor was the growth of horse and cattle ranches that competed for grasslands that had once been the exclusive domain of bison.

Some examples of academic scholarship on these transformations include: Willard Rolling's study of the Osage; Peter Iverson's research on the Navajo; and Alexander Harman's work on Puget Sound. These scholars worked on the impact of settlers on Indigenous peoples, especially with the imposition of the Indian Removal Act that brought in plough agriculture, Christianity, and Western forms of governance, along with the treaty-making process and reservation system. These eventually facilitated the development of new political institutions with the assistance of the Bureau of Indian Affairs. Playing Indian politics became a game of Indian Roulette, as discussed in detail by Francis Paul Prucha, who outlined that the American desire for a homogenous republic, Protestant Christianity and equality unleashed American greed, racism and imperial ambitions on Indigenous peoples.

The Indigenous Resistance That Ended in the Trail of Tears

In this section, we focus on the history of the removal of Indigenous communities from the southern states. Indigenous removal was considered a benevolent step, as we have already discussed, based on the argument that they tended to acquire White vices rather than virtues of 'civilisation'. Indigenous resistance to westward expansion made the settlers more determined to move them. A variety of justifications were developed for this: legal (numerous laws that validated the White settlers' control over land), and moral (Indigenous people were characterised as mere hunters who did not know how to use the land). Using Western common law practice, the settlers justified the expulsion of Indigenous people because their right of discovery was more important than the 'limited right of temporary occupancy' of the Indigenous groups.

Five major Indigenous communities lived in southwest America:

(*i*) The Chickasaw sacred land comprised western Tennessee, northern Mississippi, and northwestern Alabama.
(*ii*) The sacred land of the Choctaw included central Mississippi and Alabama.
(*iii*) The Creek Confederacy lived in Alabama and Georgia.
(*iv*) The Cherokee lived in northwestern Alabama, eastern Tennessee and southwestern North Carolina.
(*v*) The Seminole consisted of Creeks, Florida tribes and runaway African enslaved people.[30]

While each of these groups had a distinct identity, together they comprised the Indigenous Mississippian culture. They had developed a complex web of cultural traditions over centuries, with permanent village systems, an agricultural economy, a hierarchical political system based on chiefdoms, and a lifestyle rooted in their own cultural norms. They had already come in contact with European explorers, traders, colonial agents, and soldiers. Still, the pressure of expanding European settlers began to be felt only by the end of the eighteenth century. This pressure came from the French, Spanish, and British competing for colonial control over the continent. During the process of the colonisation of America, the British implemented several alien acts that aimed to curtail their right of self-determination, control over their ancestral land, freedom of movement, limit their political autonomy, criminalise their Indigenous practices, and help the colonists to relocate them to uninhabitable spaces. This included forcible assimilation, conversion to Christianity, and so on. The same concept continued to be applied by the American government after the American Revolution, in a process of internal colonisation.

In the first phase of colonisation, the British established military alliances and trading relationships with the Indigenous groups inhabiting the Mississippian region. The largest share of European immigrants came from Britain, and initially, they were involved in establishing forts, trading missions, and isolated settlements. Then,

FIG. 5.1: *American Progress*, by John Gast, oil on canvas (1872) *Source*: Wikimedia Commons.

they discovered 'virgin lands' suitable for cultivating tobacco and rice. This led to the beginning of land surrender treaties that impacted the internal structures of Indigenous societies and eventually led to their dispossession and marginalisation. This also marked the beginning of 'frontier' history in America.

After the American Revolution under the Articles of Confederation Constitution (in operation from 1781 to 1789), the Congress established a loosely structured '**Indian Policy**'. During the deliberate removal of Indigenous peoples from their sacred lands, two methods of appropriating lands in the West were pursued by the federal government. The first was based on the Western premise that the settlers had the 'right of discovery', so land and associated resources now belonged to the White settlers. Thus, the Indian policy asserted the federal government's right to regulate trade within the Indigenous nations. Since the White settlers had 'discovered' North America, all Indigenous peoples living in the Northwest and in the old Southwest were living on 'occupied' land that belonged to the federal government.

In the second process, Indigenous people were projected as 'savages' and, therefore, uncivilised people who needed to be 'saved' via assimilation into Western lifestyles, traditions, language, and religion. The civilisational process was promoted with the appointment of 'Indian agents' who taught the 'savages' the proper economic use of land through the development of commercial agriculture, animal husbandry, and a settled lifestyle. The federal government provided funds to missionary societies to encourage religious conversion to Christianity, which was considered a 'civilising' process, along with the introduction of Western education.

While religious conversion and assimilation through the schooling system was not universally successful, the so-called Indian agents were successful in persuading Indigenous groups to abandon their traditional economies and settle down in isolated homesteads, thereby opening up vast tracts of land for the settlers. These agents would then survey the appropriated territory and sell it at a minimal price to incoming White settlers, who then introduced the Western system of using land and its resources for capitalistic gains. The figure of the 'progressive Indian' was deliberately deployed so agents and trade commissioners could use it during treaty negotiations, leading to further dispossession of Indigenous communities.

Those who placed their faith in Indigenous systems shunned alcohol and refused to participate in the Western credit system. They did not gamble on horse-racing like other 'civilised Indians' who, they feared, were falling to 'civilised' vices. When existing measures failed to remove them, President Jefferson enacted a new removal policy with the Louisiana Purchase of 1803, which moved the Indigenous groups to the west of the Mississippi River, where they would eventually be 'civilised'—this period marked the beginning of the official and deliberate policy of removing Indigenous people from their sacred lands.

Beneath the guise of this civilisational process emerged the Cherokee removal crisis of 1838–1839, when the federal government exploited the discord between the groups inhabiting eastern Tennessee and western North Carolina on the one hand, and those living in Alabama and Georgia on the other. The former were more amenable to assimilating into White 'civilisation'. The federal government exploited these internal fissures to negotiate land cession treaties.

Around this time, the Cherokee, Chickasaw, Creek, and Choctaw began to adopt Western political, social, and economic systems in an effort to secure the support of the Indian agents and Christian missionaries. This marked the beginning of a new type of Cherokee resistance from 1808 to 1810, when the Cherokee established a national police force, created an executive committee to conduct business between council meetings, and made murder a federal crime within the Indigenous system of blood vengeance. In 1829, a law was enacted that treated the cession of Indigenous land as a capital offence. The Creek, too, had enacted the same directive in 1811, and when the pressure for the cession of their lands increased considerably, they shifted this responsibility to a national council. Many Creeks opposed the Westernisation of political institutions and the role of their elected chiefs, who had become puppets of the federal government. This led to the **Civil War of 1813** (also known as the **Creek War**), which allowed the federal government to ally itself with friendly Creeks against the 'Red Sticks' who 'opposed Western cultural transformations'. After their defeat, many Red Sticks migrated south and joined other Indigenous groups in Florida as well as runaway enslaved Africans, to form the Seminole Confederacy. This Confederacy continued to operate under older political systems. Those who chose to ignore the religious propaganda, mission schools, and their new elected chiefs, and instead continued to follow their traditional systems and lifestyles, were branded as 'recalcitrant savages'.

The federal government's attempts at deliberate removal thus encountered resistance, as very few tribes agreed to be removed. In 1810, about 1,000 Cherokees moved to Arkansas. Another Cherokee emigration occurred in 1817–1819 when one group ceded land in the Southeast to compensate the federal government for the additional land the Arkansas Cherokee had settled. In 1820, the Choctaw signed the **Treaty of Doak's Stand**, under which they relinquished one-third of their eastern domain for a larger tract in Arkansas. However, this treaty was renegotiated due to protests by White settlers in Arkansas. As a result of re-negotiations in 1825, the Choctaw received a new parcel of land in present-day southeastern Oklahoma. In 1826, the Creek acceded to an exchange of land in Georgia for a tract north of that held by the Choctaw. The consequences of these exchanges were very different from what Jefferson's removal policy had envisaged. As most members of the Indigenous groups that moved to the West were 'civilised Indians', it deprived the federal government of 'friendly Indians' who would be willing to negotiate land cession treaties with the federal government. Those left behind were 'troublesome Indians' opposed to their forceful removal. In the Jeffersonian era, that is, until 1829, no president followed the policy of forcefully removing Indigenous groups to the West against their will.

Another problem was brewing in the southern states of America. Cotton prices had increased in the international markets. This led to expansion of cotton cultivation and slavery in the southern states; consequently, there were growing demands in the region to liquidate Indigenous land titles for agricultural development. Georgia pressured the federal government to comply with the **1802 Compact**. Under this agreement, the state relinquished its claim to its original charter's western land, which became Alabama and Mississippi, in exchange for the federal government's promise to extinguish Indigenous land titles within the state at some unspecified time. In 1826, the Creek gave up their remaining land and withdrew to Alabama, but the Cherokee remained on their ancestral lands.

By 1827, the Cherokee had established a republican government with a written constitution fashioned after the US Constitution. The Georgia government saw this as a violation of its sovereignty and demanded that the federal government extinguish Indian land titles. In the meantime, the state legislature enacted a series of laws to establish state control over the Cherokee nation and completely marginalised them so that they would leave their ancestral lands. The state created a special militia force, the Georgia Guard, to enforce Georgia law within the Cherokee nation. The state passed laws prohibiting Indians from mining gold and testifying against White people in court, preventing Cherokee leaders from speaking in public. It also formulated plans to survey and divide Cherokee lands in preparation for distribution by lottery to White settlers. Other states began to follow Georgia's example and impose state laws to displace Indigenous peoples from their ancestral lands.

When Andrew Jackson came to the President's office in 1828, with a long experience of fighting and negotiating with southern Indigenous groups, he wanted White settlements to be established in all the Indigenous lands in the Southeast. In his message to Congress in 1829, President Jackson gave two alternatives to Indigenous groups—they could become subject to the discriminatory laws of the states, or move West and continue with their governments. This was followed in 1830 by the Indian Removal Act that authorised the President to negotiate the exchange of territory and provided him US $500,000 to achieve this task. The funds were to compensate the Indigenous groups and assist them in moving to the West.

In 1830, a group of Choctaw ceded their land in the Southeast under the provisions of the **Treaty of Dancing Rabbit Creek**. In return, the federal government promised them transportation to the West, subsistence for one year after removal, and an annuity to support education and other services. Traditionalists among the Indigenous people were against this treaty, but with dwindling numbers, they could pose little threat. In 1831, the first group of Choctaw left Mississippi. The War Department had allocated supervision of this group to the Indian trader George Gaines, who conducted them to the Mississippi River. Control was then handed over to Francis Armstrong. However, these men subcontracted their responsibility to agents guided by corruption and greed. They appropriated the funds instead of providing rations and medical assistance that were meant to help the communities overcome the problems of migration, relocation, and the harsh winter. Military officials conducted the two other Choctaw removals in 1832 and 1833, and by 1834, approximately 13,000 to 15,000 Choctaws were removed had been their ancestral lands.

Only about 7,000 Choctaws remained in Mississippi; they were either heads of households who had registered to receive an allotment or those who were prevented from leaving the state as they had to pay back borrowed money. Most of those who had to stay behind were pushed into extreme poverty and were marginalised; they became a minority and gradually fell victim to land speculators. The federal government did not assist those who were victimised by the unlawful acts of White settlers.

In 1832, the Creek chiefs agreed to cede much of their land in Alabama; some Creeks were permitted to receive the remainder in allotments. White land speculators later defrauded many Creeks of their grants, and some Creeks who had no land or farms refused to move west. This led to tension between two opposing communities and erupted in violence. This forced the War Department in 1836 to use military force to remove thousands of Creeks, many of whom died during their westward journey. Others died on sinking steamboats, or of disease, hunger and exposure, and only 14,500 made it to their new home in the West.

The Chickasaw also suffered from corruption and fraud during their removal. Under the terms of the **Treaty of Pontotoc**, the Chickasaw ceded their eastern homeland, but officials could not find suitable land for their relocation. In the meantime, their territory was opened to White settlements, defrauding defenceless Indigenous people of their lands. Desperate Chickasaw agreed to buy a tract of land from the Choctaws, and in 1837–1838, about 4,000 Chickasaw migrated beyond the Mississippi.

Learning from these experiences, the Cherokee turned to the US Supreme Court for a ruling on whether Georgia law could be extended over that part of the Cherokee nation that lay within the chartered limit of Georgia. In *Worcester v. Georgia*, the court ruled that Georgia could not enforce state law within the Cherokee nation. The state refused to comply and continued to harass the Cherokee. Finally, in 1835, the **Treaty of Echota** was negotiated, which provided for exchanging Cherokee territory in the Southeast for a tract of land in present-day northeastern Oklahoma. All 15,000 Cherokee opposed this treaty and signed a petition against it. In 1838, the federal troops seized thousands of Cherokees and made them march westward, which led to the death of about 4,000 Cherokees and is known in history as the '**Trail of Tears**'.[31]

The Seminole also resisted their removal. In 1832, they signed a provisional removal treaty in which they agreed to relocate west if they found a suitable area. When a group of them were sent along with the Indian agent, he made them sign a removal treaty from Florida by 1837. The Senate ratified this treaty, and President Jackson ordered its enforcement. The federal government believed that since the Seminoles had once been part of the Creek Confederacy, the two groups could be reunited in the West. The Seminole resisted this attempt, and in 1835, Seminole warriors ambushed federal troops, leading to the **Second Seminole War** (the first war occurred under Jackson's military leadership, in 1812). The warriors began to use guerrilla tactics and took the fight into the swamps of southern Florida. The federal government was forced to send 40,000 men and spent about 40 million dollars to defeat the Seminoles, with the war finally ending in 1842.

By now, only a fraction of Indigenous people lived in their ancestral land, below subsistence level, and were utterly marginalised. The state and federal governments began to ignore them entirely, and a new issue was now emerging on the horizon: the Nullification Crisis. As discussed in Chapter 4, the crisis began to loom over the issues of slavery and tariff rates in the southern states, threatening the unity of the young nation and diverting attention away from the Indigenous peoples.

The Indigenous Revitalisation Movement as a Form of Resistance: Case Study of Tecumseh and the Shawnee Prophet

Territorial expansion from 1800 onwards, driven by American squatters, settlers, and the federal government, resulted in their inward movement west of the Appalachian Mountains. This led to the rapid marginalisation and decimation of the Indigenous population, which in turn sparked **Indigenous resistance**. According to Eric Foner, this led to the emergence of an 'age of prophecy' from 1800 to 1812—an attempt by the 'original peoples' to protect their Indigenous identity, culture, and land, especially among the Creek, Cherokee, Shawnee, Iroquois, and many others.[32] This resulted in violent conflicts, leading the federal government to enact two crucial legislative measures: the **Land Ordinance Acts of 1785 and 1787**, respectively, followed by the **Treaty of Greenville** (which demarcated the boundary line between Indigenous peoples and American settlers in the region of Ohio). Despite these administrative measures, White settlers and squatters continued to advance due to a rapid decline in wild game, adversely impacting the fur trade. The Indigenous peoples became a marginalised group on their sacred lands, and the struggle for their survival pushed them to steal livestock from the Whites.

Indigenous communities, in the meantime, were plagued with the problem of alcoholism, a manufactured disaster that emerged from their encounter with settler society, reflecting the heavy toll of diseases, conflicts, and a disruption of social norms and ethos. The high disease burden on Indigenous populations, due to the rapid spread of influenza, smallpox, and other diseases against which they had neither immunity nor medicine, resulted in widespread health issues and high mortality. Removed from their ancestral lands, plagued by internal problems, and with an erosion of their social institutions and structures, their families were broken up and their world appeared to vanish.

In this period of rapid marginalisation and displacement, two brothers from the Shawnee Nation emerged as influential figures. Tecumseh was a Shawnee chief who had opposed the Treaty of Greenville in 1795, along with his younger brother, Lalawethika ('Makes a Loud Noise' or 'Noise Maker'). The latter had struggled with alcoholism in his youth, but after a vision in 1805, he transformed into a spiritual leader. He took on a new name, Tenskwatawa ('The Open Door'). Tenskwatawa became a religious prophet, advocating a return to traditional ways of living to resist dispossession at the hands of White settler society.[33] His approach combined Indigenous cultural revival with a complete separation from the world of White settlers.

To unify various Indigenous communities, the **Shawnee brothers** frequently referred to a story of Indigenous warriors who, during their journey, had crossed the Great Water. During their journey, a water serpent came in their way, but it was killed. Still, parts of its body were saved by a witch and contained in medicine bundles—these represented evil being passed on from generation to generation. The present situation, they argued, resulted from that evil that had not been defeated.³⁴

This narrative was masterfully woven into a tool of resistance by the Shawnee brothers as they began to propagate the belief that they were chosen by 'the Master of Life' to bring harmony. They used a sacred bundle possessing powerful medicine and enacted a series of holy laws. These laws were to be implemented in Indigenous societies to provide strength and motivation to remain faithful to their traditions. The brothers associated the mythic water serpent with the sea. Their ancestors had warned that pale-skinned people would emerge from the water to cause evil and conflict.³⁵ To bring various warring factions together, Tecumseh opposed any form of violence in Indigenous society and began to preach against the consumption of alcohol, which he considered to be a 'poison' and 'curse' unleashed by the White people. Instead, he began to emphasise Indigenous family values—maintaining the sanctity of marriage and reviving the 'warrior spirit of brotherhood' through community living—with the argument that adhering to them would end the White tradition of private property. **Tenskwatawa's 'purification movement'** advocated a return to traditional dietary patterns (which included using Indigenous instruments and cooking methods), traditional attire, hairstyles, and religious practices centering the masters of life. He began to instigate his followers against Indigenous converts to Christianity as well as their European colonisers (particularly the British, French, Spanish and Americans), as he believed all of them to be children of the great water serpent.³⁶

This movement quickly became widespread and began to unify the scattered Indigenous groups in the region, with the result that by 1805, from Ohio to Delaware, massive conflicts led to mass killings of those Indians who had converted to Christianity. By 1807, Tenskwatawa's popularity had spread to adjoining communities. Those who were alarmed at this growing violence understood the anger and Indigenous action differently. For the Americans, it was not a 'revitalisation movement' as claimed by the Shawnee brothers, but a cleverly crafted British policy to prevent American expansion.

Therefore, they termed Tecumseh a 'British agent'.[37] French and Spanish missionaries became alarmed at this growing violence against their 'benevolent' efforts to 'civilise' the 'barbarians'.

Meanwhile, to strengthen Indigenous resistance, Tenskwatawa initially tried to befriend American officials William Henry Harrison and John Johnston. However, in 1809, Harrison signed the **Treaty of Fort Wayne** with the Potawatomi, Delaware, Miami and Eel River leaders, which brought three million acres of land under American control for just two cents per acre (in present-day Indiana, Illinois, Ohio, and Michigan). Tenskwatawa opposed this treaty, and with his brother Tecumseh, he initiated political and military resistance against the American expansion. This marked the beginning of open conflict between the White settlers and the Indigenous Confederacy established by the Shawnee brothers.[38]

In 1810, Tecumseh planned an attack on American frontier settlements, timed according to Tenskwatawa's prediction of a solar eclipse. He told his followers that he could bring back the Sun's radiance. These predictions helped fuel Indigenous resistance against the advance of White settlers on Indigenous lands in what came to be known as the **Battle of Tippecanoe (1811)**.[39] At this juncture, the spiritual leader's influence was on the wane, and his followers lost the battle.

In 1812, with the US and Britain engaged in the war, Tecumseh, with his confederate tribal army, sided with Britain in the **Battle of Thames**. The battle led to his death in 1813 and ended in an American victory. This defeat accelerated American westward expansion at the cost of the further marginalisation and displacement of Indigenous communities from their ancestral lands and the complete eclipse of the Prophet, who later died in 1834 in Kansas, bringing to an end Indigenous resistance based on a tribal confederacy.

Notes

1. Larry J. Zimmerman and Brian Leigh Molyneaux, *Native North America* (Oklahoma, 1996), pp. 8, 14, 15–17.
2. Ibid., pp. 8, 20.
3. Ibid., pp. 14–15.

4. Ibid., pp. 38–41.
5. Ibid., pp. 44–45.
6. Ibid., pp. 46–49.
7. Ibid., pp. 50–51.
8. Ibid., pp. 52–55.
9. Ibid., pp. 58–59.
10. Ibid., pp. 60–63.
11. Archana Ojha, 'Federal Policies and Governance of First Nations in Canada', PhD diss. (New Delhi, 2003).
12. Paul S. Boyer, et al., *The Enduring Vision: A History of the American People, Vol. I: To 1877* (USA, 1990).
13. William L. Barney, *The Passage of the Republic: An Interdisciplinary History of Nineteenth-Century America* (USA, 1987).
14. Robert F. Berkhofer, Jr, 'The White Advance Upon Native Lands', in *The White Man's Indian: Images of the American Indian from Columbus to the Present* (New York, 1978), pp. 207–211.
15. Ronald N. Satz, *American Indian Policy in the Jacksonian Era* (USA, 1975), pp. 159–175.
16. Alfred A. Cave, *Abuse of Power: Andrew Jackson and the Indian Removal Act of 1830* (2003).
17. Robert V. Remini, *Andrew Jackson and His Indian Wars* (New York, 2001), pp. 222–237.
18. Berkhofer, Jr, 'The White Advance Upon Native Lands', pp. 207–222.
19. Remini, *Andrew Jackson and His Indian Wars*, pp. 222–237.
20. Berkhofer, Jr, 'The White Advance Upon Native Lands', pp. 207–222.
21. Satz, *American Indian Policy in the Jacksonian Era*, pp. 160–161.
22. Ibid., pp. 161–163.
23. Richard White, *It's Your Misfortune and None of My Own: A New History of the American West* (Oklahoma, 1997).
24. Frederick Jackson Turner, 'Significance of Frontier in American History', in *Frontier and Sections: Selected Essays of F. J. Turner*, ed. Ray Allen Billington (New Jersey, 1961).
25. The Gold Rush refers to the series of gold rushes, or the discovery of gold deposits, that generate intense public interest and prompted settlers to move to Oregon, Utah, Colorado, and other areas.
26. Arthur E. Bestor, Jr, 'Patent-Office Models of the Good Society: Some Relationships between Social Reform and Westward Expansion', *American Historical Review 58* (1953), pp. 505–526.
27. Tiziano Bonazzi, 'Frederick Jackson Turner's Frontier Thesis and Self-Consciousness of America', *Journal of American Studies 27* (2), pp. 149–171.
28. Ibid.
29. Ibid.
30. Eric Foner, *Give Me Liberty! An American History*, third ed. (New York, 2011).
31. For a detailed account of the removal of Indigenous peoples in the South, see Theda Purdue, 'Trail of Tears: Removal of the Southern Indians in

the Jeffersonian–Jacksonian Era', in *'They Made Us Many Promises': The American Indian Experience, 1524 to the Present*, ed. Philip Weeks (Illinois, 2002).
32. Foner, *Give Me Liberty!*, p. 311.
33. R. David Edmunds, 'Tecumseh, The Shawnee Prophet, and American History', in *Retracing the Past: Readings in the History of the American People*, vol. 1, ed. Gary B. Nash (New York, 1990), pp. 204–205.
34. Ibid., pp. 203–204.
35. Ibid., p. 204.
36. Ibid., pp. 205–206.
37. Ibid., p. 206.
38. Ibid., pp. 207–208.
39. Ibid., p. 206.

Chapter 6

The War of 1812

Background

The struggle of the Thirteen Colonies for independence was not just a struggle for freedom, but the catalyst that established the enduring principles of victory that would shape its foreign policy, leaving a profound and lasting impact on the nation. The War of American Independence was meant to defeat Great Britain, the military superpower of the eighteenth century, and formally declare America's status as a sovereign nation. In the end, the USA achieved a comprehensive political-military victory. This paved the way for what became known as the **Monroe Doctrine**, under which it was clearly stated that the United States would not tolerate interference in the Western hemisphere from other nations. George Washington first expressed this foundational principle of American foreign policy in his Farewell Address on 19 September 1796, where he warned against 'the insidious wiles of foreign influence'.[1] According to Washington, the nation was formed because of the colonists' 'abiding distrust of external danger [and the prospect of] ... frequent interruption[s] of their Peace by Foreign [European] Nations'. The '**Proclamation of Neutrality**' that President Washington issued on 22 April 1793 declared that the United States would 'adopt and pursue a conduct friendly and impartial' towards Britain, Netherlands, and Spain, united in their efforts against revolutionary France.

The first few years of the US as a new republic were times of prosperity and growth. The main reason behind this economic prosperity was the **Napoleonic War**, which continued with few interruptions from the 1790s to 1815. France and Britain were preoccupied with warfare, so a portion of the trade that they would generally have carried fell by default to America as a neutral power (see Chapter 3). As the most significant trading neutral power of the age, America had much to gain, but also faced some risk—both European powers, time and again, created conditions and situations that could have pushed America into this vicious conflict.

Emergence of Political Groups in American Politics

During the Federalist era, George Washington and Alexander Hamilton sought to transform the developing nation into a 'commercial empire' through an informal alliance with England. The party was pro-Britain in orientation and elitist in its political assumptions. However, they made a fatal mistake in 1798–99 by levying heavy taxes (such as the whisky tax and tariff policy) to execute a potential war with France. The Federalists lost to the Democratic-Republicans in 1800 who charged them with being a pro-British party that supported elements of tyranny, militarism, and taxation.

Democratic-Republicans, on the other hand, led by President Thomas Jefferson, sought to make America 'an empire of liberty', which resulted in the Louisiana Purchase of 1803 and the War of 1812. The former represented tremendous agricultural expansionism that would primarily benefit small farmers who produced for the export market. However, the export market had to be opened up, based on the principle of free trade. Otherwise, the US would become economically dependent on any foreign power with the naval capability to control the flow of international commerce. Therefore, Jefferson pursued the policies of territorial expansion, securing commercial and neutral rights, and the two-hemisphere concept, and he aimed to achieve this without war. However, the Napoleonic Wars forced him to alter his stance. Jefferson's diplomatic policy was based on his experiences as Minister to France and Secretary of State in the 1780s and 1790s, and he had supported the French Revolution during this period. Britain, in contrast, was seen as a colonial power that had exploited America, and which used its naval power to control the seas and pose obstacles to American free trade. In his electoral campaigns, Jefferson promised a new governance system free from corruption and the practices of the 'Old World'. This new system would be premised on the application of economic and diplomatic pressure, rooted in an uncompromising faith in the doctrine of natural rights and the virtuous character of the American people. During Jefferson's presidential term, the federal government's neutrality policy facilitated the expansion of American commerce and allowed for the Louisiana Purchase from Spain. The government also promoted the export of agricultural goods in the trans-Appalachian West and Florida.[2]

External Scenario

On the other side of the Atlantic Ocean, in Europe, the Peace Treaty of Amiens collapsed between Britain and France (1803), and both nations resumed their **Continental War** (1803–1815). While the US remained neutral, many European nations joined the fray. While France quickly gained control over the land, Britain was master of the sea. Its powerful navy was capable of impacting the American flow of international commerce. The situation was complex: as Reginald Horsman has explained, Britain required sailors to operate its navy, but these soldiers were defecting in large numbers due to the nation's prolonged involvement in numerous conflicts.[3] Britain's contempt for American neutrality stemmed from its view of America as a weak nation and Jefferson as a pro-France president. While Britain was locked in a struggle against Napoleon, the US was prospering at its expense.

Jefferson displayed marked differences between his political ideology and his decisions as a leader during the Napoleonic War. His failure to prioritise the balance of power and emphasise neutral rights, along with his anti-British posturing, led to antagonism between America and Britain, thwarted diplomatic initiatives, and eventually forced both countries onto a path of economic collision that would go on to trigger the War of 1812.[4]

In the meantime, from 1790 to 1810, the tonnage of American ships nearly tripled; American ships carried sugar and coffee from French and Spanish colonies in the Caribbean to Europe. This trade provided Napoleon with supplies and, by adding to the glut of these commodities in the world markets, drove down the price of sugar and coffee from the British West Indies. This led Britain to conclude that it was the one paying the price for America's commercial prosperity.

The basis of American prosperity was the **re-import trade**, an American adaptation to the British rule of 1756, which stipulated that businesses closed in times of peace could reopen in times of war. The ingenious American response to the power of 1756 was to formulate the 'broken voyage' system. As we discussed in Chapter 3, American ships would carry products from the Spanish and French West Indies to an American port, unload them and re-export them to Europe as American produce. From 1795 to 1805, the British tolerated broken voyages, but thereafter they chartered a new course. Horsman contends that the war between Britain and France had assumed commercial proportions by 1805.[5] Britain sought ways to strangle French commerce and defeat Napoleon's armies.

In 1805, a British court declared the broken voyage illegal, and in 1806, the nation imposed of a series of restrictive trade regulations known as **Order-in-Council**, which established a naval blockade around Europe. In theory, this regulation softened the **Essex Case** (see Chapter 3) by allowing American vessels to trade with French possessions as 'long as they carried their cargoes to Britain rather than to a continental port controlled by France'. Napoleon responded with his **Berlin Decree in 1806**, which proclaimed a blockade of the British Isles; any ship attempting to enter or leave a British port was now subject to seizure by France. The British answered the Berlin Decree with another Order-in-Council, requiring all neutral ships trading in the blockaded zones of Europe to stop at British ports to secure licenses. Napoleon retaliated with his Continental System and the **Milan Decree in 1807**, which proclaimed that any ship submitting to British regulations or allowing itself to be searched by the British Royal Navy was subject to seizure by France.

Internal Scenario

These proclamations and counter-proclamation outlawed virtually all international trade for America. Both Britain and France seized American ships, but British seizures were far more humiliating to Americans. France was a weaker naval power than Britain; much of the French fleet had been destroyed by Britain in the **Battle of Trafalgar**, in October 1805. As a result, France generally only seized American ships in European ports, where American ships were lured by Napoleon's often inconsistent enforcement of his Continental System. In contrast, British warships stopped and searched nearly all American vessels just beyond the American coast, in what was seen as an insulting exercise that challenged America's territorial integrity.

Many American merchant ships employed British sailors—these sailors had deserted the Royal Navy due to discontent and because Americans paid them better salaries. British sailors were desperate to leave their war-torn country. Britain, however, did not recognise such desertions as legitimate. Horsman has explained that there was an urgent need to bring back deserters in order to fill the ranks of the British navy.[6] This imperative led to the **Chesapeake–Leopard Affair in 1807**, when a British warship, HMS *Leopard*, attacked the American frigate USS *Chesapeake* and seized four supposed deserters. For Jefferson, this was a worse affront than the events of 1775. He sought negotiations with Britain to gain redress for the *Chesapeake* affair, but to no avail; subsequently, the American government imposed the **Embargo Act** as a means of 'peaceful coercion'.

By restricting French and British trade with the US, Jefferson hoped to pressure both nations to respect American neutrality. One can argue that the impasse between America and Britain arose because Jefferson was unwilling to surrender the keystone of his political philosophy. He felt that economic independence was essential for maintaining national sovereignty, but at the same time, he (like many Republicans) was extremely wary of urbanisation and the growth of factories in America. In the absence of domestic industries, trade with Europe was crucial, and Jefferson had to resist British interference with American markets in Europe. The acquisition of land and the sale abroad of what 'virtuous' farmers produced in America were two sides of the same (Republican) coin. Without free markets in Europe, the American ability to finance imported manufactured goods with exported agricultural goods would be hampered. Unless both nations respected American neutrality, the Republican leader would be forced to give more importance to the growth and development of factories and cities in America.

Ultimately, the episode demonstrated the country's political and diplomatic immaturity at the international level. Jefferson aimed to avoid war and adopted a policy of 'peaceful coercion', but these measures failed; moreover, they adversely impacted American commerce and its agricultural economy. Historians Bradford Perkins and Donald Hickey opined that Jefferson's policy was both anti-British and overly confrontational.

James Madison, also a Republican, became President in 1809. On assuming office, he found that the American army and gunboat navy had to be expanded to rebuff the British navy. In line with Jeffersonian policy, Madison applied economic pressure on Britain and France in his first two years in office. The **Non-Intercourse Act** opened American trade to all nations except Britain and France. Congress authorised the President to restore business with either country if it ceased to violate neutral rights. In 1810, **Macon's Bill No. 2** replaced the Non-Intercourse Act: it reopened trade with Britain and France, with an additional offer that if either nation repealed its restrictions on neutral shipping, the US would stop all commerce with the other. France responded to this by lifting all sanctions against America; Madison, without understanding the hidden agenda at play, readily imposed sanctions against Britain. France had never intended to respect American neutrality—it aimed to trick the latter into a posture of hostility toward Britain—and they continued to seize American vessels in French-controlled ports. After a series of conflicting and confusing economic sanctions, first against both Britain and France later only against Britain, the US embarked on a **'Second War for Independence'** against Britain. The War of 1812 was a Republican war, as not a single Federalist in the Senate voted in support of it.

America Marches into War

The war was precipitated by a highly complex set of factors, and debates on these factors continue among historians. It was the first war America fought against Britain after the War of Independence in 1776, and therefore, as mentioned earlier, it was also known as the 'Second War of Independence'. In this sense, the war consolidated the American Union that had emerged in 1776. This war has also been termed '**The American War**' and characterised as a 'forgotten war' in American history.

In his war message, President Madison listed **impressments**[7] along with the continued presence of British ships in American waters, British violation of neutral rights, and British incitement of the Indigenous peoples as factors for war. For this reason, many who opposed the war, as well as some scholars, have termed it 'Mr. Madison's War'. The President declared that Britain's 'hostile acts' were meant to strangle American trade and eliminate the US as a trading rival. These were seen as a violation of the sovereignty of the US and the neutrality rights of its ships. Moreover, there was the British policy of encouraging Indigenous peoples to settle in Canada and the Northwest with an aim to prevent American territorial expansion. In other words, Madison wanted to protect the 'principle of sovereign authority' of the US, even though it was far weaker militarily than Britain.

For Americans, it was a strange and chaotic war. Massive strategic blunders and poor communication prolonged the war, with neither America nor Britain managing to control its momentum or secure a decisive upper hand. A dangerous precedent was set during this war when, in 1814, delegates from three states—Massachusetts, Connecticut, and Rhode Island—met at Hartford, Connecticut, to discuss the possibility of seceding from the Union as they opposed the war. Fortunately, a sudden end to the war meant that this plan did not take off.[8] The Treaty of Ghent, signed in 1814, completely ignored the issues that had fuelled the conflict. According to Alan Taylor, this war demonstrated that the Americans were not militarily prepared to fight, and it was sheer luck that they were able to remain independent and avoid becoming a British colony.[9]

The War of 1812 was a watershed moment in American history, jostling uncomfortably between the early national period and the era before the Civil War. By interpreting the war as a victory, Americans felt they had established their sovereignty vis-à-vis the rest of the world for the first time. Now, their economy was no longer a pawn in European diplomacy. Turning inward to expand the Union across the breadth of the continent, Americans discovered that the Federalist and Republican political groups had outlived their usefulness. The political vacuum thus created would later enable Andrew Jackson's emergence as a Democratic Party leader, splitting the Republican Party and additionally creating an oppositional group known as the Whigs. More importance was now given to internal improvements through federal funds, tariff protection for the new industries that had developed during the Embargo Act, the establishment of the Second Bank of the US, and the expansion of the American standing army and navy. However, these changes proved temporary when sectional tensions emerged with the **Missouri Compromise**, culminating in the beginning of the American Civil War in 1861.

Interpretations of the War

Historians have analysed the causes of this war from the perspectives of national honour, territorial expansion, neutral rights, problems with Indigenous peoples, and territorial insecurity, as well as the economic recession that plagued the southern and western states from 1808 to 1810 due to Britain's economic blockade.

Till the nineteenth century, the dominant view among historians was that America had fought the war to maintain its 'national honour' and secure 'neutral maritime rights' in the face of British aggression. America also wanted Britain to give up the Orders-in-Council and impressment policies. However, by the early twentieth century, new scholarship emerged that focused on the 'Indigenous problem' and sectionalism (that is, growing differences of opinion between states that supported the war and those that opposed it) as factors in the war.

A host of competing theories explore territorial acquisition as a cause of war. Henry Adams, writing in 1895, believed that the primary purpose of going to war was the 'conquest of Canada'. In 1911, Howard T. Lewis believed that aggressive frontier expansion by Americans, who sought to satisfy their hunger for rich agricultural lands and eventually cast their eyes on the British colony of Canada, was a significant factor. Historian D. R. Anderson, in 1913, viewed the war as one rooted in problems with Indigenous groups, which could only be resolved by expelling Britain from the whole of North America. Edward Channing's interpretation focuses on regional variations that are somewhat in variance with these theories. He believed that the West wanted to 'solve' the Indigenous problem, while the South sought to conquer Florida and Canada. According to him, the North was opposed to this war because they believed that the number of slave states would increase and slavery would become more widespread. J. W. Pratt, drawing from the work of both D. R. Anderson and Edward Channing, suggested that the American Northwest wanted to conquer Canada to subjugate the Indigenous peoples and gain control over extensive farmlands. In contrast, the South sought to annex Florida: this would fulfil the strategic reason of maintaining a balance of power with the Northwest, and offered agricultural and commercial advantages. Donald R. Hickey has suggested that the war was an attempt by America to force Britain to withdraw from Upper and Lower Canada.[10] According to Hickey, the war was '… a turning point, a great watershed that shaped the young Republic's politics, military and diplomatic future'.[11] At the same time, according to Troy Bickham, for the British the war was their last attempt to control the North American continent and retain British hegemony in the Atlantic World. Britain wanted the US to become a 'client nation'.[12]

Historians developed other evaluations based on new primary sources and cues from J. W. Pratt's analysis. They began questioning why New England and Boston opposed this war while states like Georgia supported it. Louis M. Hacker believed the West had neither economic nor national interest in maritime rights. He stated that even the 'Indigenous problems' were not so profound that they would push the western states into joining the war. The problem was that in the western states, primitive agricultural techniques were used to produce commercial cash crops, which led to a decline in soil fertility and rendered lands unsuitable for the farm economy. This internal problem forced them to look towards Canada, which had 'virgin' fertile soil. In other words, Hacker supports the 'land hunger theory'.

J. C. A. Stagg, in *Mr. Madison's War*, argued that it was President Madison (and not Congress) who led America into war. Madison wanted to protect overseas commercial interests from the threat posed by Britain's policies. The United States, according to Stagg, long considered Canada as a 'hostage' that they could use to secure concessions from Britain. Therefore, Madison's threat was meant to put Britain in a difficult position—the fear of losing Canada would force Britain to acknowledge American commercial rights. In this way, Stagg characterised the War of 1812 as a conflict to protect American commercial liberties. However, Madison failed to understand that Americans still prioritised their local interests over national ones. For this reason, New England refused to support the war and even issued a threat in 1814 to secede from the Union. It was pure luck that Napoleon's escape from prison in Britain, coupled with some major American naval successes on the Great Lakes, forced Britain to withdraw from this struggle. This, in turn, effectively thwarted New England's threat of secession. American merchants began to scout for markets in Central and South America and invest at home in the growing manufacturing industries. Stagg's analysis is crucial because it highlights the close relationship between domestic and foreign affairs, a dynamic that came to the surface after the war.

Other scholars have focused on ideological issues: preserving American honour, and upholding national prestige, and defending American rights in a war-torn world. Yet others point to the political origins of Jeffersonian Republicans, who used this war as a platform to establish unity in their political group, preserve national power, and sideline the Federalists. Some of these factors fuelled the growth of a group of leaders in Congress known as 'War Hawks', who were led by Henry Clay and had the support of politicians representing the southern and western states. The War Hawks called for the expulsion of Britain from Canada and Spain from Florida. The western states had long accused Britain of deliberately instigating indigenous groups in Canada to rebel against America. Other historians have given greater weight to the issue of national honour and maritime violations as the chief cause of this war. Some historians shifted their focus towards territorial expansion, arguing that the US wanted to use Canada as a bargaining chip against Britain. In contrast, some scholarship suggests that the Republican political group feared that America would wither away if the European powers did not respect its economic policies. The worst-case scenario, for them, was the return of the Federalists to political power.

According to Eric Foner,[13] the War of 1812 was a two-front struggle, first against the British and second against the Indigenous communities who allied with the British. The war resulted in the defeat of Tecumseh, who was killed at the Battle of the Thames in 1813 by the federal army commanded by William Henry Harrison (see Chapter 5). Moreover, by 1814, under the command of Andrew Jackson, who had increased his army's strength by recruiting Cherokees and Creeks who supported assimilation with the White settlers—the rebellious Creeks (known as the Red Sticks) were defeated at the Battle of Horseshoe Bend in Alabama. This brought 23 million acres of 'virgin land' under federal control. President Jackson was again successful in 1815, when he repulsed the British attack on New Orleans; for this campaign, he had also managed to recruit freed Black people.

According to Robert V. Remini, Americans learnt significant lessons from this war under the leadership of Henry Clay. One outcome was the establishment of a new political group named the Whigs, which introduced internal improvements, government banking and protective tariffs to stimulate American industrial growth and expansion.[14] Alan Taylor has analysed the War of 1812 as a multifaceted war: it was a contest between rival visions for North America, in which the differences between loyalist and Republican elements played an essential role.[15]

The Americans fought this war for their self-defined postcolonial independence, which included the right to self-determination in trade and expansion, sovereignty for citizens, and equal treatment by the European nations. The war, therefore, marked the rise of America as a world power.

Consequences of the War

Immediately after the war, America witnessed the rise of a new spirit of nationalism. This was reflected in the reconstruction of the Presidential Palace, now known as the White House, which was given a white coat of paint to erase the memory of it being set ablaze by British forces in the War of 1812. Francis Scott Key composed the new national anthem, 'The Star-Spangled Banner'. The war also saw the rise of Andrew Jackson in politics after becoming a military war hero. The Republicans learnt many lessons from this war, and they began to adopt many policies of the Federalists, mainly in terms of providing federal funds for internal improvements, the development of transport and communication networks, and the increase in tariff rates to encourage the process of industrialisation and urbanisation. They also established the Second Bank of the US. All these factors

FIG. 6.1: Engraving showing the burning of Washington, by Warner J. Barber (1827)

Source: Wikimedia Commons.

combined to fuel the growth, development and expansion of the market revolution in post-war America.

The war and its interpretations revolve around three main issues: impressment, trade, and the status of Indigenous groups. All three issues were presented as internal and domestic issues, while impressment was a denial of the individual rights of American citizens. The consequences of war were multifaceted and long-lasting. It shaped the nation-state and its relationship with Britain. It also allows us to understand why American expansion after 1815 was towards the South and West but not the North. With burgeoning nationalism, new symbols were accorded greater importance: the Star-Spangled Banner, 'Uncle Sam', and 'Old Ironsides'. The fact remains that America was still at a nascent stage of its formative years with little experience in international politics, and different political groups could not put up a united front in this war, which created more confusion and mismanagement.

The Economy

The War of 1812 resulted in the rapid economic progress of the US from 1815 to 1820 and saw the growth of the money-market nexus. It also led to rapid westward expansion as Indigenous groups were displaced and marginalised (see Chapter 5 for a detailed discussion). This process of dispossession led to phenomenal growth for White settlers in many new states. It sparked the rapid movement of planter classes from South Carolina, Virginia, and Georgia to the new frontier states. One consequence of this was the expansion of slavery. In the aftermath of the war, America also strengthened its financial foundations by establishing a new National Bank (the Second Bank of the US) and an improved supply of credit facilities and investment opportunities.

Democratic-Republicans continued to dominate American politics till the election of Andrew Jackson. For the first time, federal funds were used to construct and develop a national system of roads and canals. The judiciary became more independent and active due to many landmark judgments. Significant changes were brought about in the **Land Act**, and the credit system was abolished for buying land; instead, land prices were lowered, and now only 80 acres of land were given in the West. As William Barney states, the period witnessed mass migration to the West. Over time, there was also a decline in farm labour and increased manufacturing employment. These economic changes brought demographic pressure as there was an increase in fertility rates, and the need for out-migration began to be felt as the concentration of population in some areas had become very dense. The South began to experience problems associated with soil erosion, leading to the rapid expansion of small planters to the emerging Deep South. The West offered inexpensive land with strong economic motivation for independence and upward mobility.

America remained isolated from European affairs to project itself as a country of freedom and democracy. According to Barney, one of the main consequences of this war was an increase in American naval defence forces with the induction of more naval ships to protect American commerce. War had also made the manufacturing process seem 'patriotic', so a substantial increase in tariff duties was imposed on British textiles to encourage economic self-sufficiency. Another consequence was that Britain closed all British West Indies ports for American ships after the Continental War. America began protracted negotiations that ultimately resulted in an agreement between the two nations in 1830. Even though this island trade was not so crucial for America, it initiated lengthy negotiations to show the world that America was a moral nation. This became a hallmark of American nationalism. The post-war period also witnessed the Missouri Compromise of 1820, which led to sectional crisis and gradual rise of southern opposition against increased tariff rates, and in turn the rise of new political parties.

During the War of 1812 and even afterwards, the US had shown great interest in acquiring the region of Florida from Spain. During the Presidencies of Thomas Jefferson and James Madison, some parts of Florida had already come under American control. In 1811, Congress passed a resolution that later became a precursor to the Monroe Doctrine. It aimed to deny Europeans the right to establish colonies in the Western hemisphere. Spain was already depleted of energy after the Continental War and, therefore, desired a peaceful resolution on the premise that the Mississippi River would be the boundary line between Mexico and USA. From 1810 to 1815, the federal government sent special missions to learn about actual conditions in Latin America, and monetary assistance was provided to the rebels to overthrow Spanish colonial rule and establish republican governments. After the War of 1812, America substantially increased its trade with Cuba. The southern states desired to form an 'American System' in the region based on grouping different Latin American nations that would take their command from Washington. However, at this juncture, the Union was still cautious in its approach towards Spain and Europe for fear of causing problems for America in the Western hemisphere. President Jackson's unilateral military action to capture Spanish territory in 1818 led to a shift in America's approach. After lengthy negotiations, in 1821, Spain finally agreed to cede Florida to the US in exchange for five million Spanish dollars. The acquisition of Florida was significant as it signalled the decline of Spain as a colonial power and led to the rise of independence movements across Latin America. To prevent this, Spain began a counter-revolution to restore its colonial rule.

At this point, America continued to pursue the 'isolationism' policy and wanted to be known as 'the beacon on the hill', providing a guide for those struggling in the world 'below'. For Henry Clay, Latin America was a land of despotism, enslaved people, inquisition, and superstition. The conversion to Catholicism had destroyed their cultural heritage, and the colonial encounter had led to racial intermixing.[16] (Here, it is important to note that while a racial hierarchy was certainly operational in Latin America, there was no 'anti-miscegenation policy' such as those instituted in the United States.) White settlers in the US widely subscribed to theories that the climate of South America made people so lethargic that they neglected neglecting the proper use of their natural resources. Even after becoming independent, such thinking went, Latin American people would simply waste their newfound freedom. Gradually, America began its expansionist programme to extend American influence and reduce Europe's control over this region for its commercial benefit, under the pretext of 'spreading the light of republicanism' throughout Latin America. Congress provided funds to establish diplomatic missions in Argentina, Chile, Colombia, Mexico, and Peru, and ambassadors were appointed in 1823. America formally recognised Mexico in 1822, and Brazil's independence was accepted in 1824. President Monroe believed that American institutions were so strong that they should utilise their superior legal and moral position to prevent European powers from establishing their dominions in Latin America, thereby assisting America in exercising its right of self-preservation. In the light of these developments, the United States developed an internal policy of expansion known as Manifest Destiny, and an external foreign policy known as the Monroe Doctrine.

Monroe Doctrine

This external policy reflected the evolution of nationalism in the US and increasing expansionism, its push for diplomatic independence, and its demand for an end to European interference in the Western hemisphere. As we have discussed, following the acquisition of Florida from Spain in 1821, Americans began to harbour ambitions of further expansion into the Latin American region. This was articulated as a vision to make Latin America a region of democracy, liberalism, and governed by Protestantism. Simultaneously, the US turned towards Alaska, which Russia and Britain controlled. In the later years, Britain withdrew, allowing the Americans to sign a treaty with Russia in 1867 that brought Alaska under US control. Monroe's Doctrine was thus premised on ending European colonisation of the Americas; in return, the US would adopt an isolationist policy of non-intervention in European affairs. This became the cornerstone of US foreign policy.

Monroe's Doctrine was concerned with the **American Declaration of Diplomatic Independence**, and its cornerstone was a preoccupation with Latin America and American nationalism based on the non-colonisation principle. On 2 December 1823, James Monroe sent a message to Congress that later became the 'Monroe Doctrine', which openly declared that the Western hemisphere was no longer open to European colonisation and political intervention.

Britain was concerned about Canada and wanted to acquire Alaska from Russia. Russia claimed the territory south of the 51st degree parallel and ordered America not to cast its eyes. Still, America ignored all warnings, and in a series of meetings in 1819 and 1821, America told Britain that it should not aspire to have a hold over North America. America also informed Russia that it would contest any Russian claim on North America.

Interestingly, even as America declared its policy of non-colonisation, it denied the right of self-government to Indigenous nations. This was even as it challenged powerful European countries so that it could force upon them the policy of non-intervention in Latin America. In 1818, James Monroe signed a treaty with Britain, recognising the 49th degree parallel up to the Rocky Mountains as the boundary between Canada and USA. In 1799, Russia established an exclusive claim to commerce and fisheries up to the 55th degree parallel parallel. In 1821, Tsar Alexander I extended this claim to the 51st degree parallel and forbade all foreign trade and ships, and to enforce this, Russia deployed its naval ships. In 1824, the US recognised Russian claims on the Pacific coast up to the 54th degree parallel. Meanwhile, in 1823, British Secretary George Canning supported the idea that the Latin American political situation needed complete separation from Spain, and he approached Richard Bush, the American minister in London, with a proposal to issue a joint declaration termed by George Canning as a 'great flirtation'. The proposal stated that forming an Anglo-American union would end all continental European attempts to intervene in Latin America, and this process would also strengthen Anglo-American ties.

John Quincy Adams opposed this proposal as it would make America look weak and like a junior partner; moreover, by doing so America would get sucked into European politics. Hence, he preferred that America deal with Latin America independently, without any assistance or support from Britain. Russia continued its effort to control the Pacific, forcing the US to adopt the policy of non-intervention in both North American and European affairs. The approach that began to be pursued by the US became known as an **isolationist policy**.

In this manner, the Monroe Doctrine came to be based on three primary principles: (*i*) non-colonisation in North America and Latin America; (*ii*) non-intervention of the US in European affairs, and; (*iii*) the policy of isolationism from world politics. At the time of the implementation of the Monroe Doctrine, it seemed that it would have an adverse impact—as Latin American countries gradually became independent, they established monarchical governments rather than republicanism. Also, American trade with Latin America declined considerably while Britain's trade increased, and Britain continued to dominate the Southern hemisphere. Therefore, neither American trade and institutions, nor the Monroe Doctrine flourished in Latin America. However, this doctrine established a workable and functional foreign policy for the American government over time. Working within its parameters, America expanded and consolidated its territory, surviving controversies over neutral rights and conflicts with Britain and France, the two mighty European powers. Its neutral stance assisted in developing and accepting American diplomatic ideas and actions.

For this reason, the Monroe Doctrine is also described as 'a diplomatic declaration of independence' that assisted in developing the 'American identity' enshrined in the Declaration of Independence. According to Dexter Perkins, the aim of the Monroe Doctrine was twofold. The first objective was to prevent a Russian advance on the Northwest Coast of America, and the second was to prevent European involvement in Latin America. Elaborating on this, William Appleman Williams writes that the Monroe Doctrine achieved three significant successes: (*i*) it assisted in the commercial and economic expansion of America and the process of internal colonisation in the westward region; (*ii*) it expanded American influence over the Western hemisphere and made the US the predominant power in the region; and (*iii*) America began to intervene in European politics in a manner so it could stay out of it. In other words, the doctrine established a 'balanced' expansionist mission that would assist America in maintaining its economic supremacy and block European nations' colonial ambitions in the Western hemisphere. At the same time, with internal colonisation, more states joined the Union, strengthening the powers of the federal government.

Manifest Destiny

This internal policy was in effect from 1815 to 1860, with the primary aim being territorial expansion of the US from the Atlantic to the Pacific Oceans. Americans came to believe that it was manifest (unmistakable) and an inevitable destiny that they would eventually take over Oregon, Texas, and all the territories controlled by Mexico. In his article 'Annexation', John L. O'Sullivan coined the term 'Manifest Destiny', stating that it was God's will for America to expand. The article offered a three-fold rationale: (*i*) the need to expand liberal American values; (*ii*) the mission to spread American institutions, and; (*iii*) God's will to destine this process. This rationale developed into what has been termed 'American Exceptionalism' that manifested into attempts to control territories under Mexico, Indigenous societies and British Canada. Sullivan wrote another article where he emphasised a moral ideal, a kind of higher law and a higher mission based on the will of God (Providence) given to the US to spread republican democracy not by war but by the spread of the 'Anglo-Saxon race' that would eventually take over Texas, Oregon, California, and Canada. The Democratic Party included this in its agenda from 1845 to 1855, but it was not supported by the Whigs and the Republican parties. It was an ideology that assisted in the promotion of westward expansion that came to be known during the time of Jefferson as the 'empire for liberty' and Jackson, as 'extending the area of freedom'. Abraham Lincoln would later go on to assert that the twin foundations of American republicanism—freedom and democracy—are 'the last best hope of Earth'. For the adherents of Jacksonian democracy, America needed to expand from 'sea to shining sea', an idea that was given the term '**continentalism**'. This popular expansionist notion was in line with the logic of American exceptionalism and Romantic nationalism, and within these concepts was embedded a notion of 'Anglo-Saxon' superiority.

According to Frederick Merk, Manifest Destiny was based on federalism, where local affairs, such as slavery, were left to be resolved by the states. At the same time, the national government concentrated its energies on national interests. He believed that this prevented the federal government from becoming tyrannical, granted freedom to people, and, with the protection given to state rights, made the concept of Manifest Destiny extremely attractive to both people and politicians. It contributed to the establishment of a free, confederated, self-governed republic on a continental scale. The 'Republic', in this context, meant not only what Thomas Paine had cocneptualised during the American Revolution, which would give rise to a new and better society, but also freedom from class restrictions, monarchy, and established churches, paving the way for a classless society and religious freedom. 'Democracy' meant not only political and economic freedom but also the space for the American people to achieve higher goals, eventually leading to good governance, better utilisation of natural resources, and a union of 'virtuous' people. Under this theory, the occupation of land was recast as a moral force that redefined America as a haven for those who wished to escape the tyrannies of Europe and fulfil their desire for liberty and self-government.

Within America, debates about the outer limit of this expansion kept evolving. At the time of the American Revolution, it was the Mississippi. By 1803, it became the Rocky Mountains; by the 1840s, it was the Pacific Ocean and the entire Western Hemisphere. Territorial expansion became necessary to ensure that Americans lived peacefully, free from European interference. At the same time, Americans would 'educate' the 'backward people' of the North and South American continents, ultimately aiming to establish the hegemony of the White or Anglo-Saxon race. The expansion process was also facilitated by technological advancements, particularly in transportation and communication. The invention of steam engines, railroads, telegraphs, and electricity brought the Pacific region, integrating it with the Mississippi Valley and the Great Lakes region. These changes ushered in the market revolution that led to a phenomenal increase in commercial and manufacturing classes who began to clamour to secure new markets.

The **Cushing Treaty of 1844** opened Chinese ports in the Pacific region for American commerce. A series of economic depressions in 1837, 1839, and 1849, along with soft cotton, corn, and hog prices, propelled migration to new regions; there were internal pressures from young Americans who were clamouring for political and social reforms. The period also saw the development of the printing press, telegraph lines, journalism, and, more importantly, the rapid growth of the penny press, which contributed to the creation of a culture of sensationalist reportage and news. James K. Polk, the youngest American President till that point at 49, encouraged the removal of all hurdles to individual advancement. Moving to the West became a hallmark of egalitarianism as the region offered economic independence and political sovereignty. In the South and North, increasing financial and demographic pressure forced many to move to the West to secure inexpensive lands. Manifest Destiny was, therefore, the product of many elements that got woven together into an integrated unit, including rising nationalism, state rights, and availability of cheap land to ease demographic pressure elsewhere, along with the freedom to develop an independent society on the lines of religious freedom, trade and political peace with no interference from Europe. However, this freedom came at the cost of the rise of sectionalism, as Manifest Destiny gave greater credibility to expansionists who upheld the importance of state rights over the federal government's powers.

Till 1837, Americans made many futile attempts to take over Canada and ultimately signed a treaty with Britain agreeing not to interfere in the region, thereby demarcating the boundary between the two. At this juncture, Americans sought to capitalise on armed rebellions for political and governance reforms in Lower and Upper Canada in 1837 and 1838. The rebellion was successfully brought under control by the British. Still, in America, it led to the rise of **filibusters**, a category of irregular military adventurers who would invade foreign lands for financial profit without getting any government sanction for their actions. These adventurers attempted several military expeditions into the Caribbean, Mexico, Central America, and Canada.

Oregon was a British colony where American settlers had spread, forcing the two to sign the **Oregon Treaty** between in 1846. Oregon came under American control, making the 49th degree parallel the boundary between the two countries and bringing six territories under American control—Missouri, Kansas, Nebraska, Wyoming, Idaho, and Oregon. After the **1848 American-Mexican**

War in which Mexico was defeated, three new states were added to the US—California, New Mexico, and Utah—and it became a continental nation. It was from here on that America began to harbour ambitions to bring Cuba too under their control. There was presumptuous fear in America that Cuba would come under British rule, so President Polk offered to buy Cuba from Spain in 1848 for a hundred million dollars. Later, Presidents Zachary Taylor and Millard Fillmore attempted to prevent unauthorised activities of the Hunters' Lodge or the Patriots, secretly known as the Society of Filibusters, from taking over the region. President Franklin Pierce offered a sum of 130 million dollars to buy Cuba, but this faced intense opposition in the North due to growing apprehensions about the spread of slavery. In the meantime, a secret document known as the **Ostend Manifesto** stated that Cuba would be taken over by force if not bought by the US. However, before this could be carried out, the outbreak of the Civil War ended this grand expansionist agenda.

Conclusion

The War of 1812 was an extremely significant event that had definite consequences for the future of the USA. Scholars have pointed to the consequent changes in political and economic ideology, initially within the scope of Jeffersonian democracy but eventually fuelling the rise of Andrew Jackson and the Democrats. The war cemented the foundational principles of the Union and provided the impetus to outline a set of moral and ethical values that justified internal expansionism. It also allowed the US to project itself as a beacon of hope and light with a divinely ordained agenda to spread American values of democracy, nationalism, and liberalism across the Western hemisphere.

Notes

1. 'George Washington's Farewell Address: To the People of the United States', 106th Congress, 2nd session, Senate document no. 106–21 (Washington, 2000), p. 25.

2. John M. Belohlavek, 'American Expansion, 1800–1867', in *A Companion to Nineteenth-Century America*, ed. William L. Barney (New York, 2006), pp. 89–91.
3. Reginald Horsman, *The Causes of the War of 1812*, (Philadelphia, 2016), p. 26.
4. William H. Barney, *The Passage of the Republic: An Interdisciplinary History of Nineteenth-Century America* (Lexington, 1987), p. 91.
5. Horsman, *The Causes of the War of 1812*, p. 27.
6. Ibid.
7. This term was used when American sailors or seamen were 'impressed' or forced to serve in the British Royal Navy. The Congress began the practice of issuing citizenship documents for its sailors to protect American citizens from being captured by the Royal Navy, but British sailors, too, began to forge such documents to escape being pushed to participate in a long war with France.
8. Allen C. Guelzo, *Fateful Lightning: A New History of the Civil War and Reconstruction* (New York, 2012), p. 20.
9. Alan Taylor, *The Civil War of 1812: American Citizens, British Subjects, Irish Rebels* (New York, 2010), p. 46.
10. Donald R. Hickey, *The War of 1812: A Forgotten Conflict*, revised ed. (Chicago, 2006).
11. Donald R. Hickey, *The War of 1812: A Short History* (Illinois, 2012), p. 3.
12. Troy Bickham, *The Weight of Vengeance: The U.S., the British Empire, and the War of 1812* (New York, 2012), p. 11.
13. Eric Foner, *Give Me Liberty! An American History*, third ed. (New York, 2011), p. 313.
14. Robert V. Remini, *Henry Clay: Statesman for the Union* (New York, 1991), pp. 136–137.
15. Alan Taylor, *The Civil War of 1812*, p. 12.
16. See Randolph B. Campbell, 'The Spanish Aspect of Henry Clay's American System', *The Americas 24* (1), pp. 3–17.

Chapter 7

American Exceptionalism
Chattel Enslavement

Introduction

The term African American refers to the descendants of approximately 10 million Africans transported to the New World by force in a period spanning about two centuries. Initially forced to work as indentured servants, they were later enslaved. European anthropologists theorised that Black people were a completely different race from White people—this theory of racialised classification has since been thoroughly disproven. The word 'Negro', today considered a racial slur, was derived from the word Negroid and coined in the eighteenth century by anthropologists.[1] African American ancestry can be traced to nearly 40 ethnic groups from 25 kingdoms in Africa. In 1619, approximately 19 Ndongas from modern-day Angola (on the west-central coast of southern Africa) were brought to Jamestown, Virginia. They became the founding generation of the Black labour system, whose enslaved descendants later developed a composite identity shaped by a common legacy of slavery and its shared experiences. Some scholars describe this process of trafficking, enslavement, and colonisation as the **'Black Holocaust'** and use the term **Maafa**, which means 'disaster' in Kiswahili. African slavery was constructed out of a cultural and historical legacy shaped by intra-group cooperation (between themselves) and inter-group conflict (between the White and Black populations) that eventually manifested in American society as a whole and its legacy became an entrenched element in the institutions of the nation that, after 1776, came to be known as the United States of America.

Between 1620 and 1700, the African population in colonial North America increased from 60 people (1 per cent of the total) to almost 28,000 (11 per cent of the total population), in tandem with the growth and expansion of the plantation economy. In the same period, there was staggering growth in the **transatlantic slave trade**, which only ended over a century and a half later in 1858, when the last known slave ship from Africa to the US, *The Wanderer*, landed on the coast of South Carolina with 409 Africans aboard (this despite the constitutional ban on the slave trade in 1808). The Spanish, Portuguese, and Dutch empires dominated the slave trade from 1450 to 1850. They transported 10–12 million Africans to Jamaica, Cuba, and Haiti. From this figure, only about 5 per cent were brought to North America. An essential aspect of the transatlantic slave trade was that it brought more enslaved people to the Americas than free immigration from Europe and Asia. This picture began to change only in the late nineteenth century when 'others', the voluntary immigrants, began to outnumber the involuntary African immigrants.[2] Three major areas in Africa supplied the bulk of forced slave labour to the United States: Upper Guinea (the Senegambia zone to Sierra Leone), followed by Lower Guinea (the Gold Coast to the Bight of Benin), and Congo-Angola.

The journey from ordinary life to indenture and later enslavement was carried out in three stages. The first stage consisted of capture and a forced journey to the African coast. Free Africans were captured, sold, and resold through various processes evolved by European slave traders. The second stage was an oceanic voyage from Africa to the Americas, known as the 'Middle Passage', which took one or two months depending on weather, season, and the distance to be covered. This stage often proved life-threatening as ships were packed with enslaved people who were provided no proper sanitation, food, or even clean drinking water. Under such conditions, these 'slave ships' frequently became host to diseases. Enslaved women were sexually exploited, and both men and women who survived this catastrophic journey landed in a completely alien and hostile environment, causing many to suffer from extreme forms of depression, shock, and even insanity. The cruelty of this process is borne out by the high mortality rate of about 15 to 20 per cent of the enslaved people on the ships in the seventeenth century. In the third and final stage, those who survived the arduous journey, alienation, and dislocation were sold in slave markets and initiated into enslavement. This was a brutal socio-economic system that inflicted unmitigated levels of exploitation and oppression on their body, minds, and esteem.

The Birth of American Slavery

The White settlers who colonised America developed a 'peculiar' labour system between 1619 and the 1820s. This came to be known as the system of 'chattel' slavery ('chattel' meant property), which expanded from Maine to Texas, keeping pace with frontier expansion over two centuries. This eventually led to the institutionalisation of a labour system that continuously mutated to adapt to evolving ideologies of racial difference. The practice of racialised slavery was widespread well after the birth of the United States, across the southern, northern, and later the western regions of the country.

The history of mutation from indentured labour to slave labour constitutes an integral part of the African American experience and history.[3] In its initial phase before 1700, its growth was only as a labour system. At this time, the distinction was not between free men and Black labour. Black people were regarded as racially different, but American colonies had not developed racial legislation or restrictions on the movements of Black people. In this phase, American colonies were importing enslaved people only in small numbers. However, by the eighteenth century, once the southern states had discovered the market value of cotton and other cash crops, the importation of enslaved people increased and their internal population correspondingly grew.[4] A standardised form of chattel slavery began to develop in this period, and it became entrenched, exponential, and discriminatory in its nature and character.[5]

During the Enlightenment period (primarily the eighteenth century in the West), a set of 'scientific' theories emerged that were based on the notion that human beings can be categorised based on 'race', and this idea became ingrained in the American colonies. Colonial society was constituted of three racial groups—the Indigenous, Black, and White populations—this differentiation based purely on an arbitrary distinction between White and non-White. This forced three alien cultural worlds to collide, sailing in an ocean of mutual suspicion, rife with exploitation, and marked by perpetual conflict. White settler society evolved a well-crafted notion of 'racial purity' of the White person. In contrast, any person of colour was seen as racially inferior: someone 'sub-human', innately dependent on and subordinate to the White man, and only capable of parasitic or imitative behaviour. This logic eventually led to the evolution of the 'one-drop rule', which stipulated that a person who had any non-White ancestry at all was of 'black blood', effectively placing a taboo on any mixed-race relations, especially sexual relations.[6]

The New World continued to evolve new norms based on Western cultures. Thus, it was important to proselytise and convert enslaved people to Christianity to maintain the appearance of a 'missionary zeal'—this was the beginning of internal colonialism, as it projected the idea that the White man was 'civilising' the Black and Indigenous 'savage'. The process of colonialism, predicated on racial bias and the exploitation of non-White people, created a new labour system based on hierarchical gradations of exploitative enslavement. The exact workings of chattel slavery remained flexible, transforming according to the needs and requirements of the enslavers, market forces, and historical circumstances. However, what is significant is that enslaved people had no social existence except as an integral part of the institution of slavery. Interestingly, to secure the labour of enslaved people, White populations were forced to acknowledge the slaves' humanity—this became unavoidable as enslaved people began to speak the same language as them, worship the same god, and adopt Western habits of dress. Despite their oppressive and dehumanising circumstances, enslaved people slowly started to carve out their distinct cultural world. They established Black Christian congregations, developed musical traditions, and shared common value systems. Their independent identity created psychological tension that ultimately led to resistance and revolts.[7]

Evolution of Chattel Slavery (1619–1776)

At the time of colonisation and expansion of the British American colonies, settlers felt the need to evolve a labour management system, since extensive labour was needed to ensure the settlers' own survival and success. They were faced with a failure to enslave Indigenous peoples, and needed to compensate for the diminishing number of White indentured servants. The management of labour evolved in the garb of a civilising mission, where Black people were not only forced to be disciplined and obedient, but also were to be assimilated into the White settlers' framework of cultural norms and internalise their supposed inferiority. This eventually was codified into a carefully crafted politico-legal code of bondage that reduced them to mere commodities—hence the use of the term 'chattel'. Slavery became a virtual laboratory for White enslavers to practise new techniques of discipline and punishment—Black people were stripped of any natural human rights and therefore had no protections. Enslavers implemented slave codes and legal systems to institutionalise enslavement as an entrenched labour system, which, in turn, assisted the settler society in normalising the colonisation process as a slave labour force established a dominant and subordinate racial structure. Enslaved people were stereotyped and dehumanised to create and reinforce racial boundaries; such stereotypes also assisted in validating this inhuman institution.

With rapid economic growth at the end of the seventeenth century and a gradual decline in the English birth rate, the colonies of Virginia and Maryland were expanding on the back of a boom in tobacco cultivation, but not getting enough White indentured servants from the 'mother country'. To encourage indentured labour, various inducements began to be given that established a sharp distinction between White 'freedom' even for indentured labourers, and Black 'bondage'. Competition for better land created differences between established farmers on the one hand, and younger men

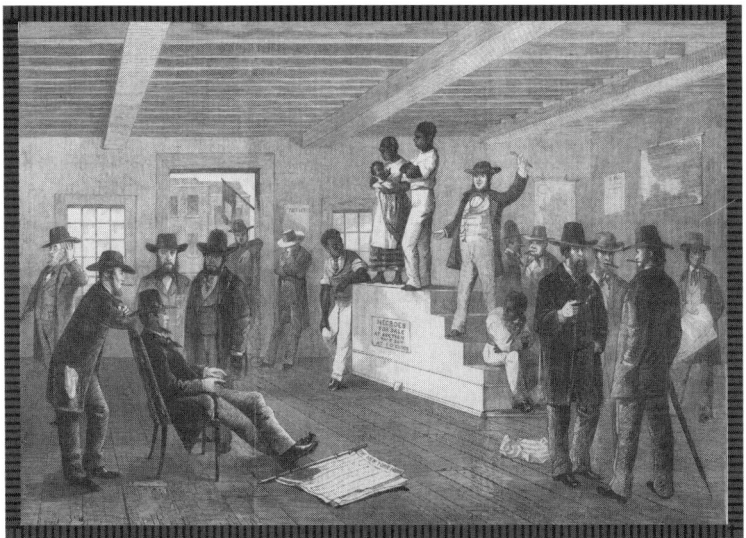

FIG. 7.1: A Slave Auction in Virginia, *The Illustrated London News* (1861)

Source: Wikimedia Commons.

as well as recent immigrants on the other—both groups required labour to work on their grounds. To ease this growing tension in the White community, Black labour began to be explored as a 'better option' compared to dwindling indentured labour.[8] However, the indentured servants and enslaved people had certain commonalities. They were both required to work with no avenue of leave or payment. Nevertheless, the difference was that enslaved people were costly, and long-term usage made enslaved labour 'better' than indentured labour. This transition was discerned by historians in the period from 1680 to 1710 in particular.

By 1720, Black slaves outnumbered White workers on large farms. This motivated settlers to implement legislation to restrict movement of Black people and ensure their subjugation and, therefore, this labour system relied on systematic racial discrimination and exploitation, but this was obfuscated by the layers of paternalism and religious missionary zeal that emphasised the importance of transforming the 'savages' and 'uncivilised' barbarians. Peter J. Parish has suggested that the **Royal African Company** had accelerated the process of bringing Africans to the Americas. This pace slackened when the company's monopoly was broken in 1698 as the British Parliament, in pursuit of its free trade policy, passed the **Trade with Africa Act of 1698**.[9] Chattel slavery in the American colonies took shape in the form of laws and judicial decisions, beginning with Massachusetts, which became the first colony in 1641 to give legal recognition to slavery. This was followed by a law passed in Virginia in 1662 that added a crucial element into the system: children born to an enslaved mother would also be enslaved for life. This single statute made slavery both permanent and hereditary. South Carolina enacted slave codes in 1690; these were revised in 1696, and made much more stringent by 1712, with every aspect of an enslaved person's life now controlled and limited by colonial laws. Virginia codified its slave rulings in 1705. By the middle of the eighteenth century, slavery had taken a form and structure that came to be identified with Africans and their descendants, that is, race ideology was fundamental to it. As Winthrop Jordon has asserted, chattel slavery was based on a logic of racial inferiority that accorded Black people slave status in order to control their labour for life.

The institutionalisation of slavery gave rise to racial tensions, with increasingly blatant and inhuman forms of coercion, exploitation, and oppression of Black people. These tensions gradually materialised into the beginning of numerous small, localised slave agitations, resistances, and rebellions. These aberrations established the need to impose even greater politico-legal control over this labour force. **The Negro Act of 1740** was a set of comprehensive laws implemented after the **Stono Rebellion** to bring all aspects of slaves' life under the control of the master, restricting their independent status as human beings. The period before the American Revolution was, therefore, earmarked by the growth, expansion, and crystallisation of this system of slavery, along with the beginning of the geographical spread of slavery.[10]

Slavery took root in three distinct geographical areas of the South. In the process, many significant and specific features of southern slavery emerged that established a White man's democracy.[11]

According to Eric Foner, enslaved people began to produce sugar, rice, coffee, and tobacco, all 'mass consumer goods' traded by Americans in external markets.[12] The first of these regions was in the Chesapeake Bay (the southern borderlands), encompassing Virginia, Maryland, and later Kentucky (beyond the Ohio River), where slave labour was used to produce tobacco that brought immense profit to enslavers. Continuous cultivation led to a decline in soil fertility. An **internal slave trade** developed to sell enslaved people in the new emerging Middle South, which consequently became the second geographical zone under discussion. This zone developed in the 1670s in the coastal settlements of North and South Carolina and later Georgia, Arkansas, Louisiana, Tennessee, and Mississippi, where slave labour was used to cultivate crops like rice and indigo. This became the most fertile agricultural belt in the US, especially with the beginning of cotton and sugar cultivation. The result was that from 1740 to 1760, there was a staggering increase in slave imports from Africa. The third geographical zone emerged in the region bordering the Gulf of Mexico and the South Atlantic coastline—this came to be known as the Deep South, spanning the area from New Orleans to Charleston. Charleston became an important slave trading port.[13] In the same period, there was a marked natural increase in the population of enslaved people, and the economic importance of their labour grew as it generated wealth through trade in commercial cash crops.[14]

It was around the 1740s to 1760s that enslaved people began to develop a distinct socio-cultural world based on the amalgamation of their African heritage and their experiences in America, giving birth to specific family systems, kinship networks, and shared community experiences. White people had colonised America and instituted slavery; in turn, enslaved Black people were transforming the dominant White society. In the words of Duncan MacLeod, the mid-eighteenth century marked 'the transformation of the southern colonies from societies with slaves into slave societies'. Apart from the three geographical zones outlined above, slavery also developed in northern colonies like New York, where enslaved people and free Black people together constituted 15 per cent of the total population, and their labour was used in urban environments.

Slavery and the American Revolution

The New World's first revolution in 1776 led to the founding of what was quickly touted as the 'first democratic nation', based on ideas of liberty, individualism and democracy. It was felt that the founding of the United States gave rise to a 'New Man'. However, regardless of these grand stated principles, the Union created new forms of colonialism by denying the same freedom and space to its enslaved people as the bonded labour generated power, wealth, status and prestige to now 'free' Whites. The American Revolution and its ideals rendered the institution of slavery a 'peculiar institution'. Duncan MacLeod has argued that the Revolution established a 'more white society than its colonial predecessor'. In 1774, in the colony of Philadelphia, **Quakers** wanted an end to slavery, and in 1776 they decided to disown those who refused to give freedom to people they had enslaved. Similarly, from 1778 and through the 1780s, Quakers in Maryland and Virginia adopted the same policy. In 1790, Quakers in Pennsylvania, together with the Pennsylvania Abolition Society, petitioned Congress to announce emancipation from slavery at the national level.[15] The **Northwest Land Ordinance Act of 1787** was initiated to prevent slavery from entering the territory north of the Ohio River. In 1808, a federal ban was imposed on the importation of enslaved people. In 1790, the first federal census estimated a figure of 650,000 enslaved people in the southern states, against a White population of 2 million in the US.

All of this notwithstanding, nobody questioned the 'economic value' of slave labour. The same period saw the beginning of a westward movement that also led to the expansion of the slave population and slaveholding into the frontiers of a new nation that otherwise claimed to be the torchbearer of democracy.[16] Slavery, therefore, became more widespread than ever. Meanwhile, overuse of agricultural lands led to the onset of environmental problems like soil erosion and a decline in the prices of commercial crops. Decreasing soil fertility meant that the labour of the enslaved could not be exploited as effectively, and the period saw increased revolts. George Washington remarked in 1794 that enslaved people were becoming 'a very troublesome species of property' as the dynamics of slavery generated mutual fear and hatred. According to Kenneth M. Stampp, slavery became a moral and social concern.

The War of 1812 accelerated westward expansion and the attendant expansion of slavery. In 1820, the **Missouri Compromise** banned slavery from the territories acquired from the Louisiana Purchase (1803). The rise of the abolitionist movement in the northern states (by the 1830s)[17] forced some righteous political leaders to gradually initiate the process of limiting this institution, seeing as it was not, in the words of George Washington, 'dying a natural death'. Stampp, in his analysis, writes that at this juncture, racism was becoming an entrenched ideology.

Rise of the Plantation System

Frontier expansion coincided with the spread of slavery, as we have noted earlier, from the **Upper South** to newly emerging territories of the Lower South. This region, also known as the **Deep South**, had vast, agriculturally productive lands for the cultivation of commercial cash crops, in particular cotton (the South's 'white gold'), which brought immense wealth, power, and social prestige to southern farmers, enabling their transformation into the planter class. This was the class that, in the blind pursuit of expanding their plantation system, made slavery an entrenched labour system.

Cotton planters gained influence after 1790 due to the rise of textile industries—both in Europe and later in the US—which led to an increase in the demand for cotton cultivation. Also significant was the invention of the cotton gin machine by Eli Whitney in 1793. This made cotton production mechanically simple and economically profitable and, therefore, lowered the cost of production beyond the coastal areas. It led to a dramatic increase in the demand for enslaved people. Additionally, new strains of cotton were being developed, and the forceful removal of Indigenous groups brought 'virgin' lands under US control. In the aftermath of the War of 1812, there was an exponential spread of White settlements in the frontier regions, especially in Alabama and Mississippi.

With all these factors interwoven together, a cotton boom emerged. It quickly became the most profitable crop. Cotton was transported to markets by intermediaries who also provided credit and managed the supply of enslaved people to the planter class. This process contributed to the rise and importance of southern cities such as New Orleans, Mobile, Savannah, Charleston, and Memphis, as well as the northeastern cities New York, Boston and Philadelphia. To meet these demands, enslavers expanded and continuously evolved new methods of controlling, subjugating, and increasing the population of enslaved people, further increasing the demand and economic value of their labour. Slave labour on cotton plantations increased total output and income, which meant that planters could buy more land and, consequently, more enslaved people. By the beginning of the nineteenth century, cotton constituted 50–60 per cent of America's total exports. These factors led to the redeployment of about one million enslaved people from the Upper to the Lower South through the establishment of a well-organised internal slave trade. Most enslaved labour was deployed to produce an agricultural surplus.[18] However, there were exceptions and variations, based on the fact that until the beginning of the Civil War, there were also thousands of enslaved people in urban areas of the US.

The development of an internal slave trade, along with the movement of enslaved people into the newly acquired region and transplantation of associated institutional slave support systems, brought economic prosperity for the **enslaver-planter class**, to the extent that by 1830, southern politicians were beginning to evolve distinct politico-administrative-legal strategies to preserve their master-slave society. Slavery, by now, had grown from a labour system into a profitable and economically dominant system of social control that gradually became fundamental to the distinct regional identity of the South. Chattel slavery became the foundation of southern politics, society, economy, and cultural traditions, and as a result the South became increasingly defensive and sensitive to outside attack. At the same time, internally, public discourses reflected uncertainties and contradictions. Stampp has termed the plantation system 'an arena of persistent conflict'. To Stanley Elkins, it was 'an oppressive institution' based on inherent internal problems.

These hidden tensions reflected a deeply divided hierarchical social practice that had developed in the South, where landownership and the exploitation of enslaved people gave enslavers wealth, power, and social standing, and additionally became a cultural symbol of their perceived racial superiority. The process of Eurocentrism that was in practice during the colonisation of America was applied in a new form, based on racist ideology, recasting the cultural hegemony and successful dominance of White settlers as an act of God.

The South began to develop multiple apprehensions—fear of slave insurrections, and the loss of political, social, and economic prestige if slavery were to be abolished. In the Upper South, where land had become unproductive due to overuse, enslavers were concerned about how to 'use' enslaved people. This goes to show that the racist logic of slavery was deeply entrenched, with enslavers constantly looking to maximise profits and perpetuate the subjugation of Black people.

This trajectory makes it evident that there were some paradoxes at the heart of this system. The entire institution of slavery was racially determined, based on skin colour; bondage was for life and hereditary, with almost no scope for **manumission** (a term used for the release of an enslaved person from bondage). Even as enslaved persons were dehumanised, exploited, and deemed inferior, it was their labour that powered the economy. The other paradox was the continuous increase in the enslaved population, primarily through the external and internal slave trade. Enslavers camouflaged the brutality of the institution in the garb of paternalistic benevolence, encouraging the enslaved to convert to Christianity and maintain a stable family life to ensure the birth of more enslaved children. This paternalistic relationship meant that the enslavers considered them both as human labour and personal property, establishing over time a peculiar southern institution based on double standards.

On the one hand, enslaved people were essential for producing commodities for the market, like cotton, hemp, tobacco, rice, and sugar, which were exported to Britain. This economic importance of the enslaved people meant that they were valuable 'property' that could be bought, sold, mortgaged, inherited, insured, and even used as collateral for business transactions. The system ensured that they never become part of the consumer class. For the master, the system revolved around a need for profits, paternalism, economic interest, and social standing. For enslaved people, it was characterised by a sense of resignation and accommodation to slave life, and resisting exploitation however they could, including resistance and open rebellion.

Historians have also considered regional variations that existed within the plantation economy. Sugar and rice plantations required elaborate irrigation systems and machinery for grinding and threshing, which was done only by the planter class, giving enslaved people more autonomy concerning their work schedule. They could tend their kitchen gardens and were given space to sell their vegetables in the market. In the Upper South, there was a shift from tobacco to wheat production, leading to less supervision of enslaved people, culminating in their manumission. For example, half of the Black population in Maryland was free by 1860. The Upper South also employed White agricultural workers and unskilled Black labourers, who were given food and cash. In Charleston and New Orleans, mixed-race children (the term 'mulatto', then in use for biracial or multiracial people, and most commonly for children of Black and White ancestry, is now considered a pejorative) on attaining adulthood began to operate schools, churches and other institutions. They were free Black individuals who played an important role during and after the Civil War.

In this way, enslaved people, in political terms, provided status, authority, power, and prestige to the enslaver classes; in economic terms, they represented commodities; in social terms, the very existence of enslaved people established class division in White society. Culturally, since the enslaved people were considered a sub-human species, White society could project itself as superior, more robust, and the epitome of 'civilised living'.

Slavery: An Economic Institution

As we have discussed, slavery gave the southern colonies and later states a distinct identity based on the social and economic hegemony of the enslaver-planter class, who laid the social, economic, political, and ideological foundations for a separate slave-based capitalist economy. Analysis based on this has moved along two different lines of interpretation. The first presents the pre-Civil War southern states as primarily an agrarian society that faced continuous assault from the industrial capitalism of the northern states. This explanation focuses on the idea that while the South was a source of capital accumulation, making the enslaver class extremely rich, it was also dependent on the growth of northern industrial centres as markets for their agricultural products. Thus, the fact that the North was developing a modern capitalistic economy and was critical of the slave labour system created pressure on the South. Other scholars have advanced a second line of interpretation. According to them, the southern planter class produced for international markets. The profit they secured was invested in buying more 'virgin' lands and enslaved people, for which they also borrowed from financial institutions, thereby making the southern economy capitalistic. In contrast, the North was moving towards industrial capitalism.

Scholarly analyses have sought to understand the South and its distinct identity from various vantage points. According to Lewis C. Gray, the South initially evolved on the foundations of British society, and over time republican ideas, a sense of liberty, and growing individualism created conditions of self-growth based on commodity production. This led to the development of a prosperous and influential economy that was independent of British control and separate from the northern colonies, with slavery becoming the cornerstone of its rural, economic, and social structures. Pioneering sociologist Max Weber has asserted that slave labour leads to retarded economic growth and creates conditions of social instability and economic backwardness. Another important marker for growth in a capitalistic economy is that due to intense economic competition, profits are reinvested in production by applying new technologies. However, in a slave economy, profits are invested in buying more enslaved people and land, which marks quantitative growth, not qualitative growth. The question then emerges: How did the South become rich and powerful?

ECONOMIC SURVEY OF THE SOUTH AND COMPARISON WITH THE NORTH

Soon after its initiation, slaves became the most lucrative 'item' of trade between the colonies of New England and the West Indies. As we have seen, enslaved people were the producers of agricultural commodities that generated huge capital profits for their enslavers and assisted in the economic development of not only American colonies but also Britain, where textile mills emerged during the period of the Industrial Revolution that spun raw fibre into yarn and then converted the same into fabric. After the American Revolution, the invention of the cotton gin machine assisted in separating stiff, short-staple cotton from seeds, converting slave-produced cotton to industrially-produced fibre that was in high demand. The growth of the cotton economy secured profits for both the southern and northern regions, and so in economic terms, slavery became a national institution. This was accompanied by the development of textile manufacturers, insurance companies, shipping industries shipbuilding, banking institutions and a host of intermediary groups to create a web of interdependent economic relations.

Broadly, Black people were categorised as either enslaved or free people. Enslaved people were generally agricultural field hands, domestic servants, and urban labourers. Slavery was premised on unpaid labour, so in effect, enslaved people were producers but not consumers or accumulators of capital resources. They were prevented from acquiring other skills, including education, to restrict any avenues of social or economic mobility and thereby ensure their continued and perpetual subjugation.

The very existence of chattel slavery created an extreme spectrum of differences between wealth and poverty. At the bottom were the enslaved people, whose hard labour produced wealth based on the non-wage system. At the top were the wealthy enslavers. Ironically, even as the institution of slavery grew, between 1830 and 1850 the number of enslavers holding five or fewer enslaved Black labourers was higher when compared with less than 40,000 who had 20 or more enslaved people, and only about 2,000 planter families had more than a hundred. Yet, the use of slave labour gave them immense profits. Till about 1850, the planter classes, along with the merchants, were some of the wealthiest classes in the country.[19]

The southern economy depended on three interlinked factors: plantation-style farms, the one-crop system (or monocropping), and enslaved labour. In this society, the enslaver class played the dominant role, and their efforts initiated the quantitative growth of the southern economy. The profit earned was ploughed into an aristocratic lifestyle and the acquisition of enslaved people and land. For this reason, southern politicians both at the national and regional levels opposed the federal policy of high tariffs, homestead funds being used for internal development, and a balanced division of power between the states and the Centre. The South incessantly complained about the North's industrial progress and economic expansion. It constantly blamed the North for the latter's 'aggressive' capitalism and exploitation of natural resources, identifying this as the reason behind the South's economic stagnation, declining capital resources, and avenues for capital investments, without acknowledging that the South depended on the North and Britain. Ultimately, this resulted in a drain of wealth from the South and became the reason for backward markets in the region, creating a paradoxical picture.

The North represented the competitive spirit and qualitative growth, with the capacity to accumulate capital invested in industries, apply new technologies, and explore new markets and avenues for modern education. More northerners lived in urban areas, which raised the land prices, and only 5 per cent of the population was illiterate.[20] For these reasons, the North sought to utilise federal funds for the economic unification of the country, which would facilitate economic progress, generate employment avenues, and open up previously closed markets and spaces. These factors attracted immigrants to the region, led to an internal increase in population, and provided northern politicians, intellectuals, and abolitionists with political, ideological, and social arguments to oppose the institution of slavery.

Limits of the Plantation Economy

The presence of the planter class reflected the rise of capitalism in the southern economy, based on the prevalence of credit, finance, banking, and extensive commercial activities. The plantation economy developed structured linkages with the world market, integrating cotton producers with merchants. This interdependence tied merchants to slave production and enslavers to secure their profit and sustenance.

It created a dichotomy as there existed a significant White population who did not enslave people in the South, like yeomen farmers and a small number of industrial classes. They had neither the purchasing power to initiate industrial development, nor any avenue for growth, as the planter class purchased their luxuries from abroad. The enslavers required only rudimentary markets for items like inexpensive clothing and agricultural tools for their enslaved people, which indicates that market relations had no transformative avenue to usher in an agricultural revolution.

Even the southern banking system functioned under the norms set up by the master planter class, as it extended credit to them for cultivating staple crops and to purchase more fertile 'virgin' land based on relatively easy credit policies, leading to the expansion of cotton production and consequently overproduction of cotton, which resulted in a decline in the price of cotton but increased the cost of enslaved people. Banks also assisted the planters in the shipment of cotton and supply of capital to purchase food materials from the American West in cash, which led to the interdependence of banks on the planter-master class and vice versa. In the process, the banks further augmented the interests of the planter class, thereby making this class look more pre-capitalistic and quasi-aristocratic, reflective of southern economic and financial backwardness due to the overdependence of financial and commercial activities on the master-slave system.

Another problem was the South's failure to develop industries, as the planter class was suspicious of industrialisation and urbanisation. They opposed the imposition of income tax and rejected state aid.

There were insufficient home markets in the South to develop industries, and those regions bordering the North had avenues of economic growth but were overwhelmed by a vibrant northern economy. There was also a lack of transportation networks in the South, which hindered industrial development. In fact, by 1850, the total railroad mileage in the South accounted for only a quarter of America's railroad network. Its manufacturing capacity was only 1/5th of the total national capacity, with significantly low levels of education and an illiteracy rate of 40 per cent.[21] Another class that could have initiated an economic transformation in the South was the non-slave farmers. However, they lived at the margins of the southern economy. Although self-independent, they were dominated by the enslaver class that wielded all the political, economic, and social powers and authority.

Nature of Slave Labour Force

Enslaved people had no incentive to produce efficiently, and they were routinely deprived of basic necessities. Labour hands were divided into '**gangs**', each commanded by a Black driver and further sub-divided into task hands, and each unit performed an assigned task. This **gang labour system** required constant supervision, and the use of enslaved labour prevented the application of new techniques. In terms of agriculture, continuous production and monocropping led to soil erosion, and consequently planters needed more capital to purchase chemical fertilisers. Most plantations produced vegetables and reared livestock for personal consumption, thereby depriving local markets of growth avenues for such products.[22]

The development of the domestic or internal slave trade, after the Atlantic slave trade was outlawed in 1808, created alternative economic avenues for the enslavers. The first was the division of enslavers' property after his demise and using enslaved people to pay off debts and settle the accounts of estates. The second was witnessed in Virginia and South Carolina, where the enslavers sold their slaves to the Lower South (the Deep South). There was a high demand for enslaved labour to clear land and forests along the Gulf of Mexico, and the result was the rise of slave markets in most of the towns of the southern states. The capital secured in such a manner was used to purchase fertiliser, agricultural equipment, and livestock. Due to environmental reasons, it was no longer productive to use enslaved labour in the Upper South. The reduction in the slave labour force saved money in the region. However, it led to the development of a regressive economy: Slaves were now sold off in the Deep South, creating a pattern of internal slave trade. This could have led to the decline of slavery, but the reality is that the internal slave trade in itself became so profitable that slavery continued to exist and expand exponentially. In turn, this demand was dependent on continued westward expansion and the expansion of slavery to new regions.

The problem was that the South needed to diversify its economy, and its total dependence on cotton cultivation created multiple issues requiring systematic intervention. Many in the South warned about an economic slide, and advocated the development and expansion of railroads, steamship lines, seaport facilities, banks, factories, and market enterprises. But those who dominated the southern economy and politics ignored these ominous warnings, and the proposals.[23]

Political Ideology of the Enslaver Class

The system was based on multiple layers of subordination that relied on possessing enslaved people and agricultural lands. Both gave the planter class politico-military honour, prestige, and power and gave southern society a distinct 'civilisational' character. The planters also extended their semi-paternal relationship with the non-slaveholding South. Planters took extreme pride in preserving localism, plantation economy, and enslaved people as their unique form of libertarianism. In other words, dependence on enslaved peoples' labour brought the independence of the enslavers. To understand this ideology, it becomes essential to understand how the enslavers established the enslaved people's society.

Social Structure of Enslaved Communities

Information gleaned from various sources, including southern American magazines, newspapers, articles, diaries and personal records of the enslavers that discussed slave management, comparative studies of accounts written by educated or free enslaved people, have assisted scholars in piecing together the history of this dark period. From these sources, it is evident that gradations of inequality marked slave society. Even compared to other forms of bonded labour and enslavement, **chattel slavery** was extremely interventionist and intrusive, dictating nearly every aspect of existence for enslaved people. As such, Black people lived in the shadow cast by systemic discrimination and deprivation. Black children born into the system were given names by their enslavers—once again reflecting the idea that enslavers 'owned' the enslaved individual right from birth. These names were purportedly based on their attitude and character; in practice, many of them were racist and had deeply pejorative connotations. According to Orlando Patterson, Black childhood was extremely traumatic, as children had to witness the psychological dehumanisation of their parents on an everyday basis, a form of social exploitation that never seemed to end.[24] Enslaved people generally experienced, during their lifetime, different owners and working environments depending on the enslaver's behavioural patterns. The system was also highly diversified, leading to the social stratification of enslaved people into skilled, unskilled, educated, and illiterate categories.

Although there was only one 'class' of Black people within the racial paradigm, it had various sub-divisions: free people, enslaved people, and biracial or multiracial people. In the 1850 census, 11.2 per cent of Black people had mixed racial ancestry. The figures varied from region to region. In the South, 10 per cent of the non-White population was identified as mixed-race; in the North, the corresponding figure was 24.8 per cent, and in the West it was 23.4 per cent. By the end of the eighteenth century, Black people constituted a significant minority in North America, indicative of the scale of the looming problem that would eventually manifest in a full-blown civil war.

Preachers, magicians, herbal medicine practitioners, midwives, and enslaved people skilled in folk art, music, and song were considered important as they were the torchbearers of Black material cultures. Enslaved people who plotted against White enslavers were held in high regard, as were older enslaved people—both women and men—who cared for the children, maintained the vegetable gardens, animal stock, stables, and yard, mended and washed clothes, looked after the sick, did spinning and weaving on the loom. Bondsmen like carpenters, blacksmiths, brickmakers, stone masons, shoemakers, weavers, millers, landscape practitioners, and domestic enslaved people like coachmen, laundresses, seamstresses, cooks, footmen, butlers, nursemaids, and personal enslaved servants usually acquired skills essential to survival and made themselves indispensable, and thus were highly regarded.

Urban Slavery

The urban slave population in the South was on the rise till the 1830s. This was still a relatively small demographic: a spurt in the demand for enslaved people on cotton plantations meant that by 1860, only peripheral regions bordering the coast or the southern border, like New Orleans, Charleston, Savannah, Richmond, and Memphis, had a population of more than 10,000 inhabitants, while states like Mississippi, North Carolina, Arkansas, and Florida did not have a single town with a comparable population. Enslaved people in urban areas with tasked to work as drivers, porters, roadmen, handymen, and shop assistants. Some worked in the rudimentary industries of the region. Barbara Jeanne Fields has proposed that the reason there were few enslaved people in the urban areas was that slavery was the 'antithesis' of industrial development and, therefore, could never thrive.[25] Urban areas were also home to White labourers, who resented the enslaved people as their presence put stress on their wages and employment opportunities.

The South developed a market for skilled 'hired labour' like carpenters, blacksmiths, or mechanics. They were referred to as 'slaves virtually free' by John Hope Franklin. However, they were different from 'free Blacks'. In the mines, free Black people worked on wages, since enslaved people were 'expensive commodities' who were too valuable to be exposed to the risk of mine explosions. Another example given by Michael Johnson and James Roark in their book *Black Masters* offers a detailed history of 'free Black' people who were characterised by the writers as generally non-confrontationist and accommodationist in their approach. Black people in urban America constantly feared being sucked back into slavery, and most lived in complete poverty. In Maryland, by 1860, the number of enslaved people and free Black people had almost become equal, and, as explained by Barbara Jeanne Fields this made the White population defensive and nervous.[26] Therefore, they often exerted harsh control over both to keep them under control, which clearly showed that slavery was neither a static nor uniform institution in the southern region. Slavery was, therefore, in the words of Peter J. Parish, based on 'variations, exceptions and paradoxes' because, as Orlando Patterson asserts, slavery may be defined as a deliberate, 'violent domination' by the enslavers on the basis of an entrenched system.[27]

The System of Bondage and White Democracy in the South

The institution of slavery created class divisions amongst the White population in the South. Overall, a paradoxical relationship emerged between the institution of slavery and the notion of liberty—it was primarily to preserve the institution of slavery that the South established practices emphasising individual liberty and championed the rights of the states. Thus, it was the quest to protect an institution of systemic 'unfreedom' that eventually produced a southern prototype of White democracy.

The scholar George Fredrickson termed this a 'herrenvolk democracy', based on an ideology of the racial inferiority of the enslaved people that granted enslavers the power of social and racialised control. James Oakes, who similarly focused on the racialised system of slavery, emphasised the predominance of small and medium-sized slaveholdings and the entrepreneurial and profit-hungry spirit of the enslaver classes. Randolph B. Campbell, in his study of one Texas county, categorised White southern society into five classes:

(*i*) Large planters controlling 20 or more enslaved people;
(*ii*) Small planters controlling 10 to 19 enslaved people;
(*iii*) Yeomen farmers (including White farmers with small landholdings and non-slaveholders);
(*iv*) Poor White people (tenant farmers and farm labourers); and
(*v*) Non-farming classes living in urban areas.

Yeomen farmers formed the 'middle class' and were divided between possessors and non-possessors of enslaved people. However, in White society, there was ample scope for mobility between the classes. In other words, the system was not rigid for White people. Moreover, by the nineteenth century, with the rise of the Deep South, the practice of enslavement expanded. As a result, more and more White people were tied politically, economically, and socially to the institution. With slavery being seen as beneficial to the geographical mobility and social status of White people, it acquired greater strength and power as an institution.

Eugene Genovese has understood this dynamic in terms of '**planter-dominance**' by relying on Marxist and Gramscian perspectives. He analyses the South as a pre-capitalist, seignorial (that is, feudal) society that slaveholders and the planter class dominated. This class created a paternalistic master-slave relationship, and also established a hegemonic relationship between themselves and the wider White society, based on their economic power and influence. The planter class extended loans to poor White families and gave their slaves on hire to them. They also assisted other White farmers in the marketing, transportation, ginning, and milling of commercial crops. Steven Hahn, looking at the same phenomenon, arrived at some different conclusions: He argued that through these practices, slavery assisted in reducing class differences and conflicts within the White southern community, with the planter class offering support to other White people to maintain their social status and political power. The planters invested in local churches, schools, and cultural activities to demonstrate the 'unity' of White people. This interdependence was essential to prevent slave rebellions and resistance and stall the abolition of slavery—opposition to the latter was reinforced by fears that abolition would spark racial conflict, economic decline, and social upheaval. Scholar J. William Harris has defined this as 'shared interests and shared fears' that formed ligaments of a community in the White South, which indicated that southern states had their notions of democracy, probably based on Jeffersonian ideals of rule by the aristocracy, as explained by William J. Cooper in *Liberty and Slavery*. In the South, liberty was committed to the institution of slavery. Edmund Morgan has further elaborated this point in *American Slavery, American Freedom* (in the context of Virginia, which dominated American politics till the beginning of the Jacksonian era). During colonial rule, the White population experienced the tyranny of the executive power of the Crown. Therefore, after the Revolution, they ensured that the role of the government remained confined to the protection of liberty and property of the citizens.

Out of the first five presidents of the United States, four were from Virginia, including George Washington and James Madison. They had all enslaved people at some point or the other, and they all believed in ideals of republican liberty, which used racial justifications to validate the existence of slavery. This brand of American liberalism was based on a firm belief to hold on to White freedom, which was sustained by the exploitation of the enslaved, and which gave a distinct identity to the South. It prevented the possibility of conflict arising between capital and labour, since an entire racialised group had been confined to performing unpaid hard labour that was necessary to sustain the new nation. William J. Cooper stated that from 1820 to 1850, the South supported national political parties as they protected southern interests. However, with the rise of the Republican Party in the North that promised to keep Slavery out of the western territories, the South declared secession. Cooper also suggested that when the abolitionists attacked slavery as a moral evil, they threatened the cherished southern ideals of liberty and honour. To Kenneth Greenberg, honour meant having the power to extract respect and discipline from others by creating a system of dominance. In other words, for the White population to become powerful, they had to ensure that Black people remained powerless, and this represented the fundamental contradiction in the enslaver-enslaved relationship.

It was only from the 1830s that the South grew defensive about slavery, since they faced a serious challenge from the North. To counter the abolitionist 'attack', they projected the enslaver-enslaved relationship as 'organic' and 'liberating', drawing on evangelical beliefs that recast slavery as a 'divinely ordained' system for regulating the relationship between so-called superior and inferior races. Enslavers claimed that the southern economy was not backward, as it made huge profits. They also highlighted that they paid high salaries to White workers.

Genovese concluded that the southern model of slavery was based more on class and social hierarchy than race or racial superiority. In constrast, many others, like George Fredrickson, asserted that slavery was based on racism and the perceived racial inferiority of Black people, based on the dominant psuedoscientific beliefs prevalent in the West at the time.

The Enslaved Economy

The problem in the South was multifaceted. Urban centres needed to be economically diversified. Dependence on enslaved peoples' labour meant that there was no application of new technology, and the complete dependence on cotton forced the South to import manufactured goods from the North or from abroad, which in turn meant that they were compelled to mortgage their second crop to northern manufacturers and bankers in order to secure capital to purchase the cotton gins, tools, and other associated products. Another problem was that Britain paid for the southern cotton in bills and drafts were deposited in northern banks, causing the South spiral into a vicious debt cycle.[28]

Southern 'paternalism', the aristocratic lifestyle of planters, and the dehumanising ideology that justified slavery, all fuelled discontent, resulting in the rise of the abolitionist movement, as well as the Free-Soil agitation (which opposed the expansion of slavery) of the North. The northern states had witnessed an increase in their population, accumulation of capital, and rapid economic development from the 1830s and particularly in the 1850s. In the West, there was a demand for technically advanced agricultural tools and machinery and the gradual growth of capital-intensive farms, so the North and the West were ready to capture the southern markets with better farm products and quality cotton textiles. On the other hand, the declining White population in the South made the region more insular, and fearful of the changes taking place in the rest of the country as well as of its consequent impact on southern society and economy. According to Elizabeth Fox-Genovese and Eugene D. Genovese, the unique and deeply conservative cultural paradigm of the South, which revolved around the aristocratic aura of the enslaver class and the perpetuation of slave labour, was a carefully nurtured mythology that imbued the planter class with a powerful sense of masculinity and hegemony against the rapidly advancing and progressing northern economy and capitalism.[29]

Scholars who question the economic preponderance of the North and West argue that industrialisation in these regions would not have been possible without the agricultural advancements in the southern states. To support their view, they cite the widely accepted fact that till 1860, cotton exports constituted 75 per cent of total US exports, while in the same period, the North was largely dependent on its home markets. However, for E. D. Genovese, what this really proved was that American slavery was embedded in the capitalist world economy that had emerged in this period. It created a unique form of social relations and a new, distinct way of life that was different from that of the North. It established a hierarchical society based on 'paternalism', which linked dominant and subordinate classes in a complex pattern of mutual responsibilities and obligations; the spirit of individualism was absent. It was a semi-feudal economic setup in which all activities of the plantation economy were closely tied to with the institution of slavery. To comprehend the plantation economy within a capitalist framework, according to Genovese, one needs to analyse how agricultural capitalism created barriers to industrialisation.

In recent years, scholars have begun to examine the economic dimension of the controversy surrounding Robert Fogel and Stanley Engerman's *Time on the Cross* (which attempted to prove the profitability of slavery based on plantation labour), scholars have begun to look deeper into the economic dimensions of the institution. Fogel and Engerman had discussed slavery as a mild, efficient, and profitable institution based on an in-depth study of slave life that included their food, living conditions, sexual preferences, religious traditions, and individual mobility. Enslavement brought immense profit, based on a few crucial factors: efficient management capable of extracting the right amount of labour, and a high market demand of crops that tilted the scales in favour of enslavers and made the southern economy more robust. Historians are now beginning to place slavery at the centre of America's phenomenal economic growth, and stipulate that there is a need to look afresh at the role it played in assisting the industrialisation of the North. Slavery is no longer considered a sectional economic issue, but rather a national concern. The issue is no longer whether the southern economy was capitalist (this is now considered an old and outdated debate), but how interdependent the two economies of the North and South were in the first place. The rise of the Republican Party shattered the 'balance' that was established on consensus and 'the rule of law' that provided support to the institution of slavery, respect for 'private property' and governance structures that legitimated slavery at the federal and state legislative levels.

Historical evidence indicates a significant increase in cotton production after 1793, from 8 million pounds in 1795 to 48 million in 1801, and by 1806, the figure had reached 80 million pounds. This was possible as enslavers developed innovative business models, new models of calculation, and well-oiled systems to manage the enormous agricultural business based on the bonded labour system, which was now a commodity that led to the development of new business practices and market capitalism, assisted by the Deep South's emergence. The process can be traced back to when slave traders maintained account books of the Atlantic slave ships, based on quantification and abstraction that converted African people into units of exchange and made them racialised subjects for sale in the

Americas as commodities. Drawing from such analyses, scholars have also begun to emphasise enslaved women's reproductive labour as a mechanism of wealth creation for the enslavers.

Dale Tomieh terms the process '**second slavery**', where after the War of 1812, the South began to develop a new governance system to protect their '**labour commodity**' and consolidate their power and authority in the region and the national government. Historians term this the '**Second Middle Passage**', which brought shipbuilders, captains, and investors from the East into the Deep South, linking all the regions in an interconnected American capitalist system. They used new technologies like steam engines to process and transport agricultural commodities and enslaved people to internal and external markets, and this led to the rise of trading companies in the cities of Baltimore and Richmond and the movement of enslaved people to New Orleans, where they were sold as consumer goods on credit, linking the southern economy to banks and bondholders in the East. This new form of human private property (the enslaved) represented a new business enterprise based on the tenets of 'modernity' and 'progress'. They were the new big business corporations that practised a regimented gang labour system, evolving a disciplinary management system based on the 'violence of whip' and a daily quota of picking cotton that was measured individually with mathematical precision, increasing the working capacity of the enslaved people. Thus, the system was highly capitalistic and paternalistic (in contrast to the interpretations of Fox-Genovese and Genovese). The planters utilised the accounting techniques developed by Thomas Affleck, who standardised and pre-printed plantation record books, which made it possible to calculate 'depreciation' of slave assets by combining multiple tabulations into a simple bottom-line total. The planters had established hierarchical reporting structures by appointing overseers and managers to maintain annual production targets, which were measured according to quarter, half, and full 'hands' that were put into labour. Another invention, the reaper machine, assisted Richmond capitalists in the vertical integration of processing, packing, shipping, and sale of white flour to Brazil.

In the plantation economy, bonded labour was used physically and financially as it could be transferred, stored, given as collateral, dowry, or even bequeathed. Therefore, in the 'Second Slavery', scholars now discern the introduction of American industrialisation, bureaucratisation, mass migration, nationalism, and imperialism as a consequence of the American enslavement system. After 1803, all territorial expansion and state-formation in America was established on the backs of the labour of enslaved people, giving rise to a form of capitalism fundamentally reliant on slavery, and the wider politico-economic system was manipulated so as to create an undisputed space for the institution of slavery within national politics. Also, the sons of most wealthy planters were educated in the northern Ivy League universities, and later, some went on to become faculty members in the southern universities, but they never questioned these ideas of human capital. Most northern higher education institutions, hospitals, and religious institutions were getting huge donations from wealthy planters, integrating the so-called two regions into a single, unique capitalistic economy that brought immense prosperity and made the US different from the European continent.[30]

Historiography

Slavery shaped American history right from the early days of colonisation to the post-revolutionary era when the framers of the Constitution incorporated the ideology of freedom and equality. They denied the same to the Indigenous and Black peoples. Therefore, when the US emerged, it was a democratic nation with half its population living within the chains of colonisation and bondage. This dichotomy prompted scholars to undertake research a few decades after the Civil War to analyse the institution of slavery and the reasons for its expansion. In initial assessments, American scholars focused on slave-based plantation systems, the economic importance of slavery, the nature of the master-slave relationship, the social-cultural life of the slaves and different forms of resistance to the institution—these broad areas were generally studied using a top-down approach that centred White perspectives. In the second phase of assessments, with the growth of African American voices in the academy and greater focus on Black history, scholars began to work on understanding slave experiences and narratives, cultures of the enslaved, and forms of resistance, now from the perspective of the enslaved person and not from the accounts of the enslaver. This constituted a bottom-up approach.

SLAVERY AS A BENEVOLENT INSTITUTION?

Early historical accounts demonstrate a clear distinction between scholars who condemned slavery, and those who saw it as legitimate. James Ford Rhodes, in the seven-volume *History of the United States from the Compromise of 1850* (1893–1906), concluded that the plantation economy was an immoral and inhuman institution based on the exploitation of Black labour by White men. Ulrich B. Phillips, in *American Negro Slavery* (1918), presented the institution as a labour system based on benevolence and patriarchy that benefited both the enslaver and the enslaved person. His focus was on the aspects of treatment of the enslaved, the significance of the slave economy, and an analysis of the effectiveness of the slave labour system.

Historians earlier relied heavily on diaries of White enslavers, newspaper reports, and other sources written exclusively by White people. The pioneering work of Herbert Apetheker and Harvey Wish was the first scholarly criticism of the romanticisation of the slave-based plantation economy and society. The two scholars contended that earlier historians failed to understand the inherent contradictions between the two communities and resistance by Black people, even on slave ships. In fact, there were continuous attempts to overcome oppression and exploitation through revolts and resistances. They present historical evidence of major slave resistances that spanned over a period that also witnessed the growth, expansion, and entrenchment of the institution of slavery. This is also highlighted in the works of Raymond and Alice Bauer: they argue that the hidden contradictions of enslavement came out in the form of discontent among the enslaved and the use of indirect forms of resistance. This included a deliberately slow pace of work or destruction of the master's property, including tools, storage, and livestock; spreading rumours about White masters and their families; pretending to be sick or pregnant, self-injury; and even killing their children or dying by suicide. These varied acts were termed by the southern Whites as reflective of the 'racial backwardness' of the Black person, but were in fact very conscious, deliberate acts of resistance against exploitation and inhumane conditions.

Kenneth M. Stampp, in *The Peculiar Institution* (1956), presented the slave institution as economically backward but still profitable and yet extremely brutal and degrading to both the (White) exploiter and the (enslaved Black) exploited. In a marked engagement with U. B. Phillip's interpretation, Stanley Elkins in *Slavery: A Problem in American Institutional and Intellectual Life* (1959) finds that the institution manifested as a psychologically damaging, repressive system. These effects were never questioned. During its initiation, the system of slavery enforced a child-like 'sambo' personality on enslaved people and established conditions comparable to Nazi concentration camps in World War II. This line of thought invited criticism from Earl Thorpe, who believed this comparative study was useless and used the wrong set of analytical tools.

Nevertheless, Elkin's theory shifted scholars' attention towards studying slave communities and personalities and understanding their culture. In a more methodological and critical approach, Eugene Genovese asserted that this personality type existed in all slave societies. However, such an approach alone fails to explain why enslaved people resorted to destroying, undermining, and weakening the institution of slavery through revolts, resistances and rebellions. For Genovese, slavery was based on a feudal system that was pre-bourgeoisie in nature and structure, based on class exploitation in which enslaved people still managed to maintain their distinct identity and uniqueness, creating their cultural world.

Genovese used new types of sources, like slave narratives, in his book *Roll, Jordon, Roll* wherein he described slavery as a paternalistic institution that aimed to establish a system of hegemonic control over the 'physical' and 'mental' world of the enslaved, establishing a shared relationship based on 'organic' experiences that became both 'conflictual and paternalistic'. Enslaved people were the 'paternal' responsibility of the enslaver, but simultaneously they resorted to varied methods to overthrow this authoritarianism under the garb of responsibility. Paul D. Escott highlighted another dimension—slave narratives brought to light the existence of two different worlds and cultures, and an emotions gulf between the two. Therefore, paternalism was a tool to extract labour from enslaved people and maintain White domination on the plantation. For enslaved people, this institution was defined by feelings of suspicion, anger, and hatred due to injustice and prejudice that had generated multiple layers of inequalities, which were so extreme that they denied the humanity of enslaved people. The outer world of Black existence as enslaved people was very different from the inner world of Black culture and identity that enslaved people created for themselves.

Focus on Economic Dimensions

According to Peter J. Parish, enslavement was not an efficient institution, as there was excessive exploitation of labour, land, and natural resources, including the tendency to monopolise products and markets by the planter class. Profits were based on the usage of slave labour, too, which had wide variations when compared with the Upper South to the Deep South, from the Atlantic seaboard to the lower Mississippi Valley and in plantations producing cotton, sugar, or rice. Yes, the fact remains that the institution was based on the foundations of economic interest. However, slavery was also an instrument of social (racial) control that brought status, prestige, and power to those who enslaved people. Therefore, it became necessary for scholars to take a broader perspective of slavery beyond just economic interest.

On the other hand, according to Gavin Wright, it is essential to understand that the maximum utilisation of slave labour was primarily on cotton plantations, followed by rice and sugar, respectively. This meant that cotton determined the value of enslaved people as it generated the greatest profit. For the enslaver, it was essential to balance out the maximisation of profit and self-sufficiency in a manner that did not wholly exhaust enslaved people and push them towards an early death.

There have been debates on whether the slave economy was driven by capitalism or not. According to Fogel and Engerman, a capitalist instinct guided the enslavers, not paternalism. Contrary to this, Eugene Genovese claims that the southern economy was situated in a pre-capitalist society that utilised banking, credit institutions, and the merchant class to run their business, and therefore, the social relationship in the South remained paternalistic, where securing enslaved people became essential to sustain the position and power of the enslavers. Another scholar, James Oakes, has challenged this dominant line of thought. According to Oakes, slave-owners constituted a capitalist class guided by the acquisitive interest in securing capital profits, based on a free-market economy and commercial relationships. To guarantee material success, it became essential to possess more and more slaves. The difference between Genovese and Oakes was their definition of the planter class and the question of whether they were simply slaveholders, or capitalists. However, according to Oakes, paternalism existed only in the period before the Revolutionary War, and after that, capitalism guided the enslavers. While Genovese believed that slavery in the South was both an economic and labour system that developed on a paternalistic social structure, especially after the end of the slave trade in 1808, just when Europe ushered in the Industrial Revolution that raised the demand for cotton and assisted in the development of paternalistic slave system. Adding to this debate Peter J. Parish writes that this class was guided by economic interests and paternalism.

Another historical interpretation, by Willie Lee Rose, posits that by the nineteenth century, the South had begun to 'domesticate' enslaved people by reducing excessive punishments and began to 'rationalise' slavery as a social and psychological necessity. Parish also stated that enslavement squeezed income levels in the South, which created a stagnant economy with no avenue for change or diversification. The debate then began to move towards the historically accepted fact that enslavement was already declining and in remission in the border states and the Upper South. However, according to Alfred H. Conrad and John R. Meyer, the Upper South developed an internal slave trade, selling enslaved people in the Deep South and the Southwest, bringing it considerable profit. However, this argument was challenged by Fogel and Engerman, who claim that more than the trade, enslaved people were moved forcefully into the Deep South and Southwest with the movement of their enslavers. Still, not many historians accept this line of argument. Historians are also divided on the existence of practices of 'breeding', that is, forcing enslaved people to have children.

The Creation of an Independent World of Black Communities

John Blassingame, in *The Slave Community*, has developed a different framework from such studies. He emphasised the inner strength and freedom of mind that the enslaved people developed in their agentic cultural world. Peter Wood has similarly highlighted how Black people brought their knowledge of agricultural production to America, which led to the 'taming' of land and resources and the production of cash crops in the South. Colonists perceived Black people as being immune against many American diseases, which made them more valuable than the White indentured servants. Wood also highlighted the issue of the race 'problem' and the slave resistance. His scholarly work highlighted Black pasts and its immense legacy towards the transformation of America into a 'New World'.

While there is no consensus amongst historians concerning the nature of slavery, they all agree on one essential point: the very existence of slavery was the leading cause for the economic backwardness of the South, as it made the southern economy rigid and stagnant. This factor prevented the South from experimenting with new ideas and avenues, due to low education and living standards, shrinking consumer classes, and limited internal market growth. By the 1850s, the South was reaching its saturation point in terms of territorial expansion, and the need was now to diversify the southern economy; however, since the capital was locked in the ownership of enslaved people, the institution of slavery became a veritable black hole.

The Culture and Identity of the Enslaved People

Slave culture has become an important area of research within the broader field of African American history. Stanley Elkins' work, on the psychic emasculation of Black Americans by an exploitative institution that had few societal barriers to its operation, is considered an influential early study. Elkins emphasised the '**sambo personality**' that enslaved people developed, which left them without culture and self-respect, and imbued them with an 'infantilised' personality that rendered them incapable of rebellion and created a sense of dependence on their enslavers. The term 'sambo' reflected a racial stereotype applied to plantation slaves, who were projected as docile yet irresponsible, loyal but lazy, humble yet prone to lying and theft. Their behaviour was infantile or childish.[31] Elkins' conclusions have been challenged and critiqued by later scholars, including Black historian John Blassingame, who highlighted the strength and mental independence that enslaved people developed through association with one another.[32] Peter Woods has also emphasised the importance of an African American culture that developed among enslaved people.

A new dimension was added to this line of analysis by E. D. Genovese, who combined Marxist interpretation with the study of cultural aspects. He stressed the moral independence and cultural unity of enslaved peoples; simultaneously, he also studied how enslavers physically and mentally subjugated enslaved people. He considered the relationship between the two as complex and ambivalent, premised on the logic of paternalism that was in operation while living in the world of the plantation. Paternalism, in this sense, defined the White man's point of view. As for enslaved people, the relationship was one of exasperation, anger, distrust, and hatred. A contentious gulf always separated the two. Enslaved people knew they were viewed by their oppressors as less than human and 'maintained' by their enslavers to advance their economic profits and social status. To achieve this, the gulf was created and perpetuated based on racism and a psychosocial mental abyss was created based on injustice and oppression of Black people.

From 1863 till the almost mid-twentieth century, American scholarship prioritised White perspectives, guided by an evolutionary ideology that placed the European American coloniser at the top of the civilisational hierarchy. To justify slavery, this ideology portrayed Black people as 'primitive', 'barbaric', and 'childlike' in their behaviour and, therefore, needing to be under the paternal control of the 'civilising' White society. In contrast, enslaved people in America were abruptly thrown into alien conditions and environments, and additionally found the New World to be rife with colonial modes of punishment, exploitation, and racism in its most cruel form. Over a period of time, two polarised cultural worlds began to emerge in the southern region, and with segregation becoming deeply entrenched, their social and mental worlds diverged to the point that divided racial spaces emerged, with enslaved people developing a unique culture. Lawrence Levine was the first scholar to examine this culture, and his work showed how Black people strategised against racism, capitalism, and oppression by developing frameworks of political morality. The Black cultural world evolved from a distillation of African cultural inheritance, combined with adaptations of European and Anglo-American experiences.

Paul D. Escott's work, too, points to segregation. He writes that 'two worlds' existed in the southern states. Enslaved people developed a unique cultural world not only to establish their identity as human beings, but also to cope with the burden of enslavement. By developing different value systems, codes of ethics, religious communities, their own spiritual universe, and an understanding of their environment—which were all intertwined with fragile, yet precious memories and traditions of their ways of life in Africa—they formed a community ethos that could be passed on from one generation to the next, and which would provide inner strength and an independent thinking, and agency to their community.[33] Escott identifies three sources from which slave culture derives its power: (*i*) the existential experiences of racial exploitation; (*ii*) the development of life-saving skills in the face of deprivation; and (*iii*) internal structures to help overcome racism. The beliefs, practices, and code of ethics that governed these cultural worlds were based on a sense of justice, which became an essential element in their everyday struggle against the harsh world created by White society.³⁴

White people defined enslaved people as separate, inferior, and sub-human, denying their existence as independent individuals. As a socially subjugated class, the enslaved person could rise from one form of intense labour to another without bringing about any significant rise or shift in their status, rank, or removal of bias against their racial identity. This necessitated the development of a moral system independent of White control and racial regulations. The essential elements of African American culture were, in reality, an amalgamation of African, Indigenous, and European cultures that enslaved people encountered, experienced, and assimilated for their survival in the New World. The fact remains that racial hostility, prejudice, and exploitation led to a sense of loyalty, cohesion, and cooperation within their communities to protect their personal spaces, thoughts and inner world against White interference.³⁵

The first step towards the creation of their own 'space' was in terms of their appearance, which became part of their cultural identity. The Other became the 'self' through the adoption of African hairstyles, headdresses, and clothes along with a mixture of Indigenous and European styles. This blending of diverse cultures within the Black community initiated a process of identity-building that enabled them to establish their world, distinguishing themselves from the dominant White society.

The outer appearance of difference extended further in terms of spoken language, since Black people were never educated in the Western sense. The enslaved people developed 'pidgin', using which people from different African linguistic backgrounds could communicate and transmit their cultural traditions. Sterling Stuckley believed that it was pidgin English that brought the enslaved people together, mitigating their regional differences and establishing a sense of community. According to Genovese, cultural penetration was a two-way street as enslaved people borrowed from White society and mixed it with their African heritage. Enslaved people also developed their own unique forms of oral culture through the world of sound: words spoken, chanted, or sung. The denial of Western education necessitated the development of an internal community mechanism whereby older adults within slave society became great storytellers. Their riddles, proverbs, and folktales were a powerful mode of communicating facets of their unique forms of morality and imparting training to younger generations on how to survive in an oppressive environment.

Mysteries or tales, including stories, proverbs, anecdotes, and jokes based on the African past as well as present experiences became an essential tool for the transmission of African American cultural values and education that led to memory training amongst the youngsters, developed the power of reasoning, philosophical questioning, and analytical skills. **Slave tales** aimed to provide hope for the future and were an important survival tool. They were also essential for maintaining family ties and instilling obedience to parents and elders. Such tales also served as a tool for transmitting the religious beliefs of Black communities. Trickster tales, with their multifold meanings, often showed how the weak could defeat or manipulate the mighty. The genre parodied cruel masters and the injustice, hypocrisy, and immorality of slavery as an institution. Sterling Stuckey has emphasised the importance of storytelling in transmitting slave culture across generations, as we have discussed, and noted that these were based on African storytelling traditions. According to Stuckey, it is through slave culture that enslaved people belonging to different ethnic African groups were unified in the New World, creating a distinct African American community. Enslaved people evolved songs, tales, rituals, and ceremonies to construct an African American culture. Their songs were based on nature with a solid relationship to dance and bodily movements; they allowed avenues for a kind of psychological release, and were a means of cultural self-assertion.

In this sense, Black culture grew to become source of power and strategy of resistance, rebellion, and obedience, sometimes manifesting as masterful deception.[36] Slave music was based on distinct cultural traditions that emerged from the blending of individual and community expressions. According to John Blassingame, Black music was based on an understanding and adoption of Christian imagery as well as English, along with musical forms inherited from various parts of Africa, leading to the emergence of a genre of Christian music known as '**spirituals**', an original, diasporic, and artistic creation. The genre incorporated the use of musical instruments such as the drums and banjo, which came to be used even during religious sermons. It also featured rhythmic melodies and chants that made for lively music and were seen to provide a kind of relief from the mental toll of extreme oppression. These traditions gave birth to a new genre of music that came to be known as jazz and blues music. Even their varied dance forms, often based on complicated patterns and athletic footwork (for instance, the 'patting juba') helped to release pent-up emotions and liberate their bodies, if only for brief interludes. These forms of artistic expression were in marked contrast to the extreme forms of bodily policing to which Black people were subjected.

Over time, despite the official policy of denial of education to enslaved people, the community found ways to acquire formal learning. Initially, education was restricted to exemplary individuals who, showing exemplary courage, persisted in their efforts despite discrimination and fears of persecution. One example is Maryland mathematician and astronomer Benjamin Banneker (1731–1806), considered to be among the first Black scientists, who assisted in a federal survey of the District of Columbia in 1791. Banneker published an almanac from 1792 to 1797. In an era where racist ideologies were predominant and White settlers widely subscribed to the belief that Black people were innately 'deficient' and 'uncivilised', the very existence of a figure like Banneker called racist pseudoscience into question. Abolitionists cited his mathematical ability as proof that people of African descent possessed higher mental capabilities equal to those of White people, and that slavery was therefore wrong and immoral. Banneker himself had sent his first almanac to Thomas Jefferson to persuade him to accept the equality of Black people. African-born poet Phillis Wheatley, of Boston, was known for her collection *Poems on Various Subjects, Religious and Moral* (1773). She also wrote poems on George Washington and the Methodist preacher George Whitefield. Her lyrics challenged the pervasive dehumanisation of Africans in White societies, and were an assertion of the fact that African people possessed as much humanity, if not more, than anyone else, and deserved to be slaves to no one. She also wrote a poem about Scipio Moorhead (1750), a Black artist who may have engraved the copperplate frontispiece for her book. Enslaved people brought with them their African agricultural production techniques. They taught their exploiters to cultivate vegetables and crops like rice, indigo, and cotton, develop gardens, and read weather signs. They brought with them the knowledge of how to deal with varied wildlife and animals like alligators. They created their own medicine, teas, and tonics based on ingredients found in America to cure themselves of common ailments.[37] According to Blassingame, enslaved people introduced basket weaving, wood carving, pottery, and unique musical instruments; another notable contribution of the African American experience was the use of certain architectural features developed in Africa.

THE WORLD OF BLACK RELIGION

Religion provided enslaved people with a set of ethics and a different view of the universe, providing them spiritual independence and a paradigm of justice that challenged White propaganda and oppression. By creating shared practices, they rejected the White man's religious traditions, including a system of worship that continuously reinforced their subordinate position. In the process, a distinct emotional dimension emerged within the Christian tradition. Their moral behaviour also differed when they resorted to stealing and theft. In the White world, stealing was immoral, but if a slave stole, say, food that they had produced but were subsequently deprived of, it was considered a righteous action. They did not consider that immoral, but rather a reclaiming of what rightly belonged to them. This was their ethics of justice. Religion, in this context, offered mental and spiritual freedom and a universe that was free from enslavement, supported by an ideology centred on liberation. The ethical code of behaviour that developed through faith practices supported their various forms of resistance. Similarly, the spiritual vision that defined Black religious communities emphasised faith in humanity and the dignity of human labour.

The dominant image of the spirituals—the genre of religious music discussed earlier—is that of a chosen people on their way to the promised land, and of maintaining personal contact with God. Black people maintained that the God of Moses and of Jesus did not create them to be slaves or second-class citizens. Moses typically symbolises liberation. The well-documented historical reality was that even when the slaves were converted, they did not uncritically accept its tenets, but instead used their mental freedom to rationalise the religion of Western civilisation. Christianity, for them, could be oppressive if accepted without thinking and liberating if it provided inner strength to face the day-to-day challenge of existence and survival.[38]

The early African American religion came from the bottom up. Black preachers, including some women, were not formally educated; they were community leaders who were believed to have gained their knowledge directly from God or the Holy Spirit. Another facet of African American religion was that it was multiracial and evangelical. Early Methodism and the many independent churches and sects it inspired reflect this. The founder of Methodism was the English Anglican priest John Wesley in Georgia, and the first two people he baptised were enslaved women. Methodist congregations met in homes where people of all races, genders, and social status met and narrated their own stories of personal salvation. It also led to the emergence of Black preachers like Harry Hosier, who was born enslaved (1750–1806) near Fayetteville, North Carolina and was known as 'Black Harry'. Hosier became the first Black American Methodist preacher. Another Black Methodist preacher was a woman named Isabella, born enslaved in New York State in 1797, who later gave herself a new name, Sojourner Truth. She emerged as a gifted preacher in her native Ulster County in the Hudson River Valley in the late 1820s. She later moved to New York after gaining freedom through a New York law in 1828. By the 1840s, she began to channel her power as a preacher toward antislavery and feminist movements.

The third dimension of the Black religion was organised churches. Breaking away from White congregations in the late eighteenth century, Black northerners founded their own church organisations in Philadelphia. The African Methodist Episcopal (AME) church, the first Black congregation, grew out of American Methodism. One Black preacher, Richard Allen (1760–1831), impressed Methodist circuit riders with his righteousness and preaching abilities and they permitted him to purchase his freedom. Allen later settled in Philadelphia, preaching to Black people at the St. George Methodist Episcopal Church. As African Americans were subjected to stringent regulations, Allen and his colleague Absalom Jones (1746–1818) established the Free African Society of Philadelphia in 1787. In 1794, they left the White-dominated church and set up their own Bethel African Methodist Episcopal Church. After years of struggle with St. George's Church over control of Mother Bethel, Allen joined forces with Daniel Coker (1780–1846), the leader of Baltimore's Black Methodists and other Black Methodists from Salem, New Jersey, and Attleborough, Pennsylvania. Together, they formed the African Methodist Episcopal Church connection in 1816, which became the first Black denomination.

Daniel Coker was the son of an indentured White woman and an enslaved Black man. He spent the years from 1820 to 1821 as a pioneer in the newly established Maryland colony of Liberia and subsequently spent most of his life in Sierra Leone. This region was founded by free northern Blacks and formerly enslaved people who had joined with the American Colonization Society to create the new colony of Liberia in West Africa in 1820. In Sierra Leone, Coker published several articles opposing slavery.

The roots of the African Methodist Episcopal Zion church can be traced to the northern city of New York in the late eighteenth century. Here, the Black Methodists belonged to the John Street Methodist Church, where the congregation was about 40 per cent Black in 1793. Black church members formed an African Chapel known as the Zion Church in 1796, under the leadership of Peter Williams (1763–1836). The African Chapel became independent in 1801 and gained the status of a separate denomination between 1820 and 1824.

The independent Black churches offered ample opportunities to Black men but did not welcome women preachers. They, too, obeyed St. Paul's stricture against women speaking out in church, even though most members were women. While women Black preachers were extremely gifted, they were illiterate, and literacy is an essential requirement for the clergy. Some gifted female preachers were Jarena Lee (1783–c. 1850s) and Zilpha Elaw (c. 1790–c. 1850s). Black communities began developing distinct art forms based on Christian motifs during this time. Hagar's figure, Abraham's servant and bearer of his child Ishmael, appeared in most Black writings as African Americans could see parallels between her situation and that of enslaved Black women and single parents. Black women also made quilts, like Harriet Powers (1837–1911), who made figures of her people and quilts with Biblical motifs.[39]

Therefore, for African Americans, religion became a form of mental resistance and defence against physical oppression. It taught them community values, a sense of compassion, and the ability to critically comprehend their masters and reject the ideological rationale for their enslavement.[40]

On the other hand, southern White communities stressed the importance of individual piety rather than social regeneration as southern politicians, intellectuals, and religious leaders aimed to curtail any space for social experimentation. When compared to the North, which was witnessing the 'era of reform' through the growth of utopian socialism and trade unionism, feminism, pacifism, and abolitionism, this is especially stark. Southerners criticised the development of such 'isms' as they preferred conservatism, order, and tradition. Despite such an atmosphere, enslaved people rejected the interpretation of Christianity as propounded by their masters, for the White religion emphasised obedience, humility, and a release from suffering in an afterlife rather than in this world. Enslaved people viewed themselves as a chosen people. From the Bible, they were drawn to the stories of people who overcame adversity, like Daniel escaping the lion's den, David slaying Goliath, and Moses leading his people to a promised land of freedom. In religion, Black people found a vehicle for surviving the experience of enslavement with their dignity intact, and in the church they found a space to develop a leadership independent of White control.

Eugene Genovese believed that religion was the centrepoint of the slave world. Black communities used it as a tool of resistance and spiritual comfort and for psychological relief from the pressures of enslavement, providing them with a means of endurance. They developed a distinctive African American religion that included conjurers, magicians, and Christian preachers who emphasised faith, love, and not rigid doctrine or formal structure. These were amalgamated with certain rituals that were in continuity with the long-lost African heritage of the enslaved. These rituals were based on beliefs in the living dead, conjuration, ghosts or apparitions, faith in magic traditions, and the art of interpreting dreams.[41] Luck was important within this spiritual framework—perhaps a fallout of the precarity and uncertainty in the lives of enslaved people. They made their religion a space of happiness and peace that inspired, according to Albert Raboteau, a strong sense of community. According to Lawrence Levine, it provided them with alternative religious standards by creating space with the help of which they prevented legal slavery from becoming spiritual slavery. One well-known (if frequently misunderstood) alternative practice was the tradition of 'voodoo' or vodou, an Afro-Caribbean faith system; conjurers influenced the slave community and developed, in Blassingame's terms, a **syncretic African Christianity**. He states that the Black church was the 'single most important institution for the "Americanization" of the bondsman'. Christianity provided both spiritual release and spiritual victory, and in the words of Stuckey, it was 'Christianity shot through with African values'.

Based on the factors mentioned above, Herbert G. Gutman has asserted that the process of cultural formation among enslaved people began before the American War of Independence and continued well after the Civil War.[42] According to E. D. Genovese, American slavery was a chattel system based on material possessions that could be bought, sold, mortgaged, and rented.[43] The control of this property established a racial distinction between enslavers and enslaved persons and created an unjust social order based on cruelty and hatred. This socio-cultural world was also based on a land-plantation system where slaveholders had become entrenched as the regional ruling class. Therefore, the southern slave system was based on racism and class exploitation and the White southerners maintained a paternalistic relationship with Black people. Once made racially inferior, enslaved people were exploited to provide status, authority, and prestige to their masters. However, despite all this, enslaved people retained their self-worth and self-respect through the development of an independent world of African American culture.

Slave Rebellions: Breaking the Shackles of the White World

… All men are created equal and endowed by their creator with certain inalienable rights and among these are life, liberty, and the pursuit of happiness.

–Declaration of Independence

In the 'land of freedom', slavery grew to be a dehumanising institution, both physically and psychologically. From a tender age, enslaved people experienced forms of degradation and humiliation that generated from extreme depression, desperation, and complete apathy. Enslaved children were born into bondage, and by age seven they were made to perform domestic work in White homes; at age 10, they were brought to work in the agricultural fields. White society developed a standardised form of cruelty that aimed to create a sense of powerlessness among Black people. Generally, this either pushed Black people to create modes of community solidarity and build an invisible protective barrier; or it produced a deep-rooted nihilism, leading some enslaved people to unleash their deeply internalised anger or desperation on those more vulnerable than them, generally their children or spouses. In a bid to protect their children from this oppressive world, they sometimes even killed them in infancy. White oppression created a dark alien planet for Black people. This process assisted in the ideological construct by the White settler to project them as cold, calculating tricksters who were lazy, childlike, and oversexed.

Slavery as a labour system was applied through force, constant surveillance, and a dedicated policing system. In the period stretching from the seventeenth to the eighteenth centuries, any negligence towards assigned duties and responsibilities was met with various inhuman punishments ranging from branding, chaining, castration, muzzling, maiming, and whipping. However, as the price for purchasing enslaved people became expensive by the beginning of the nineteenth century, the standard form of punishment became whipping and chaining. The situation was much worse for enslaved women, who were essentially required to work double shifts—both as enslaved people and to feed and take care of their families.[44] Enslaved women also had to withstand the compulsion to bear children even without their consent. It was common practice to encourage enslaved women to get pregnant and fertile women slaves were termed as 'breed women' (although there is no historical consensus on whether practices of 'breeding' are borne out by the historical record).[45] They were given special treatment, good food, time to rest and relatively less work when compared with other enslaved people. Enslavers also encouraged the pairing of enslaved people to ensure an internal production system for such an expensive commodity. White enslavers who sexually exploited slave women often felt compelled to sell them to keep the sanity of their White wives, who could not bear to see biracial children on the plantation, a clear sign of White enslavers' adultery.[46] Enslaved women had to endure yet another cruelty: as the domestic slave trade became profitable, enslavers frequently broke up enslaved families, and this process picked up pace with frontier expansion as young men began to move into new territories with their share of 'slave property'.

The psychological trauma of slavery was manyfold, ranging from sexual exploitation, humiliation, punishment, and poor health conditions due to overwork, to inadequate food and clothing that shortened their life expectancy. Enslaved people paid a very high price in terms of the psychological violence unleashed on them, in the form of total obedience and submission to the dictates of their masters. Despite this cruelty, they were required to maintain a sober demeanour; this complicated the relationship even further. Those enslaved people who managed to run away were described in newspaper advertisements as 'stutterers', and advertisements carried their wound marks as signs of recognition. Historians are now of the opinion that enslaved people generally suffered from post-traumatic stress syndrome due to the hegemonic control exercised by slave-owners over their physical, spatial, and mental worlds.

Some plantations had medical doctors caring for the master's precious commodity. Still, as most plantations did not have this facility, enslaved people had herbalists and magicians who used their African knowledge to cure common slave ailments. This clearly shows that there were different levels of oppression in small and big plantations depending on the type of crop produced. With the ever-expanding Deep South, over time, people in the Upper South became relatively less cruel. While the White masters created class divisions amongst their slaves, enslaved people themselves lacked 'class consciousness' as their common outlook towards slavery united them.[47] It is an established historical fact that enslaved people worked from sunrise to sunset. Since they barely had spare time, in the words of a formerly enslaved person, they never suffered from 'mattress fever'. Extreme rules, punishments, and denial of education circumscribed their lives. The application of stringent southern social sanctions and constant physical abuse was an established practice in the South. Some particularly abhorrent practices included branding, burning of enslaved people, punishing them by placing persons inside barrels studded with nails, placing them inside small sweatboxes with only the head exposed to the sun, burning them with coals, killing enslaved people who were no longer in position to work due to old age, sickness, accident, the constant physical ailment was a common practice.[48] Perhaps enslaved people alone could never destroy the institution of slavery, but they still constantly struggled and resisted this bondage system. The house servants, due to their proximity to the master, passed vital information to other enslaved people, for example if their families were going to be sold, punished, rented out, or mortgaged. This helped the affected people to run away and escape, even if such an escape was brief.[49] The only enslaved people who belonged to neither world were the Black Drivers, who were looked down upon with suspicion by all the other enslaved people and carefully supervised even by the masters. For the enslaved people, physical punishment was the worst part of slave existence, and most enslaved people had virtually no contact with people outside their plantation. Enslaved people, therefore, lived in a carefully crafted, isolated world of existence.[50]

American Exceptionalism 211

Enslaved people knew that they were not in a position to destroy the institution, so over a period of time, they perfected the art of weakening it from the inside. Their most potent weapon was resistance, formulated and carried out in many ways to reduce their physical and mental abuse or secure better treatment. Generally, those who dared to run away knew their worth and had mastered the technique of playing the White master against the overseer, or exploiting the vulnerabilities of their masters. By resisting the institution, enslaved people not only lessened the plantation discipline and expanded the scope for their survival, but also, equally importantly, the fact that slave resistance happened continuously and in everyday existence attested to the extreme brutality of the institution.[51]

Resistance was carried out in multiple ways:

- Feigning illness, work stoppage, negligence, pretending to be 'stupid', pouring white sand on the cotton to make it weigh more, sleeping hidden among the corn fields, breaking tools, and pretending to be clumsy while handling tools.[52] Some enslaved people refused to cooperate with any form of punishment, knowing well that they were valuable as property, and sometimes violence erupted in the field itself in the heat of the moment.[53]
- Committing crimes: arson, poisoning, running away, and theft. Running away and hiding in the woods was a common form of resistance as other enslaved people provided the runaways with food, clothing, and information. **Runaways** often applied particular substances, like red pepper, mud, turpentine, or wild turnips, on their bodies, to throw off dogs from the trail. Enslaved people knew that their absence meant an economic loss to the master. Hiding was perfected into an art form, even if the runaways were often recaptured. They sometimes organised secret meetings using well-practised sounds of birds, music, or secret codes, and these were also used to help out runaway slaves. During these private meetings, they often stationed a 'raid fox', generally a person adept at giving the wrong directions to slave patrollers. Meetings were organised to plan the theft of food, animals, or other things

that the enslaved group believed they were entitled to claim. Most field hands were involved in all kinds of resistance as they were the worst exploited, followed by house servants and skilled artisans.[54] The enslaved people used music to transmit secret messages, control the pace of work in the fields, help out the weakest Black labourers, and amuse the enslaver even as they secretly mocked him.[55]

- **'Maroons'** were a group of fugitive slaves who formed independent communities in far-flung areas like Virginia's Great Dismal Swamp and Florida's Everglades. They were runaways who had escaped punishment and illness, and sometimes those who escaped so that they would not be separated from their families.[56]
- There were instances where enslaved people openly engaged in verbal abuse against enslavers, beat them up, or even killed their enslavers, White overseers, or police patrollers.[57]
- Enslaved women, too, found ways of resistance, including violence, especially in contexts of sexual abuse and exploitation.[58]

According to Herbert Apetheker, there were at least 200 slave rebellions in America from the early seventeenth century to the Civil War in the 1860s. According to Harvey Wish, the potential of slave rebellions as a tool against the institution of slavery was not realised by abolitionists. Enslavers preferred to maintain silence over the issue to prevent any social panic sparked by such clear signs of the system's inherent fallacies and to maintain their sectional pride. Even the southern press avoided writing on this serious issue, with a view to maintain the impression of racial superiority of this 'benevolent' institution. However, slave rebellions in America were smaller and less frequent compared to Brazil, the West Indies, and Sant Domingue (present-day Haiti), as the White population formed the majority in America. Moreover, slaves in America managed to establish customs and rules that would govern the conduct of their enslavers without directly challenging the institution of slavery itself. As one ex-slave declared, 'White folks do as they please, and the darkies[59] do as they can'.[60]

Major Slave Rebellions and the Underground Railroad

Rebellions began right from the inception of the transatlantic slave trade. Slave ships witnessed the first **slave rebellions**, which began as soon as enslaved people were loaded onto boats or during their journey, particularly when the ships were sailing along the Gambia River, or along specific points on the West African coast (such as Sierra Leone, Goree, Cape Coast Castle, Cabinda, and Cape Malpas). The ships bred desperation and despair: many enslaved persons died by suicide, jumping off the ship; some refused food altogether and suffered deliberate starvation, or refused to be treated medically in case of sickness, becoming delirious and uncontrollable. Generally, ship rebellions occurred spontaneously in the face of multiple suicides, or when enslaved women managed to steal and hide weapons and gave them to the men. There were occasions when enslaved people successfully took control of the ship and forced the captain to take them back to Africa. However, in the case of failure, which was the more common outcome, punishment was brutal and extreme, with leaders of the rebellion subjected to torture and eventually killed. Given the frequency of revolts, there was a provision in the West for taking insurance coverage in the case of slave insurrections.[61]

Slave rebellions were infrequent, but plots and resistances were many and localised, and most were short-lived. There was no recorded slave revolt from the time of Nat Turner to the beginning of the Civil War. According to Genovese, most slave rebellions were attempts to challenge the system and create fear in the minds of the enslavers. Enslaved people knew the futility of running away, so some became habitual runaways, seeking to live a temporary life of respite before being brought back into the system. The flight was an act of individual resistance, although sometimes it occurred in groups, like the 'maroons' that ran away to join the Seminoles in Florida. According to one estimate, by the mid-1830s, 1,200 maroons in Florida were removed to the Southwest in the 1840s. Lawrence Levine and Genovese do not characterise these as politically conscious acts—both scholars saw this opposition as 'passive' and not based on planned political action, except in the case of rebellions.[62]

Slave insurrections were common both in the North and the South during the colonial period. Harvey Wish had presented evidence that during the early period, before slavery became an entrenched institution, there were instances when White indentured servants joined hands with Black slaves against their masters. This was evident in the failed plot in Gloucester County, Virginia (1663). In the eastern county of Virginia in particular, repeated slave plots were reported from 1687 to 1730, which forced the colonial administrators to establish a designated slave patrol unit in 1726 to prevent more enslaved people from being brought in. High duties were imposed on the importation of slaves.

On 6 April 1712, about 23 enslaved persons, all of whom had been severely exploited, armed themselves with guns and clubs and set fire to houses on the northern edge of New York City, killing nine White people. Indigenous people joined hands with the enslaved people in this insurrection. Later, the rebel slaves were captured by American soldiers and brutally executed. This violent backlash to the insurrection far exceeded the mayhem committed by rebelling enslaved people.

The Stono Uprising took place in South Carolina in 1739. England was at war with Spain at the time, and a group of about 20 slaves from Angola sought to take advantage of this. They gathered at Stono under the leadership of a man named Tommy and took out a procession, beating drums to invite other enslaved people to join them. They armed themselves and crossed into Spanish Florida, killing settlers and looting or burning down their houses, but were eventually defeated by armed White people. The uprising ended with the deaths of 65 people, of which 44 were Black and 21 were White. Slave rebellions were also reported from Berkeley County and Charleston County, and these impacted slave uprisings in the colony of Georgia, from where enslaved people attempted to slip into Spanish-held territories.

Another plot was unearthed in New York in 1741. This was a mixed revolt by a group comprising both Black and White people. A White man accused of supplying weapons was executed along with his entire family; a White Catholic priest was hanged as a co-conspirator; 13 Black people were immolated, and 18 were hanged. A total of 80 enslaved people were removed from New York. To prevent such occurrences, the New York Assembly implemented a substantial increase in taxes on the importation of enslaved Black people. However, this increase was later abolished by the British authorities.

After the American Revolution, there was a surge in the frequency of slave rebellions, keeping pace with the growth and expansion of the plantation economy, the rise of the Cotton Kingdom, and the emergence of the powerful planter-enslaver class in the South. Abolitionist propaganda did not overtly influence these rebellions. However, in many instances, White sympathisers played vital roles, offering support to enslaved people who were looking to escape.

Enslaved people constantly encountered adverse situations in their day-to-day existence. These ranged from the threat of sale and break-up of their families, to humiliation, harsh punishments, and daily abuse that was deeply degrading and dehumanising. These experiences were a reminder of their subjugated status, and in this climate of mutual fear and resentment, there was little space for compromise, bargaining, and agreement.

The so-called slave leaders, who were generally family elders and preachers, typically endorsed more passive forms of resistance and instead used their energies to develop unique and functional folk culture, music, dance forms, and songs that provided psychological protection against the highly exploitative system of slavery and also assisted in the development of family and community ties. These measures helped cultivate an internal capacity to face the external pressure from the dominant White community.[63]

The state of Virginia was impacted most by the slave rebellions. Gabriel Prosser (1775–1800), a Richmond blacksmith (enslaved by Thomas Prosser) and his brother Martin, a slave preacher, started the **Gabriel Rebellion** in 1800. They were both literate. Gabriel talked to Black people regarding the **Rights of Men** and the Declaration of Independence. According to Francis D. Cogliano, up until 1763, slavery was widespread in America. However, by 1800, it had become a regional institution that began to face threats from within, as the essence of the American Revolution influenced enslaved Black people who, too, affirmed faith in human liberty.[64] Slave uprisings in San Domingo also inspired Gabriel. Martin held secret religious meetings where he used Biblical stories of Israelites escaping Egyptians' bondage to justify slave rebellions. The brothers had planned that on a pre-planned date (30 August 1800), they would march to Richmond from the surrounding plantation under the banner of the slogan 'death or liberty'; they were to plunder the armoury, burn the city, and kill all White people except for the Quakers, the French, and the Methodists (as these groups were opposed to slavery) so they could take over the town. However, sudden rains and flooding of roads made it impossible for the rebels to come together. Some enslaved people who were loyal to their enslavers exposed the plot and that ended the rebellion.[65] This was so serious that it led to the formation of the American Colonization Society in 1816. Slave patrol laws were strengthened to prevent slave rebellion plots in the future.

Despite this, from 1802 to the War of 1812, multiple slave revolts were reported. One such plot was initiated by a White man, George Boxley, who in 1816 instigated enslaved people to revolt, but about 30 of them were captured and executed while Boxley himself managed to escape. According to Francis D. Cogliano, the period from 1775 to 1815 saw the maximum number of slave resistances, in the form of armed conflict, flight, lawsuits and political pressure, which clearly showed that more than Jeffersonians, it was enslaved Black people who understood the core principles of the Declaration of Independence that stated: 'All men are created equal'.[66] During his trial, one of the rebels declared, '… I have adventured my life endeavouring to obtain the liberty of my countrymen and am a willing sacrifice to their cause.'[67]

Denmark Vesey (1767–1822) was an enslaved carpenter in Charleston, South Carolina, who acquired his freedom through money from winning a lottery in 1800. He asserted that slavery and bondage were against the teachings of the Bible, and that slavery went against democracy and the Christian faith. He also knew about successful slave rebellions in Haiti, and followed closely the Congressional debates about the potential expansion of slavery beyond Missouri. Vesey was also an African Methodist Episcopal Church member and was inspired by Old Testament accounts of Jewish enslavement and persecution. He thought of himself as a Black Moses who had been given power and insight to lead his people out of slavery. He even envisioned himself successfully securing assistance from the West Indies and Africa to establish his Black state. In 1822, along with the slaves of Charleston, he organised an attack on 14 July, Bastille Day, the revolutionary national day of France. However, he was betrayed. About 130 rebels were captured and 35 executed, including Vesey, but he never revealed how he came to plan this rebellion.

Nat Turner (1800–1831) was a slave preacher in Virginia and a visionary who believed that God had chosen him to lead his people to freedom. He was the son of an African-born slave mother and was deeply affected by the violence and atrocity of the slave system. His life experiences and the mystical visions he dreamt of during his childhood and youth convinced him that he had the prophetic power to carry out successful action against slavery. He, along with five associates, who were later joined by 80 other enslaved people, killed and burnt his master's family as well as other White people. He destroyed his enslaver's property in Southampton County, but was later captured after many weeks in hiding and executed. This led to the beginning of a debate in Virginia on whether to abolish slavery. Ultimately, the state established a set of slave codes to resolve the issue.[68]

In 1839, enslaved Africans transported illegally from Cuba captured the ship that was transporting them, the AMISTAD, and attempted to take it back to Africa. They anchored at Long Island, New York, where the US Coast Guard captured them. This case reached the Supreme Court, which granted them freedom.

As we have earlier discussed, running away was the most common form of resistance. There were famous fugitive slaves, like Frederick Douglas, William Wells Brown and William and Ellen Craft. Some of these created a unique genre of African American literature, the ex-slave narratives, inspiring others to follow in their footsteps. For many fugitives, running away was difficult as they left behind their families to escape to freedom in northern and western states and Canada. They were assisted by sympathisers who took them out through the **Underground Railroad**. This term was applied to an informal network of people from different ethnicities in the North and West who assisted runaways in walking on to the path of freedom.

This network stretched to Michigan and Canada. In the southern states, Black churches and free Black persons assisted in their escape, as did the Quakers. Those with missionary zeal to end this brutal institution also provided aid to runaway slaves. In Pennsylvania, William Still was the head of the Philadelphia Vigilance Committee; in New York, there was David Ruggles, the leader of the New York City Vigilance Committee; in Ohio, a White Quaker named Levin Coffin assisted runaway Black people in Cincinnati. These incidents puncture the claim that slaves were childlike or satisfied with the institution. The fact is that in 1850, the **Fugitive Slave Act** had to be implemented to bring back runaway slaves, and in 1851 and again

FIG. 7.2: Harriet Tubman, portrait by Harvey B. Lindsley, taken between 1871 and 1876

Source: Wikimedia Commons.

in 1854, troops had to be used to get back enslaved people from the White abolitionists, reflecting the level of exploitation and economic importance of this institution.[69]

One of the most well-known enslaved women in American history was Harriet Tubman who, one account declared, was the Moses of her people. Tubman escaped to her freedom in 1849, narrowly avoiding being sold off and separated from her husband. She journeyed from Maryland's eastern shore to Philadelphia, where she worked to muster up funds to facilitate and plan more escapes, and went back about 19 times to bring more enslaved people to freedom. She made her last rescue mission in 1860, and by then she was known as the 'Moses of her People'. These famous slave rebellions and their respective leaders became heroes to Black people and were vilified and called 'bad' by the White. In the Black world, the word 'bad' acquired a new definition, and it denoted a person of power and fortitude possessing the quality of goodness towards humanity.[70]

Slave rebellions also occurred in Florida, Louisiana, Tennessee, Kentucky and Texas, and the growing frequency of revolts and rebellions began to make some political leaders uneasy. They began to view slavery as inhuman and inconsistent with the political and economic ethos of the nation. In the meantime, in the southern states, the internal slave trade took a downward turn due to slave rebellions, and therefore, laws against free Black individuals were made more stringent, slave codes were enacted, and attempts began to be made to prevent enslaved people from getting educated. Efforts to restrict education stemmed from an understanding that most of the Black leaders were relatively privileged individuals among Black communities, like blacksmiths, free individuals, or preachers—literate individuals with an excellent knowledge of the outside world. Religion also played a significant role in all slave rebellions. Nat Turner, for instance, famously declared: 'Was Not Christ crucified.'[71]

By the 1850s, it was becoming increasingly hard to deny that the institution of slavery was evil. The Fugitive Slave Act of 1850 cast a shadow over personal liberty laws and abolitionists became determined to end this institution. The rise of the Free-Soil Party in 1848 was committed to stopping the expansion of slavery in the West. The South continued to support and protect the institution, which led to the beginning of the Civil War. The thirteenth Constitutional Amendment finally ended this institution, bringing to an end more than two hundred years of bondage, slavery, and inhuman exploitation in a country that otherwise prided itself on being the land of liberty, democracy, and individualism.

Notes

1. The English borrowed the word from Spanish. They linked it to slaveholding and placed Black people on a social hierarchy that accorded superior status to Christians and White people.
2. Peter J. Parish, *Slavery: History and Historians* (New York, 1989), p. 12.
3. Parish *Slavery*, p. 14.
4. Ibid.
5. Kenneth M. Stampp, 'Slavery: The Historian's Burden', in *Perspectives and Irony in American Slavery: Essays*, ed. Carl Degler and Harry P. Owens (Jackson, 1976), p. 155.
6. Allen C. Guelzo, *Fateful Lightning: A New History of the Civil War and Reconstruction* (New York, 2012), p. 30.
7. Guelzo, *Fateful Lightning*, pp. 30–33.
8. Parish *Slavery*, p. 14.
9. Ibid.
10. Peter Kolchin, *American Slavery, 1619–1877* (New York, 1993), pp. 12–13.
11. Guelzo, *Fateful Lightning*, p. 38.
12. Eric Foner, *Forever Free: The Story of Emancipation and Reconstruction* (New York, 2006), p. 7.
13. Guelzo, *Fateful Lightning*, p. 34.
14. Parish *Slavery*, p. 15.
15. Stampp 'Slavery', p. 156.
16. Parish *Slavery*, pp. 18–20.
17. It was around this time that Frederick Douglass, a former slave and important leader advocating for African American rights, and William Lloyd Garrison, founder of the radical newspaper *The Liberator*, began the abolitionist movement.
18. Allan Nevins, *Ordeal of the Union: Fruits of Manifest Destiny, 1847–1852* (New York, 1947), p. 466.
19. Eric Foner, *Give Me Liberty! An American History*, third ed. (New York, 2011).
20. Guelzo, *Fateful Lightning*, p. 24.
21. Ibid.
22. Ibid.

23. Ibid., p. 25.
24. Orlando Patterson, *The Ordeal of Integration: Progress and Resentment in America's 'Racial' Crisis* (Washington, DC, 1998), p. 40.
25. Barbara Jeanne Fields, *Slavery and Freedom on the Middle Ground* (New Haven, 1985).
26. Fields, *Slavery and Freedom on the Middle Ground*.
27. Orlando Patterson, *Slavery and Social Death: A Comparative Study* (Cambridge, Massachusetts, 1982).
28. Guelzo, *Fateful Lightning*, p. 25.
29. Elizabeth Fox-Genovese and Eugene D. Genovese, *The Mind of the Master Class: History and Faith in the Southern Slaveholder's Worldview* (New York, 2005), p. 313.
30. Sven Beckert and Seth Rockman, ed., *Slavery's Capitalism: A New History of American Economic Development* (Philadelphia, 2016), pp. 1–27.
31. Stanley Elkins, *Slavery: A Problem in American Institutional and Intellectual Life* (Chicago, 1982).
32. John Blassingame, *The Slave Community: Plantation Life in Antebellum South*, revised ed. (New York, 1979).
33. Paul D. Escott, *Slavery Remembered: A Record of Twentieth-Century Slave Narratives* (Chapel Hill, 1979), p. 95.
34. Ibid., p. 95.
35. Ibid., pp. 96–100.
36. John Blassingame, ed., *Slave Testimony: Two Centuries of Letters, Speeches, Interviews and Autobiographies* (Louisiana, 1977).
37. Escott, *Slavery Remembered*, pp. 102–104.
38. Ibid., pp. 112–114.
39. Nell Irvin Painter, *Creating Black Americans: African American History and its Meanings, 1619 to the Present* (New York, 2006).
40. Ronald Segal, *The Black Diaspora: Five Centuries of Black Experience Outside Africa* (New York, 1995).
41. Escott, *Slavery Remembered*, pp. 102–104.
42. Herbert G. Gutman, *The Black Family in Slavery and Freedom, 1750–1925* (New York, 1976).
43. E. D. Genovese, *The Political Economy of Slavery*. (New York, 1965).
44. James Oliver Horton and Lois E. Horton, *Slavery and the Making of America* (New York, 2005), p. 123.
45. Escott, *Slavery Remembered*, p. 44.
46. Ibid., p. 46.
47. Horton and Horton, *Slavery and the Making of America*.
48. Escott, *Slavery Remembered*, pp. 38–42.
49. Ibid., pp. 66–67.
50. Ibid., pp. 68–69.
51. Ibid., pp. 93–94.
52. Horton and Horton, *Slavery and the Making of America*, p. 120.
53. Foner, *Forever Free*, p. 22.
54. Escott, *Slavery Remembered*, pp. 77–90.

55. Horton and Horton, *Slavery and the Making of America*, p. 125.
56. Ibid., pp. 127–131.
57. Escott, *Slavery Remembered*, p. 80.
58. Foner, *Give Me Liberty!*, p. 23.
59. Generally a pejorative term, here it is deployed by a Black speaker.
60. Gutman, *The Black Family in Slavery and Freedom*.
61. Horton and Horton, *Slavery and the Making of America*, pp. 130–131.
62. Escott, *Give Me Liberty!*, p. 72.
63. John White, pp. 11–12.
64. Francis D. Cogliano, *Revolutionary America, 1763–1815: A Political History* (London and New York, 2000), pp. 182–183.
65. Douglas Egerton, *Gabriel's Rebellion: The Virginia Slave Conspiracies of 1800 and 1802*, (Chapel Hill, 1993), p. 51.
66. Cogliano, *Revolutionary America*, p. 183.
67. Egerton, *Gabriel's Rebellion*, p. 102.
68. Vincent Harding, *There is a River: The Black Struggle for Freedom in America* (New York: 1981). See also Herbert G. Gutman, *The Black Family in Slavery and Freedom, 1750–1925* (New York, 1976).
69. Horton and Horton, *Slavery and the Making of America*, pp. 136–137.
70. Ibid., pp. 137–138.
71. Gutman, *The Black Family in Slavery and Freedom*.

Chapter 8

The Civil War
Slavery, Sectionalism, and Economic Interests

Introduction

The civil war that the United States was embroiled in from 1860 to 1865 had a long history, rooted in fissures that had existed right from the inception of the nation, primarily the twin problems of slavery and sectionalism. These two factors continued to sharpen the differences between the North and the South. This came to a head since the northern states became industrialised on a free-wage labour system, even as the southern states clung to an agricultural economy dependent on enslaved labour.

The Course of the Civil War

In December 1860, South Carolina seceded from the Union, and in February 1861, Florida, Georgia, Alabama, Mississippi, Louisiana, and Texas followed suit. Together, they formed the **Confederate States of America**, with Jefferson Davis as its president. In April, Confederate troops fired on the US flag at **Fort Sumter** in Charleston Harbour, sparking the Civil War. In May, North Carolina, Tennessee, Arkansas, and Virginia joined the Confederate States of America with its capital at Richmond. The first open battle was in July 1861, the **Battle of Bull Run**. For US President Abraham Lincoln, it was essential to prevent Kentucky, Maryland, Missouri, and Delaware from leaving the Union. Maryland was critical, as then Washington, D. C. would find itself isolated in rebel territory.

Table 8.1: Events Leading to the Civil War

	Year	Historical Events
1.	1836	Texas's independence from Mexico
2.	1845	USA annexes Texas
3.	1846–1848	Mexican War
4.	1846	Wilmot Proviso
5.	1848	Treaty of Guadalupe Hidalgo + Gold found in California + Rise of the Free-Soil Party
6.	1850	Compromise of 1850
7.	1850	Fugitive Slave Act
8.	1854	Kansas-Nebraska Act + Establishment of the Know-Nothing Party + Rise of the Republican Party
9.	1856	Bleeding Kansas
10.	1857	Dred Scott Decision
11.	1858	Lincoln-Douglas debates
12.	1859	John Brown's raid on Harper's Ferry
13.	1860	South Carolina secedes from the Union
14.	1861	Abraham Lincoln's Inauguration + Fort Sumter fired upon

Source: Author.

In the South, there were regions and ethnic groups that did not support the war. The western upland counties of Virginia left the Confederacy to join the Union in June 1861 and became West Virginia in 1863. The Irish in the North were opposed to compulsory conscription in the Union army. Militarily, the economic structures of the two warring regions impacted their strategy. The North had a larger population and, therefore, a vast army that was deployed to take over the Mississippi route, invade Tennessee, and capture Richmond. The North also controlled the US Navy and easily blockaded the South, and its naval forces took control of the majority of ports and coastal regions. The war demonstrated that the Confederacy had better military generals and inflicted heavy casualties on the northern army. It was only in 1862 that the Union army successfully captured the two Confederate forts that controlled Tennessee and the Cumberland River under the command of the northern general Ulysses S. Grant. Grant was also victorious at Shiloh, near the Tennessee-Mississippi boundary, in April 1862, and Memphis came under Union control in June 1862, followed by another victory and the takeover of Kentucky. New Orleans came back to the Union by May 1862 and also prevented the Confederate attempt to take over New Mexico and Arizona.

Despite this success, President Lincoln was reluctant to declare the abolishment of slavery. In response, radical Republicans aggressively pursued the agenda of abolition; on the other hand, the president's reluctance allowed the South to claim that the war had nothing to do with the freedom of Black people, and was really about regional power. The South argued that the North was fighting this war to expand its powers and limit state rights. It was only when Lincoln issued the preliminary Emancipation Proclamation did abolition appear on the horizon. In March 1863, the Union initiated a conscription scheme, which drew a large number of African Americans into the Union army, including those serving in the Navy. This led to the South losing momentum and strategic initiative.

In the Civil War, Britain had sided with the Confederates as it needed southern cotton for its textile mills. France and Russia did not want the US to become a dominant power in the Western hemisphere. However, the preliminary Emancipation Proclamation precluded any European interference as the Union now had the moral high ground as well as the military advantage.

However, the South continued to put up a resistance until December 1864, when Tennessee and Richmond came under Union control. In April 1865, the Confederate general Robert E. Lee surrendered to Union general Ulysses S. Grant on 9 April 1865 at Appomattox Courthouse in Virginia. Union victory was, however, overshadowed by the assassination of Lincoln on 14 April 1865 by a group of Confederate supporters and sympathisers.

The war resulted in a massive loss of life, and the total loss to America was greater than those in the two World Wars combined.

Scores of Americans suffered disabling injuries, and material destruction, especially of the South, was tremendous. Many industries were destroyed, along with vital railway lines, putting the South's finances in a precarious condition. During and after the Civil War, Congress had the freedom to pass measures considered essential for western expansion, which the South had previously resisted, including the Homestead Act and the Pacific Railroad Act. Federal lands were allocated to establish new universities, and incentives were provided to promote industrialisation of the country. The Republican Party remained in a powerful position for nearly 50 years, bringing about massive economic and industrial expansion that became symbols of American patriotism, unity, and marked the gradual rise of a new global power.

BACKGROUND OF THE CIVIL WAR

There is a general historical consensus that the USA's political structure, even in the colonial period, was established in relative isolation and with a significant degree of freedom from British control. In other words, they operated as virtually independent political units (see Chapter 1). Over time, the colonies developed operational structures to regulate their own internal affairs. When Britain attempted to assert its sovereign control and regulations over the American colonies, it led to the American Revolution and the Declaration of Independence, accompanied with the establishment of the Continental Congress and the Continental Army, thereby bringing together a loosely structured political system that ensured the 'freedom' and 'independence' of each of the thirteen states. Subsequently, the Thirteen Colonies formed a semblance of government based on the Articles of Confederation, which gave equal representation to each of them in the Continental Congress but failed to establish a national government. Later, a new constitution was formulated in 1787 and took effect in 1789, granting more powers to the national or federal government to prevent the re-colonisation of the developing nation.[1]

The Emergence of Compromise Politics

The new federal government initiated the first in a series of compromises when the bicameral legislative system was established. In the lower House, that is, the House of Representatives, each state's representation was based on population. However, for the Upper House—the Senate—a settlement was reached where each state had two seats, to ensure equal representation to the interests of the states. Even the process of electing the President was not based entirely on the popular vote, given the formation of committees of state electors. When the process of ratifying the Constitution was underway, three states—New York, Virginia and Rhode Island—ensured that they had the right to 'retrieve' their powers from the national government if it was in the best interest of the state.[2] Then there was the question of slavery. Thomas Jefferson, who was himself en enslaver, was unsuccessful in his attempt to place a section in the Declaration of Independence condemning slavery and the international slave trade. Other political leaders, including George Washington and the first Chief Justice of New York, John Jay, also called for an end to slavery. They felt that enslavement was dehumanising and also negatively affected the enslavers, who began to consider the enslaved people their property. Its existence was in complete opposition to the American concept of individual liberty. However, the dominance of southern White leaders in the federal government ensured that even in the American Constitution, slavery was deemed acceptable, to the extent of protecting the rights of enslavers and allowing the Fugitive Slave Law of 1850. The Constitution of 1787 used the word 'persons held to service of labour' and it was ensured that Congress would have no authority to abolish slavery. The economically powerful southern enslavers secured political dominance in all the branches of the federal government—executive, legislative and judicial—to ensure the perpetuity of the institution of slavery.[3]

The first President of the United States, George Washington, along with Alexander Hamilton and the Federalists, began to push for the growth of manufacturing and trade, aiming to industrialise the country, along with the use of internal development funds for the construction of roads, bridges, and canals. They sought to provide financial stability with the establishment of the National Bank, a move that also enhanced the power and political strength of the federal government, and imposed a system of federal taxation for the growth of the economy.[4] As we have discussed in Chapter 3, Jefferson opposed this, arguing that it was unconstitutional, as he feared it would put pressure on American farmers to produce commercial cash crops. In his view, cultivating crops commercially would make farmers dependent on market forces rather than keeping them economically self-independent. Jefferson thus famously advocated for establishing an 'empire for liberty', inaugurating a brand of politics that came to be termed Jeffersonian democracy.[5] This phase represented the beginnings of conflict between the urban and rural economies.

Another point of conflict emerged, in 1798, when President John Adams, to prevent the growing tide of support for Jefferson, passed the Alien and Sedition Acts (see Chapter 3). Jefferson and James Madison sharply opposed this since they were of the view that the states had the right to nullify any act of the national government.[6] At this juncture, America resembled a loosely structured mishmash of a nation. Still, it was bound together by their shared cultural traits, represented through evangelical Protestant Christianity. The church also established centres of higher education that assisted in shaping American ethics and philosophy according to the structures of Protestant evangelical beliefs. They all spoke the same language, which brought about linguistic unity.[7] Another common cultural tradition was a firm faith in Republicanism, based on the natural rights of man propounded by John Locke, and an equally strong belief in Adam Smith's philosophy of free trade and commerce for the growth and development of capitalism. With the rise of the **Industrial Revolution** in Britain by the 1800s, there was a growing clamour to grow more cotton and other commercial agricultural products in America. The application of steam engines for boats and railroads reduced transportation costs at this opportune moment. This allowed American farmers to move towards producing single cash crops with high demand in the external markets.[8]

At the same time, under the presidential tenure of Jefferson and the Democratic-Republicans, America acquired land beyond the Appalachians from France, that is, the region of Louisiana, in

1803. This led to the process of a federal government-sanctioned system of admitting the new territories as states into the Union, further expanding the concept of Republicanism and providing a stimulus to the agricultural economy.[9] This contributed to the proliferation of banking institutions, the shift towards a market-oriented economy, and the exploration of natural resources, which in turn encouraged the emergence of chartered corporations. Jefferson observed these changes with great alarm as he believed they would erode the independent foundations of states and local legislatures (see Chapter 3, this volume). In 1807, Jefferson imposed the Embargo Act on all foreign trade to safeguard the young Republic from the world market. However, the result was that on the eve of the War of 1812, the American economy and the armed forces were ill-prepared to fight the war, and only luck saved the Americans from being colonised again.[10] Another significant compromise that set a dangerous precedent was at the Hartford Convention (1814–1815) held in Connecticut. Delegates from Massachusetts, Connecticut and Rhode Island assembled to examine the possibility of seceding from the Union, as they were unhappy with the decision to go to war; however, the sudden gains made by the US army prevented any such move.[11]

The lessons learnt from the War of 1812, according to Robert V. Remini, assisted astute politician Henry Clay in establishing a new political group, the Whigs, that brought within its fold the Democratic-Republicans and implemented policies to stimulate modern economic growth by undertaking programmes of internal improvement, government banking, and to impose tariffs to protect nascent American industries from European competition. This political group and its supporters began to oppose slavery and the aristocratic life of the enslavers, promoting an alternative set of values based on a free-wage labour system and emphasising hard work and self-control.[12] These policies completely overturned the political philosophy of Jeffersonian democracy. More transformations were afoot in federal politics. In 1828, Andrew Jackson laid the groundwork for the establishment of the Democratic Party. His distrust of banks, high tariffs, national debt, and use of public funds for internal improvements led to the implementation of policies that marked the beginning of a fight against the liberal, market-based economic power politics of the Whigs. This situation led to political and economic polarisation, with the northern states striving towards urbanisation and industrialisation, while the agricultural states of the South wanted the protection of their most precious 'property', the enslaved people, and to abolish high tariff rates on imports.[13] These developments were taking place at the time when the United States had embarked on the path of rapid frontier expansion and was beginning to bring in new territories, leading to questions over whether new regions would be brought into the Union as free or slave states.

These divergent trends led to an increasing divide in the demands placed by the North and the South on the federal government. A solution was found in the Missouri Compromise of 1820, which many historians would later regard as one of the immediate causes of the Civil War. It allowed for the admission of Missouri—part of the territory acquired from France in the Louisiana Purchase, and settled by southerners—as a slave state. Maine was admitted as a free state to maintain a symbolic political balance in the US Congress. This compromise split the remaining territory into free states, the dividing line running from the West to Missouri's southern border; the North of that line, except Missouri, was 'free', while the South of the line were the slave states.

In 1832, during the Jacksonian era, South Carolina began to protest the high tariff rates that aimed to promote domestic industrial growth. The state's leaders threatened to nullify the collection of tariffs within the state and issued a threat of secession if pushed by the federal government. To prevent the Nullification Crisis from escalating to a major national crisis, President Jackson was given more executive power by Congress through the Force Bill, which gave him the authority to deploy the armed forces against South Carolina. To prevent the situation from deteriorating, Henry Clay proposed another compromise based on a planned gradual reduction in tariff rates that prevented the nation from breaking apart. Even at this early juncture, Jackson had warned that the threat of secession was becoming real in the South and predicted that it would be over the issue of slavery.[14]

Slavery Becoming a Sectional Issue

The compromise formulated by Henry Clay could only delay the inevitable till the next significant event took place. In the 1840s, US army surgeon John Emerson took Dred Scott, an enslaved person who had been sold to him in the 1830s, to various postings in non-slave states. Dred Scott was eventually sent to Missouri, where Emerson's wife lived, and it was here that Dred Scott filed a petition for his freedom on the premise that he lived in free Minnesota territory. He lost the case in the Missouri state court but gained a hearing before the Supreme Court in 1857, where he eventually lost the case. The case set an important precedent, as the Court decreed that the federal government had no legal rights to abolish slavery in any part of the western territories, which meant that slavery could legally expand into any part of the West. The Supreme Court ruling also clearly stated that free Black people were not citizens and therefore had no legal rights. Both the Fugitive Slave Act and the Dred Scott case antagonised the abolitionists, and northerners came to believe that even the judiciary had become racially biased owing to the predominance of southerners on the bench. In the words of American poet William Cullen Bryant:

> Slavery, instead of being what the people of the slave states have hitherto called it, their peculiar institution, is a Federal institution, the common patrimony and shame of all states.[15]

After the US-Mexican War (1846–1848) and the Treaty of Guadalupe Hidalgo (known as the Mexican Secession), new western lands were added to the Union, which led to Texas being admitted as a slave state and California as a Free State. Pennsylvanian leader David Wilmot proposed a complete ban on all forms of coerced labour in the newly acquired territories, in what came to be known as the **Wilmot Proviso of 1846**. The House of Representatives passed this, but in the Senate, where both slave and free states were equally represented, it could not be passed. John C. Calhoun, among the most influential of the South politicians and a 'great defender' of the institution of slavery, argued for slavery to exist in perpetuity as it was, for him, a 'positive good'. There were other political leaders who wanted this problem resolved by popular sovereignty based on what people decided for their land.

Even as these debates remained unresolved, gold was discovered in California. The status of California (as a free or slave state) was a matter of intense debate, even though the territory was south of the Missouri Compromise line. This led to the beginning of an intense debate among three political stalwarts: Daniel Webster, Henry Clay, and John C. Calhoun, who shifted the debate from the specifics of the Constitution to the principles of divine law and natural justice. These intellectual debates could never bring reconciliation. It was because California wished to be admitted as free that the Compromise of 1850 took place, in which the territories of Utah and New Mexico were given the leverage to choose based on popular sovereignty to become free or slave states. Texas wanted its border to be extended westwards to Santa Fe, which would assist in making the slave states' lobby more powerful in Congress.

Supporters of the abolitionist movement, in the meantime, raised the demand to abolish the most significant slave market in North America, in the country's capital city, Washington DC—although they did not demand an end to the institution itself. This new crisis too was resolved with yet another Compromise of 1850 that was formulated by Clay ('The Great Compromiser') in association with Webster, Calhoun and Stephen Douglas. It aimed to establish a balance of power between the North and the South by granting the territorial legislature the right to decide on the remaining land acquired from Mexico. The boundary of Texas was fixed, and the rest of the territory claimed by it came to be known as New Mexico Territory, which later became the states of Utah and New Mexico. The issue of free versus slave state was left to the popular sovereignty. The federal government assumed the debt of US $10 million of the state of Texas. This compromise further strengthened the 1793 Fugitive Slave Act that permitted enslavers to capture runaway enslaved from the northern states, and now the federal agencies were required to assist in the process. The law also stated that anyone who aided an escaped slave or interfered with the capture of a fugitive enslaved was liable for criminal prosecution. This compromise was ominous for the nation: California elected pro-slavery representatives, and both

New Mexico and Utah enacted slave codes that opened pathways for these new states to expand slavery. The compromise offered no permanent political solution to sectional interests. It only provided a temporary solution to avert political rupture.

Northerners refused to obey the Fugitive Slave Law, and mob violence followed whenever attempts were made to capture slaves. At this juncture, Harriet Beecher Stowe's novel *Uncle Tom's Cabin* came out, further creating a divide between the North and the South. In 1854, William Lloyd Garrison publicly burned a copy of the US Constitution in Massachusetts, clearly indicating that the federal government was no longer in a position to control the South.

In 1854, Congress passed the Nebraska-Kansas Act under pressure from Senator Stephen A. Douglas of Illinois. This Act revoked the Missouri Compromise. His motive was to gain the widespread support of southern enslavers for his Presidential campaign. It was becoming clear that any new territory acquired by the US would determine its status vis-à-vis slavery based on the state representatives. Soon, the issue began to spark open protests and fights among supporters and opponents of slavery, particularly in Kansas between 1854 and 1859, where violent confrontations led to the popular moniker 'Bloody Kansas' or 'Bleeding Kansas'. The passing of the Nebraska-Kansas Act strengthened the support base of the Republican Party, and in 1860, Abraham Lincoln became the first Republican President.

The northern abolitionists became aggressive as this Act would mean an expansion of slavery into new territories and thereby strengthen the slave lobby. John Brown, a radical abolitionist, focused on efforts to arm enslaved people and establish a Free State in the mountains of Virginia and Maryland. Brown had been active in Kansas where, in response to an 1856 attack on Lawrence by pro-slavery raiders, he, along with some of his followers, had entered the slaveholding territory and kidnapped five men and later killed all of them. On 16 October 1859, Brown led a raid on the federal arsenal at Harpers Ferry, Virginia. He aimed to capture weapons, but the attack ultimately failed and culminated in the death of ten attackers; Brown was arrested and convicted of murder and treason.

He was hanged on 2 December 1859, becoming an instant hero for the northerners and a villain in the eyes of the southerners.

With the election of Abraham Lincoln in 1860, the South decided to secede from the Union, beginning with South Carolina. Abolitionists rejoiced at the secession of southern states, as it meant that all the slave states were now out of the Union. They believed war was necessary to end slavery and abolitionist leaders like William Lloyd Garrison, Wendell Phillips, and Frederick Douglass wanted the federal government to stop trying to prevent secession. However, the President had no intention of dividing the Union. According to historian James M. McPherson:

> The basic Garrisonian argument for disunion was a simple one. Under the Constitution, the national government was pledged to protect slavery. The number of slave states had increased from six to fifteen during the existence of the Union. Since the adoption of the Constitution, the slave power had marched on from one victory to another until, in 1857, a southern-dominated Supreme Court had declared that Negros were not citizens of the United States.[16]

Slavery, therefore, instead of dying a natural death, was becoming all-pervasive and gained further ground with the rise of rudimentary industries (ironworks and hemp factories) in the South that, according to Allen C. Guelzo, would have led to the emergence of industrial serfdom in the South.[17] According to Robert William Fogel, the fact remains that by the 1850s, slavery, instead of being a 'dying institution', was not only aggressive, dynamic, and mobile but was creating further racial divisions. By 1860, in terms of economic wealth, the South was behind only Britain, the fourth greatest economy in the world, and was quite ahead of France and Germany.[18] On the other hand, by 1860, new types of mills and factories emerged in the North, where a wage labour system was applied, including employment given to women workers (for instance, at Lowell Textile Mills). These changes meant that slave labour remained an exclusive peculiarity of the South.[19]

The South wanted an expansion of slavery into western states; abolitionists wanted to end slavery. In contrast, northern politicians wanted to limit the institution. After 1850, the westward expansion of the USA was complete. No more compromises could occur. The balance could no longer be maintained between free and slave states. According to Guelzo, three distinct factors pushed the country towards the Civil War. *First*, there were cultural differences between the two regions, with the North being 'economically aggressive'. *Second*, the country's political foundations had been weakened by numerous compromises. *Third*, by 1860, the North had only free Black communities, and with the opening up of the West, this region wanted to prevent the spread of slavery. The third factor showed that slavery was becoming a sectional issue that ultimately pushed the nation towards the war.[20]

The Abolitionist Movement

William Lloyd Garrison of Massachusetts founded the *Liberator*, an abolitionist newspaper in 1831, and in 1833 he established the American Antislavery Society. Wendell Phillips also joined Garrison and was among the most vocal abolitionists, demanding not only emancipation but also citizenship and full civil rights for Black people. Theodore Weld and other abolitionists desired a gradual end of slavery through legislative action, especially in the South; Garrison and Wendell opposed this plan and wanted an immediate end to the practice. On 4 July 1954, Garrison termed the Constitution a 'covenant with death' and an 'agreement with Hell' before burning a copy, and added, 'So perish all compromises with tyranny'.[21] Various strategies were proposed among abolitionists: some advocated the abolition of this institution by the President or Congress, while others advocated encouraging enslavers to free their enslaved. Radicals like John Brown believed that enslaved people should be assisted to rise in revolt and take their freedom by force.

Interestingly, none of them put forward the suggestion that a constitutional amendment be brought about, as this would have required the approval of three-fourths of the states at a time when half the American states were slave states. However, aggressive posturing by the abolitionists did manage to put forward this message to 11 seceded southern states, including Virginia, Mississippi, Tennessee,

Louisiana, Arkansas, and Texas, that slavery would be eventually abolished in the United States. However, when the Civil War progressed, it became clear that the northern politicians had no intention to abolish slavery. Their prime motive was to prevent its expansion and to reunite the divided nation. According to Ira Berlin:

> With President Abraham Lincoln in the fore, federal authorities insisted that the nascent conflict must be the war to restore the national Union, and nothing more. Confederate leaders displayed a fuller comprehension of the significance of slavery, which [Confederate] Vice-President Alexander Stephens called the cornerstone of the Southern nation.[22]

The Rise of the Republican Party and Abraham Lincoln

The Republican Party, under the leadership of Abraham Lincoln, had no intention of giving freedom to enslaved people as he was neither an abolitionist nor anti-slavery. However, his electoral success was met with anger and secession of the southern states. Florida, Alabama, Georgia, Louisiana, Texas, Virginia, Arkansas, Tennessee and North Carolina elected Jefferson Davis, a wealthy slave planter from Mississippi who had earlier served as the US Secretary of War, to the post of President of the newly established **Confederate States of America**, a seceded nation. According to Frederick Douglass, Lincoln's priority was preserving the Union and not the freedom of Black people. For this reason, northerners called this war a 'White man's war'. Black people were made to join the Union Army only when the war became prolonged and the Union needed more troops to fight the battle. It was evident, according to Guelzo, that the President wanted to save the Union without going to war, and he did not want to escalate the issue of slavery. He also believed that the Constitution had not given his office the power to abolish the legally sanctified institution of slavery in the 15 southern states. The President's dilemma was this: How might one prevent the expansion of slavery in the newly acquired western territories, while being fully aware that this would mean the end of this institution, which would not be acceptable to the South?[23]

The reason why President Lincoln was reluctant to end slavery was that he wanted continued support from four slave states, Missouri, Kentucky, Maryland, and Delaware, that were still with the Union. Therefore, he only initiated gradual steps towards disbanding the slave system. In the first step, to overcome the Fugitive Slave Act of 1850, which made it mandatory to return runaways to their enslavers, enslaved fugitives were termed as 'enemy property'; therefore, as 'contraband of war under the First Confiscation Act of 1861', the Union army was empowered to retain enslaved people and not hand them over. Under the provisions of the second Confiscation Act of 1862, 'contraband' (as enslaved Black people were known in the northern states) could be 'seized' from Confederates and thus freed. In the meantime, the President explored the possibility of deporting Black people to Haiti; however, this was abandoned as the war progressed. The Union began to lose White men in large numbers, and simultaneously, there was a real threat that Great Britain and France may give political recognition to the Confederacy. The two countries had an ulterior motive: buying cotton from the South, and selling required war-related materials to it. This grave threat forced the President to reconsider, and prompted the **Militia Act of 1862**, which empowered the President to enlist African American men into war service.

These events make it clear that wartime necessity transformed the nature of the Civil War, which was fought for the Union's preservation, but eventually could only be resolved through a crucial step to end slavery. Hence emerged the **Emancipation Proclamation**. There were two proclamations; the first preliminary Emancipation Proclamation, issued in September 1862 but later merged with the second, applied only to the seceded states, and four slave states still in the Union were spared. The final Emancipation Proclamation applied in January 1863 included provision for enlisting freedmen into military service to fight for the Union and was applied only to the southern seceded states. Nevertheless, the Union Army became a 'liberation army' that gave freedom to enslaved people, and it began the process of recruiting freedmen into the Union Army.

The emancipation proclamation was the central, most significant aspect of the Civil War and turned the tide in favour of the Union Army. The declaration wrought social transformation that impacted the South and other regions of America. According to Ira Berlin, this single step provided the energy that gave freedom to African Americans and brought the Union victory. The states of Maryland, Kentucky, and Missouri remained with the Union; enslaved people joined the army to attain complete freedom. According to Philip S. Paludan, the proclamation was a masterstroke of legislative action that assisted in preserving the Union and bringing in the much-needed number of Black soldiers to the cause of the Union. It granted freedom to Black people, but without giving them equality or rights. The experience of being free profoundly impacted African Americans, who tentatively began to collectivise for education, fairness, and equality. This gradually led to the rise of African American leaders and movements during the Reconstruction era.[24]

The Significance of the Emancipation Process

As the war dragged on, emancipation became an essential goal for the North due to political and military reasons—it was the only way to build up a moral base to undermine the legitimacy of the South's primary source of labour and to hit them economically where it hurt the most.

Slavery also existed in the North, but the number of enslaved people was neither significant nor widespread as in the South. At the same time, even in the North, many White people considered free Black workers as their competitors for jobs and farmlands.

By 1860, enslaved African Americans constituted a third of the southern population, which in total was approximately 9 million; in the North, the free Black population was half a million out of a total population of 23 million. In the South, cotton production, along with rice and tobacco, assisted in the spread of slavery. Cotton constituted 60 per cent of all exports, and America supplied 80 per cent of the world's cotton. In 1857, when the North was experiencing an economic depression, the South continued to enjoy economic prosperity. But the fact remains that only 1,800 plantation owners owned more than 100 slaves, while the remaining 350,000 slave-owners had fewer than five enslaved people. Enslaved people were expensive and not all White southerners could afford them. Still, the reason for widespread support for the preservation of this institution was, according to Steven E. Woodward:

> [White southerners] considered [slavery] a beneficial and indispensable feature of the great order of the universe. They fully approved of the South's 'peculiar institution' and hoped to make it into the slaveholders' ranks someday. They might have relatives who were slaveholders and felt connected to the slaveholding strata [class] of society by many ties, not the least of which was their common whiteness.[25]

Most southern Whites believed that the Bible justified slavery and that God had ordained it. Slavery, they argued, had existed from time immemorial, right from the Greco-Roman world, and they even asserted that compared with the conditions of northern workers, the enslaved were much better treated. Proponents of slavery went as far as to claim that it provided Black people with security and brought them within the Christian fold. As we saw in Chapter 7, racist stereotypes were prevalent, and so many believed enslaved people to be 'childlike' and incapable of governing their own lives; hence the idea that most enslaved people justified their condition and status.

In the meantime, free Black people began to organise themselves. The National Negro Convention was formed in Philadelphia in 1830, and Black-led organisations such as the American Society of Free Persons emerged as well. Some prominent Black abolitionists were William Wells Brown, Sojourner Truth, and Harriet Tubman. David Walker, a free Black man from North Carolina migrated to Boston and in 1829 published his influential 'Appeal'. In this Appeal, Walker encouraged Black people to resist slavery and kill those who exploited them. Although William Lloyd Garrison supported the Appeal, he opposed Walker's violent methods.

White enslavers feared slave rebellions, especially after Nat Turner's Rebellion, also known as the Southampton Insurrection, in 1831. Nat Turner, who led the revolt, was educated and a preacher—many southern states passed laws preventing enslaved people from learning to read and write, and further restricting their civil liberties, including the right to assembly. From the 1780s, attempts to escape enslavement in the South culminated in the development of the 'Underground Railroad', an organised system of safe houses and secret routes that assisted those seeking freedom to escape to the North or Canada. Harriet Tubman became famous for helping many enslaved people through the Underground Railroad movement (see Chapter 7).

Frederick Douglass, a self-taught fugitive slave, was asked in 1841 to describe his experiences as an enslaved person. It was then that he discovered his knack for public speaking. He later wrote an autobiography, *The Life and Times of Frederick Douglass*, which became one of the most significant antislavery works in pre-Civil War America. *The Life and Times and American Slavery, as It Is*, by Theodore Weld, became extremely popular in 1839 and provided a vivid account of slave life. Another book that captured the imagination of the North was Harriet Beecher Stowe's novel *Uncle Tom's Cabin*, published in 1852. In the novel, Stowe's slave hero, Uncle Tom, suffers cruelly at the hands of his owner, Simon Legree. This novel led many White readers to become champions of the abolitionist movement. With abolitionist leaders' help and through literature, the issue of slavery was kept alive in American society, leading to the formation of the Free-Soil Party (1848–1854), who wanted the West to be developed only through free labour.

Even during the Civil War, Black people who joined the Union Army were neither given equal pay nor permitted to become officers. In the aftermath of the Civil War, not only did the status of formerly enslaved people change, but also the American political economy saw a massive restructuring, with more powers now allocated to the federal government. The war also brought about significant constitutional amendments, bringing to an end a long era of domination by a 'slavocracy', as abolitionists called it, in American politics and the judiciary. In the period before 1860, a significant part of the office of the President was controlled by the southern slaveholder class, including their stringent hold over the Supreme Court—out of a total of 35 justices till 1861, 20 came from slave states of the South. It was Chief Justice and slaveholder Roger Taney of Maryland who had passed the decision on the *Dred Scott Case* that declared African Americans as non-citizens.

Another aspect of the Civil War that began to catch the attention of American historians was the ground reality that the South had divided loyalties, with yeomen farmers who remained loyal to the Union. In Virginia, they established a separate state of West Virginia in 1861, and a similar pattern was observed in Eastern Tennessee. As the war progressed, internal friction between the different social groups of the South came to the surface, creating social conflicts and further powering anti-war emotions. The Confederate States of America, to maintain their unity and support of the big planter class, made the slave laws more stringent and imposed war taxes like the **conscription law**, which was disliked by most yeomen farmers, who began to see it as 'a rich man's war and a poor man's fight'. As the Union Army gained significant victories, enslaved people started to leave plantations, agricultural lands were destroyed, and the southern frontier states were now ruined, to the extent that most enslavers became tenant farmers.

The Civil War and Recent Interpretations

The Civil War raised several questions about America's national identity, the relations between local and federal authorities, and the place that Black communities occupied in American society. For decades after the Civil War, the issue of slavery was predominant in studies of the period. However, from the 1960s, the focus shifted to the impact of emancipation and how it changed the course of the Civil War, based on the narratives of enslaved people, enslavers, and free Black persons. Scholars began to concentrate on how the Civil War transformed the northern and southern regions, exacerbating their mutual differences and leading to new types of conflicts that became evident in the Reconstruction era. At the same time, contemporary scholars have also highlighted that White society in the North did not accept the freed Black persons as their equals as racism remained a deep-rooted issue; the South, similarly, continued to re-formulate its strategies and structures to keep the Black population 'under their firm control'. In this sense, both the North and the South presented a picture of old wine in a new bottle even after emancipation. Despite these limitations, enslaved people strategically made use of the Civil War: When the Union army began to push into the territories of the Confederacy, they crossed over to join the Union army to search for family members sold to other enslavers. The Civil War allowed them to become 'free' even before Lincoln's Proclamation.

From 1960 onwards, historians brought in a new set of connected issues. Slavery was no longer seen as a peculiar institution that existed only in the southern states. Historians credited the growth and development of slavery in the South with the American Revolution, the settlement of the West, and industrial expansion, which created a sectional crisis culminating in the Civil War.

New Political historians have presented the Civil War in terms of an ethnocultural conflict between Protestants and Catholics, who represented different political cultures. In doing so, they highlight a complex network of social and cultural relationships that challenge any single interpretation of the Civil War. New Political History used a new methodology that incorporated statistical analysis of quantitative data and a distinct model of historical explanation. However, this type of analysis places excessive emphasis on one aspect, either religious or cultural. These two factors are unidimensional concepts that cannot account for the influences of time, place, or other associated factors.

Joel Silbey's article, 'The Civil War Synthesis' was the most important among the writings of the New Political historians. He criticised earlier historians for emphasising the aspect of slavery too heavily while completely ignoring questions of nativism. He presented an argument on the premise that a vast gulf existed in the political culture of different anti-southern political elites. Moreover, the majority of voters had more interest in the issues of immigration and the Temperance Movement rather than delving into issues of slavery and sectional conflict. Lee Benson argued that a small group of southern conspirators, taking advantage of the 'irresponsible character' of the political system, caused the war. To Eric Foner, the kind of interpretation advanced by Silbey betrays an inherent elitist bias as it assumes that 'large portions of the electorate do not have meaningful beliefs'. It also fails to account for many historical processes that are not included in this interpretation. For example, if nativism was the primary impulse driving the North, why was Abraham Lincoln, who was from the South, an opponent and not a supporter of slavery?

Another school of historians has cited the 'modernisation' process, which entailed changes in the basic structure of society due to rapid economic development, urbanisation, industrialisation, the creation of an integrated national economic and political system, and the spread of market revolution, along with changing capitalist economic relations and mental attitudes. The North underwent these modernisation processes, while the South remained agrarian and pre-capitalistic, resulting in the beginning of the conflict. In his book *The Transatlantic Persuasion*, Robert Kelly has shown how the Republicans became staunch nationalists and homogenisers who were intolerant of any social diversity and therefore attempted to impose their values on dissenting groups. Examples of this include the Temperance legislation in response to the entry of Irish immigrants, and the imposition of antislavery views on the South. Kelley's analysis of this sectional conflict is that it was a struggle between local and national institutions, primarily over the issue of slavery, which became a factor in the moral, economic, and political issues between the two sections, thereby creating sectional conflict.

According to Foner, the problem with this interpretation is that modernisation is confused with industrialisation. The theory begins to resemble Charles Beard's viewpoint that the Civil War was a conflict between industrial and agricultural economies. The reality was that the North was still industrialising itself. The only significance of this approach is that it provides a better understanding of nineteenth-century America and forces us to relate historical events in the larger context of the development of American society. However, none of these schools of historians are able to answer the fundamental question posed by David Brion Davis in *The Problem of Slavery in Western Culture*: Why did slavery, which was till that point considered normal, become unacceptable at this juncture?

Foner argues that two processes must be understood here: (*i*) changes in attitudes toward labour, and (*ii*) the conditions of the labouring classes. According to C. Vann Woodward, New England Federalists did use anti-southern and antislavery political rhetoric, and they also opposed the three-fifths clause of the Constitution and southern domination of the national government. They supported free labour and spoke about the economic backwardness of the South and differences in customs and culture between the North and the South. However, this rhetoric never came to a head as the Federalists had their allies in the South. They believed society should be based on order, harmony, and organic unity based on static and verifiable ranks and order. Therefore, for them, raising the issue of slavery in national politics would lead to the breakdown of American society.

In recent times, a new wave of scholarship has sparked fresh critical insights into the issues surrounding the Civil War. These scholars view the period extending from the 1820s to 1830s in America as an era when ideological transformations were taking place primarily due to profound economic changes, with the expansion of a market-oriented capitalist society and the onset of the transportation revolution that, in turn, created a culture of competing individuals. All these changes took place, according to Foner, during the era when Jacksonian philosophy was predominant. This philosophy gave impetus to anti-monopoly, anti-corporate and egalitarian values, which respected the concept of 'free labour', and freedom came to be viewed as the property of every individual as it provided avenues for advancement in a competitive society. Now, America was divided along sectional lines between supporters and opponents of slavery. Supporters of antislavery came to believe that freedom would enable an internalised self-discipline that would inculcate humane values of discipline, order, and restraint. From this perspective, for Lincoln, the abolition of slavery became essential for maintaining the Union's law, order, and political unity.

The reason why the Republican Party and abolitionists gained the support of the northern elites, middle classes, as well as the labouring class is due to their emphasis on land reform, a necessary step for modernisation, which came to be associated with opposition to the expansion of slavery. They supported the antislavery movement as it provided them with a safety valve and granted them economic freedom and socio-economic mobility. It is also essential for historians to study the related social changes in nineteenth-century America and the growing number of people participating in the electoral process, which affected American mass culture as well as its political culture.[26]

After the Civil War, slavery was discontinued, the Union was preserved, and the warring regions were transformed. The quintessential image of the South as a world dominated by enslavers, enslaved people, yeomen, and White farmers was changed to landlords, merchants, tenants, and sharecroppers, both White and Black. This was, in some sense, a new contentious phase that underlined both remarkable shifts and progression that established, according to Jeffrey R. Hummel, an oppressive 'leviathan state'[27] that marked the end of Lincoln's America, dominated by small shops and family farms to an ever-expanding urbanised and industrialised economy based on racial divisions. For pro-Confederacy groups, the Union was preserved at the expense of a perceived 'loss of equality and freedom' for southerners—of course, this perspective centres White libertarian views and glosses over the entrenched unfreedom of Black and Indigenous people.[28]

In this sense, the leading cause of the Civil War was the rise of the antislavery movement at a time when America was still in the grips of Jacksonian democracy, which had fostered mass participation of common Americans in politics. This had led to the creation of two extreme sections, the North and the South, with both sides trying to influence public opinion through the use of mass media, creating sharp ideological differences. The South fought the war to preserve the world of enslavers. In contrast, the North, under the leadership of Lincoln, fought to protect the society of free, self-made men that provided economic opportunity to small traders, merchants, artisans, and farm owners. After the war, the South could no longer defend slavery, which gave poor White groups and free Black people a chance to organise their protest movements against planter control in the region. In contrast, in the North, the war led to the growth of mechanisation and industrialisation, centralisation of national institutions, and the rapid spread of capitalism, which was very different from Lincoln's vision.

According to Foner, the tragic irony of the Civil War is that each side fought to defend a distinct vision of a 'good society'. Still, this vision was destroyed by the very struggle to preserve it. An example of such a vision is visible in the now-debunked 'Lost Cause' theory. The Lost Cause was a carefully crafted theoretical portrayal of the antebellum South developed by ex-Confederate officials to obliterate the memory of their military defeat and the ignominy of losing their precious property—the enslaved people. Lost Cause interpretations revolve around the Confederate experience, based on the information collected from the memoirs, speeches, artwork and the graveyards of the fallen soldiers. This theory was formulated to positivise the establishment of the Confederacy and present to posterity a corrective image of the Civil War through their written records. It, therefore, became a form of southern propaganda to showcase the righteousness of their actions. The federal government did little to stop its spread and publication.

Historian Rollin G. Osterweis, in his book titled *The Myth of the Lost Cause, 1865–1900*, presented this theory as part of pre-Civil War southern romanticism. According to Alan T. Nolan, the Lost Cause attempted to create a formidable image of the Confederate people and an idealised image of the Confederate States of America. The supporters of the Lost Cause downplayed the role of slavery that pushed the region towards secession, instead blaming the abolitionists for both sectionalism and secession. The theory glorified the southern slaveholding social structures and the Confederate Army fighting to save the spirit of American independence, for which the sacrifices of the Confederate soldiers were exemplified. It stated that the North won only due to the availability of resources and the big army at their disposal. Moreover, books like *Gone With the Wind* by Margaret Mitchell also glorified southern culture, monuments, cemeteries of fallen soldiers, and artwork, as they all aimed to establish a distinctive identity of southern White culture.

The term 'Lost Cause' was used in 1867 by Edward A. Pollard, who published *The Lost Cause: The Standard Southern History of the War of the Confederates*. Thomas L. Connelly wrote *The Marble Man: Robert E. Lee and His Image in American Society*. Another work was by Gaines M. Foster, titled *Ghosts of the Confederacy: Defeat, the Lost*

Cause, and the Emergence of the New South, 1815 to 1913. In all these southern scholarly works, one commonality is observed: they all attempted to elide the fact that slavery was the main reason for the rise of the Confederacy, with the result that, according to James L. Roark, the South manufactured historical narratives to glorify the peculiarities of southern society, economy, and culture.

Proponents of the Lost Cause portrayed the abolitionists as troublemakers who deliberately fostered disagreements between the two sections. They squarely blamed the aggressive North for the Civil War at a time when slavery would have eventually died a natural death. At the same time, according to Jefferson Davis, the enslaved people were portrayed as a faithful, peaceful, and content labour class who desired to remain as they were, obliterating the need for the Emancipation Proclamation. To further extend their arguments, a myth was created and narrated that southerners were Norman cavaliers who had conquered the Anglo-Saxon tribes (who were equated with northerners), which made southerners a warrior race, known for their gallantry, chivalry, honour, and gentlemanly qualities. Therefore, they could have overpowered the North but for the fact that the South lacked both human resources and material resources to match those at the disposal of the North. To lend more credence to this myth, a cultural portrayal was embellished that presented the southern White people as more humane and culturally superior. The southern soldier, for example, was depicted as a heroic warrior who fought to defend the South's constitutional right; southern military generals were saintly beings, even supermen, who marched in defense of their land, culture and distinctive values and identities.[29]

President Lincoln, in his second inaugural speech, had stated that slavery was the chief cause of the war; historians also present slavery as the principal cause. James M. McPherson, for instance, has refuted the idea that the Civil War was over issues of tariffs or state rights. The main reason for secession was slavery, which led to the war. Charles Joyner concurs with this view. Interestingly, this debate has continued, and consensus still eludes historians. According to Elizabeth Varon, while slavery was an important issue, a valid question is why slavery alone proved to be the most critical factor. The reasons for the failures of sectional compromise need to be analysed. In the same line of thought, even Edward Ayers opines that slavery and freedom should be the beginning of enquiry and not its end.[30]

The old-school, classic interpretation that blamed sectional differences was unacceptable to revisionists who believed it was a contingency, chance, and even irrationality that culminated in the war. Historians have now attempted to understand this war based on the geographic and temporal parameters that led to the sectional conflict, seeking to establish a relationship between sectionalism and nationalism. Such analyses trace connections between race and class in sectional politics.

It is also important to understand the global impact of the war. Allan Nevins and James McPherson equate it with the Mexican-American War (1846–1848), or due to a transnational journey from Mexico City to Washington of the 1848 Treaty of Guadalupe Hidalgo, as stated by David M. Potter in *The Impending Crisis, 1848–1861* (1976). Linkages have been established between the Civil War and the American conquest of Texas, its ambitions in the Caribbean, and the desire to take over Cuba, all of which have been confirmed by the historical record. According to Edward Barlett Rugemer, when Americans gained access to the enslaved people in the Caribbean, it led to the rise of debates within the nation over slavery. Those who supported slavery learnt that most of the important slave rebellions that had taken place, mainly in Haiti, were due to the spread of abolitionist thought. Freed enslaved people, in their eyes, were synonymous with racial conflict and lawlessness.

On the other hand, those who supported an antislavery position believed that independence for the Caribbean would be peaceful. According to Matthew J. Clavin, proslavery supporters were alarmed by the Haitian Revolution and feared an unholy alliance between 'savages' and 'White fanatics'. For antislavery supporters, this revolution was a remarkable example to be emulated for self-liberation by the enslaved people. For abolitionists, it gave them a spark to ignite and kickstart a conflictual process to end slavery. These extremely divergent positions led to massive division and confrontation.

In the eyes of historians like Clavin and Rugemer, the struggle over slavery and the cause of the Civil War was part of a transatlantic narrative. Both historians also expanded the geographical boundaries by extending the temporal limits of sectionalism and taking their study period into the late eighteenth and nineteenth centuries.

On the other hand, historians Brian Schoen, Peter Onuf, and Nicholas Onuf situate pre-Civil War politics within the context of global trade and situate it within the parameters of economic analysis of the rise of sectionalism. According to Brian Schoen, the crux of the matter is that slavery expanded in the South at a juncture when it was disappearing from most of the Atlantic world. The reason for this was the southern dependence on the cotton crop. Schoen's analysis is thus centred around cotton and its subsequent impact on the southern political economy. The enslaver class's dependence on cotton and its marketability in Europe ultimately shaped southern politics and the practice of selling cotton, which in turn assisted westward expansion. This further solidified enslavers' endorsement of slavery and their commitment to free trade without any federal restrictions. Planters had enjoyed economic prosperity for a very long time, and this led to the illusion that they were seceding for a just cause. Onuf and Onuf put forward a similar line of thought in their research, titled *Nations, Markets, and War*, which stated that economic prosperity led to political competition between the two regions, particularly over trade policy.

The question emerges as to why these studies are essential. These scholars trace the dynamic of cotton cultivation and debates on domestic politics to the late eighteenth century, addressing how it led to political conflict between the North and South. These historians have stretched the geographical and temporal boundaries of the sectional conflict. They show that conflict emerged a decade before the Missouri Compromise of 1820. The fact remains that right from the time of the American Revolution to the end of the external slave trade in 1808, and then from the beginning of the Missouri Compromise and the War of 1812, several factors emboldened both supporters of slavery and its opponents. With relentless westward expansion, local interests became dominant. State politics became a decisive factor in America, with a dividing line emerging north and south of the Ohio River. Hammond also shows how the debate over Missouri had roots in the past. Therefore, political historians have slowly excavated a layer of political differences over whether slavery was to be expanded.

CAUSES OF THE CIVIL WAR: THE LONG VIEW

Leonard L. Richards establishes a connection between the beginnings of northern opposition to rising slave power and their attempts to control the 1787 Constitutional Convention. Southern enslavers managed to save the institution of slavery, but later, according to David L. Lightener, the North managed to impose a congressional ban on the domestic slave trade. According to Richard S. Newman, this led to the rise of antislavery sentiments long before the rise of abolitionism. Scholarly debates moved the study of the Civil War to the period when the US was founded, following an interconnected chain of events that extended to the Missouri Compromise, with a significant role played by the Haitian Revolution. They also draw links to Jefferson's Embargo Act of 1807 and the War of 1812, wherein the worst hit in economic terms were the southern White enslavers. They got infuriated when the North began to block the expansion of slave states in the newly acquired territories.

Conflict over the state of Missouri led to the beginning of a sectional conflict, which, as we have discussed, was already in the making for an extended time, and this debate was deliberately suppressed during the Jacksonian era.

Historians also emphasise the period from the 1840s to the 1850s. During this period, White society in the South began to perceive the White population in the North as their inferiors. In the North, public opinion was increasingly against the growing power of the enslavers. At the same time, the Northeast and Northwest formed an economic and political alliance that left out the South. Therefore, the late 1840s saw the beginning of secessionist patterns and, at the same time, the rise of new political leaders in both regions. It is popularly identified with the 'blundering generation', a reference to 'self-centred' politicians who came to power in 1850 and pushed for their respective positions to the point of precipitating the war. Historian Peter Carmichael has explored these aspects in his study of Virginia, where young, dominant White politicians who claimed that they were working to restore the state's lost prestige and power supported the secession process.

Some studies of the period have been based on the outline provided by David Potter's essay, 'The Historian's Use of Nationalism and Vice Versa' (1962), and have delineated inherent divergences between the nationalist aspirations of the North and the sectionalised position of the South (the latter's position did not prioritise preservation of the Union). Still, divisions were manifested on respective sectional lines. According to Susan Mary Grant, the North and South had established sectional identities by 1850. Spurred on by the rise of the Republican Party, the North became a beacon of new nationalist aspirations and goals, and in contrast with this the South appeared in a negative light. These opposing forces established two polarised arenas: the South came to represent elements of sectionalism and the North, new-found American nationalism. Thus, the South came to be seen as creating internal problems that threatened national unity.

However, this nationalist image was not necessary borne out in reality, as the North, too, had its own sectional interests at heart. Another scholar, Matthew Mason, has supported this idea: he claims that the antislavery northern crusaders were the same New England Federalists who, in 1815, had squandered the political fortunes of their political group as they worked to carve out a sectional identity in the North. It was only after the Civil War that actual reconstruction of the nation on nationalist lines began to appear. Historians now understand that the northern victory in the war obscured its own sectional aspirations, while the defeated South, with its support for slavery and its eventual defeat, emerged as the villain in the conflict.

Other historians have emphasised that from 1776 to 1860, America was still developing its political institutions; the enslavers, with their accumulated wealth, controlled the reins of the federal power structure and used this to expand their politico-economic interests. From this point of view, one cannot justify the defence of slavery as a sectionalised issue. Robert Bonner has outlined how the elite enslaver class made use of their political clout to recast the institution of slavery in a manner that fit in with the nation's identity and governance policies, and in fact attempted to blend it expertly with the American dream of territorial expansionism, republicanism, constitutionalism, and evangelicalism. However, the rise of the Republican Party effectively scuttled such efforts, forced the South to secede, and marked the end of 'proslavery American nationalism'.

In a somewhat similar vein, Mathew J. Karp has defined the southern sectionalist leaders as 'imperialists' who 'utilised' federal funds to expand American naval power with the sole purpose of protecting slavery, enhancing their wealth, and exerting greater political influence within and beyond the boundaries of the nation. Brian Schoen, too, showed how, by the 1850s, the boom in cotton prices increased the enslavers' aspirations, and they therefore began to make efforts to secure a tariff policy suitable to their needs and expand their territorial base into new westward regions. However, this process of monopolising power was halted with the rise of the Republican Party. This was an explosive development, as the southerners could not digest their declining hold over the federal power structure even as they retained economic power. James L. Huston has shown how the conflict ensued with the South attempting to 'nationalise' the institution of slavery and integrate it with a national market. This came into competition with the free labour system of the North, propagated by the Republican Party. This led to an increased polarisation and ultimately the division of the Union.

These historical interpretations make it clear that both North and South used the yardstick of nationalism and sectionalism depending on their internal situations and interests. They were 'nationalist' when they felt internally cohesive and dominant, and sectionalised when they were on weak ground. Both sections were aiming to take over or control the national government and mould it to suit their sectional interest. The existing hegemony of the South was broken by the rise of the Republican Party, leading to the collapse of the South's proslavery agenda and pushing it towards secession.

This new scholarship also highlights a unique point: Those who opposed slavery were not concerned about enslaved people or their oppression, but rather, about how much damage slaveholders inflicted on northern White groups and, thereby, on their liberty. There was asymmetry in the whole politics of slavery—the South attempted to maintain its hold over the institution of slavery to sustain the enslavers' racialised supremacy and economic interests, while the North became concerned with the concentration of power and problem of the slaveholding class. Carol Lasser has shown how, between the 1830s and the 1850s, the 'self-interest' of both sections guided antislavery or proslavery crusades. The emergence of White male farmers and workers in the North who supported the antislavery wave reflected their self-interests and not the cause of the enslaved Black population.

According to John Ashworth and William W. Freehling, the continuous conflict between the enslaved people and their enslavers pushed the latter to adopt political policies detrimental to northern liberties, and this created sectional strife. These historians have 'reintegrated' American history to weave together issues of social and political history. In the ensuing sectional conflict, elites from both sections clashed over political and economic policies that led to political and ideological differences and resulted in the Civil War. It was the continued opposition by slaves that forced the enslavers to institute gag rules, apply stringent fugitive slave laws, and support the expansion of slavery to extend their political base. It was at this point that they came into conflict with the free labour ideology of the North. Thus, it was slave resistance that forced the enslavers in the South to change their relationship with the North, and the consequence of this was the Civil War. According to Freehling, the 'militant slavocracy' that led to the rise of 'Slave Power' in the South threatened the White communities in the North, so they began to resist Slave Power, but this was not to free enslaved people, only to protect their own rights. This also swung the northern vote towards the Republican Party. In this sense, the slave resistance pushed the two sections to war, but the intention of the North was not to institute racial equality or end the widespread injustices meted out to Black people. The conflict between the two regions was over the competition for 'political power'. The fact remains that from the time of Andrew Johnson, the main issue dominating national politics were money, power, class, and democracy. Thus, those in the North were not morally charged antislavery crusaders, but White groups who were equally enmeshed in racist society and whose main goal was to protect White liberty and equality in the American republic. At the same time, one must remember that these conflicts later contributed to the notion of human equality and influenced the Reconstruction period. According to Adam Rothman, the Civil War overthrew the richest, elitist and constitutionally protected class from the corridors of national power, making this war a class-based conflict between the South and North. In recent times, scholars Sven Beckert and Seth Rockman's edited volume, *Slavery's Capitalism: A New History of American Economic Development* (2016), has overturned all the earlier interpretations to focus on how the bonded enslavement system was responsible for the use and application of new inventions, technologies, business management systems, corporate business structures, and the rise of southern urban centres that integrated themselves into complex markets, commerce, trade, education, and national politics. The institution was thus central to the creation of wealth in the USA. Enslavers came to dominate power and authority, accumulate capital, and earn profits that benefited even the northern economy and assisted in the development of a uniquely American brand of capitalism.

The above analysis suggests that this period cannot be adequately explained by traditional interpretations, and long-held views and historical opinions on the subject need to be challenged based on a more critical examination of historical facts.

Conclusion

Sectionalism, therefore, brought about sharp differences between the two regions. Still, several compromises assisted in cutting the rising tentacles of war, particularly the Missouri Compromise of 1820, followed by the Compromise of 1850 that temporarily mitigated the demands and requirements of the northern, southern and western states and their respective political economies. However, this temporary patchwork of compromises began to fall off after the US-Mexico War when 'fire-eater' southern politicians raised the banner of secession from the Union, and again in 1850 in the form of the Kansas Crisis precipitated by John Brown's raid on the Federal Armoury at Harper's Ferry, Virginia in October 1859, with a clear intention to push the cause of abolition and use armed force to this end. This was at a point when the southern politicians were demanding stricter enforcement of slave codes, laws, and a complete blanket ban on the abolition of slavery in the Congress.

Slavery as an institution had been extremely violent, and the beginning of the end of this bondage was equally fierce, resulting in the beginning of the Civil War. Even during the war, as thousands of enslaved people were rendered homeless, they were herded into refugee camps. They were disliked by anti-Black northerners and by their ex-enslavers, who used armed force to bring them back into the institution of slavery. These tumultuous events marked the rise of the Republican Party in 1856, which was opposed to the spread of slavery (but significantly was not antislavery on principle), leading to a gradual reduction in the capital price of slave property and pushing the nation towards internal conflict.

The abolition of enslavement not only galvanised national politics, but more importantly, it gave freedom to about four million enslaved people, bringing to an end one of the most brutal institutions of the modern era. The war culminated in the liberation of African Americans, thereby ushering in a 'Revolution of Emancipation' in American history. After the war, there were shifts in African American gender roles whereby free Black men became the head of the household. Black women were looked at as wives and mothers of their children, although, unlike White women, they were still expected to work to augment the family income for survival.[31] The journey from being seen as property to recognition as human beings, with the rights to establish their society and institutions marked the rise of the Free Black individual.

Notes

1. Allen C. Guelzo, *Fateful Lightning: A New History of the Civil War and Reconstruction*, (New York, 2012), pp. 6–7.
2. Ibid.

3. Michael Vorenberg, *Final Freedom: The Civil War, the Abolition of Slavery, and the Thirteenth Amendment* (Cambridge, UK, 2001), p. 9.
4. Ibid., p. 17.
5. Ibid.
6. Guelzo, *Fateful Lightning*, p. 8.
7. Ibid., p. 9.
8. Ibid., pp. 13–15.
9. Ibid., p. 12.
10. Alan Taylor, *The Civil War of 1812*.
11. Guelzo, *Fateful Lightning*, p. 20.
12. Robert V. Remini, *Henry Clay: Stateman for the Union* (New York, 1991), pp. 136–137.
13. Guelzo, *Fateful Lightning*, p. 20.
14. Ibid., pp. 20–22.
15. Quoted in Allan Nevins, *The War for the Union*, vol. 3: *The Organized War to Victory: 1863–1864*. (New York, 1971), p. 96.
16. James M. McPherson, *The Struggle for Equality: Abolitionists and the Negro in the Civil War and Reconstruction* (Princeton, 1964), pp. 31–32.
17. Guelzo, *Fateful Lightning*, p. 39.
18. Robert William Fogel, *The Slavery Debates, 1952–1990: A Retrospective* (Baton Rouge, 2003), p. 63.
19. Guelzo, *Fateful Lightning*, p. 43.
20. Ibid., pp. 41–52.
21. Walter M. Merrill, *Against Wind and Tide: A Biography of William Lloyd Garrison* (Massachusetts, 1998).
22. Ira Berlin, et al., *Slaves No More: Three Essays on Emancipation and the Civil War* (Cambridge, UK, 1992), p. 3.
23. Guelzo, *Fateful Lightning*, pp. 4–5.
24. Eric Foner, *Reconstruction: America's Unfinished Revolution, 1863–1877* (New York, 1988), p. 93.
25. Steven E. Woodworth, *Cultures in Conflict: The American Civil War* (Westport, 2000). Quoted in Allan Nevins, *The War for the Union*, vol. 3, p. 96.
26. Eric Foner, 'The Causes of the American Civil War: Recent Interpretations and New Directions', *Civil War History 20* (3), September 1974, pp. 197–214.
27. Jeffrey R. Hummel was drawing on the Hobbesian concept: a powerful state (the leviathan) must establish absolute power that can enforce laws and ensure order in society to prevent chaos and conflict.
28. Ibid., pp. 102–103.
29. Gary W. Gallagher and Alan T. Nolan, ed., *The Myth of the Lost Cause and Civil War History* (Bloomington and Indianapolis, 2010).
30. Michael E. Woods, 'What Twenty-First Century Historians Have Said about the Causes of Disunion: A Civil War Sesquicentennial Review of the Recent Literature', *Journal of American History 99* (2), September 2012, pp. 415–439.
31. McPherson, *The Struggle for Equality*, pp. 31–32.

References

Andrews, Charles M. 2018. *Colonial Period of American History*, vol. 1. Cambridge: Cambridge University Press.
Appleby, Joyce O. 1984. *Capitalism and a New Social Order: The Republican Vision of the 1790s*. New York: New York University Press.
Apthekar, Herbert. 1960. *American Revolution, 1763–1783: A History of the American People: An Interpretation*. New York: International Publishers Co.
Bailyn, Bernard. 1967. *Ideological Origins of the American Revolution*. Massachusetts: Harvard University Press.
———. 1986. *Voyages to the West: A Passage in the Peopling of America on the Eve of Revolution*. New York: Knopf.
Bancroft, George. 2023. *History of Colonization of the United States*, vols 1–3 (New York, 2023).
Barney, William L. 1987. *The Passage of the Republic: An Interdisciplinary History of Nineteenth-Century America*. Lexington: Heath and Company.
———. 2001. *A Companion to 19th-Century America*. USA: Blackwell.
Beard, Charles A. 1914. *An Economic Interpretation of the Constitution of the United States*. New York: Macmillan.
Beard, Charles A., and Mary Beard. 1927. *The Rise of American Civilization*. New York: Macmillan.
Becker, Carl L. 1909. *The History of Political Parties in the Province of New York, 1770–1776*. Madison: Wisconsin University Press.

Beckert, Sven, and Seth Rockman, ed. 2016. *Slavery's Capitalism: A New History of American Economic Development*. Philadelphia: Pennsylvania University Press.

Belohlavek, John M. 2006. 'American Expansion, 1800–1867'. In *A Companion to Nineteenth-Century America*, ed. William L. Barney. New York: Blackwell Publishing Ltd, pp. 89–103.

Berkhofer, Jr, Robert F. 1978. 'The White Advance Upon Native Lands', in *The White Man's Indian: Images of the American Indian from Columbus to the Present*. New York: Alfred A. Knopf.

Berlin, Ira, Barbara J. Fields, Steven F. Miller, Joseph P. Reidy, and Leslie E. Rowland. 1992. *Slaves No More: Three Essays on Emancipation and the Civil War*. Cambridge, UK: Cambridge University Press.

Bestor, Jr, Arthur E. 1953. 'Patent-Office Models of the Good Society: Some Relationships between Social Reform and Westward Expansion'. *American Historical Review* 58 (3): 505–526.

Bickham, Troy. 2012. *The Weight of Vengeance: The U.S., the British Empire, and the War of 1812*. New York: Oxford University Press.

Blassingame, John, ed. 1977. *Slave Testimony: Two Centuries of Letters, Speeches, Interviews and Autobiographies*. Louisiana: Louisiana University Press.

——. 1979. *The Slave Community: Plantation Life in Antebellum South*, revised ed. New York: Oxford University Press.

Bonazzi, Tiziano. 1993. 'Frederick Jackson Turner's Frontier Thesis and Self-Consciousness of America'. *Journal of American Studies* 27 (2), pp. 149–171.

Boorstin, Daniel J. 1953. *The Genius of American Politics*. Chicago: Chicago University Press.

Boyer, Paul S., Clifford E. Clark, Jr, Joseph F. Kett, Thomas L. Purvis, Harvard Sitkoff, and Nancy Woloch. 1990. *The Enduring Vision: A History of the American People, Vol. I: To 1877*. USA: Heath and Company.

Brown, Richard Maxwell. 1975. *Strains of Violence: Historical Studies of American Violence and Vigilantism*. New York: Oxford University Press.

Brown, Robert E. 1955. *Middle-Class Democracy and the Revolution in Massachusetts, 1691–1780*. Ithaca: Cornell University Press.
———. 2007. *Charles Beard and the Constitution: A Critical Analysis of an Economic Interpretation of the Constitution*. New York: W. W. Norton & Co.
Butterfield, L. H., ed. 1981. *The Adams Papers: Diary and Autobiography of John Adams*, vol. 2, 1771–1781. Cambridge: Cambridge University Press.
Campbell, Randolph B. 1967. 'The Spanish Aspect of Henry Clay's American System', *The Americas 24* (1), pp. 3–17.
Cave, Alfred A. 2003. 'Abuse of Power: Andrew Jackson and the Indian Removal Act of 1830'. *The Historian 65*. Available at https://doi.org/10.1111/j.0018-2370.2003.00055.x (accessed June 2025).
Channing, Edward. 1912. *History of the United States: The American Revolution, 1761–1789*, vol. 3. New York: The Macmillan Company.
Cogliano, Francis D. 2000. *Revolutionary America 1763–1815: A Political History*. London and New York: Routledge.
Commager, Henry Steel, ed. 1985. *Selections from The Federalist: A Commentary on the Constitution of the United States*. Illinois: Harlon Davidson.
deMause, Lloyd. 'The Psychogenic Theory of History', *Journal of Psychohistory 25* (1): pp. 112–83.
Edling, Max M. 2008. *A Revolution in Favor of Government: Origins of the US Constitution and the Making of the American State*. New York: Oxford University Press.
Edmunds, R. David. 1990. 'Tecumseh, The Shawnee Prophet, and American History', in *Retracing the Past: Readings in the History of the American People*, vol. 1, ed. Gary B. Nash. New York: Harper and Row.
Egerton, Douglas. 1993. *Gabriel's Rebellion: The Virginia Slave Conspiracies of 1800 and 1802*. Chapel Hill: North Carolina University Press.
Elizabeth Fox-Genovese and Eugene D. Genovese. 2005. *The Mind of the Master Class: History and Faith in the Southern Slaveholder's Worldview*. New York: Cambridge University Press.

Elkins, Stanley. 1982. *Slavery: A Problem in American Institutional and Intellectual Life*. Chicago: Chicago University Press.

Escott, Paul D. 1979. *Slavery Remembered: A Record of Twentieth-Century Slave Narratives*. Chapel Hill: North Carolina University Press.

Faulkner, H. U. 1960. *American Economic History*. New York: Harper and Row.

Feldberg, Michael. 1980. *The Turbulent Era: Riot and Disorder in Jacksonian America*. New York: Oxford University Press.

Ferguson, E. J. 1968. *The Power of the Purse: A History of American Public Finance (1776–1790)*. North Carolina: Omohundro Institute of Early American History and Culture and the North Carolina University Press.

Fields, Barbara Jeanne. 1985. *Slavery and Freedom on the Middle Ground*. New Haven: Yale University Press.

Fiske, John. 1888. *The Critical Period of American History, 1783–1789*. Cambridge: Cambridge University Press.

Fogel, Robert William. 2003. *The Slavery Debates, 1952–1990: A Retrospective*. Baton Rouge: Louisiana State University Press.

Foner, Eric. 1974. 'The Causes of the American Civil War: Recent Interpretations and New Directions', *Civil War History* 20 (3), pp. 197–214.

———. 1988. *Reconstruction: America's Unfinished Revolution, 1863–1877*. New York: Harper & Row.

———. 2006. *Forever Free: The Story of Emancipation and Reconstruction*. New York: Vintage Books.

———. 2011. *Give Me Liberty! An American History*, third ed. New York: W. W. Norton & Co.

Gallagher, Gary W., and Alan T. Nolan, ed. 2010. *The Myth of the Lost Cause and Civil War History*. Bloomington and Indianapolis: Indiana University Press.

Genovese, E. D. 1965. *The Political Economy of Slavery*. New York: Pantheon.

Gipson, L. H. 1936. *The British Empire Before the American Revolution*, vol. 8. Caldwell, Idaho: Caxton Printers.

Grob, Gerald N., and George Athan Billias, ed. 1978. *Interpretations of American History: Patterns and Perspectives*. New York: Free Press.

Guelzo, Allen C. 2012. *Fateful Lightning: A New History of the Civil War and Reconstruction.* New York: Oxford University Press.

Gutman, Herbert G. 1976. *The Black Family in Slavery and Freedom, 1750–1925.* New York: Pantheon.

Harding, Vincent. 1981. *There is a River: The Black Struggle for Freedom in America.* New York: Pantheon.

Harper, Lawrence A. 1942. 'Mercantilism and the American Revolution', *Canadian Historical Review 23* (1), March, pp. 1–15.

Hickey, Donald R. 2006. *The War of 1812: A Forgotten Conflict*, revised ed. Chicago: Illinois University Press.

Higginbotham, Dion. 1983. *The War of American Independence: Military Attitudes, Policies, and Practice, 1763–1789.* New York: Northeastern Classics.

Horsman, Reginald. 2016. *The Causes of the War of 1812.* Philadelphia: Pennsylvania Press.

Horton, James Oliver, and Lois E. Horton. 2005. *Slavery and the Making of America.* New York: Oxford University Press.

Jeff Taylor. 2006. *Where Did the Party Go? William Jennings Bryan, Hubert Humphrey, and the Jeffersonian Legacy.* Columbia and London: Missouri University Press.

Jensen, Merrill. 1940. *The Articles of Confederation: An Interpretation of the Social-Constitutional History of the American Revolution, 1774–1781.* Wisconsin: Wisconsin University Press.

———. 1981. *The New Nation: A History of the United States during the Confederation, 1781–1789.* Boston: Northeastern University Press.

Johnson, Emory Richard. 1915. *History of Domestic and Foreign Commerce of the United States.* Washington DC: Carnegie Institution of Washington.

Kammen, M., ed. 1986. *The Origins of the American Constitution: A Documentary History.* New York: Penguin.

Katz, Stanely N., John M. Murrin, and Douglas Greenberg, ed. 1993. *Colonial America: Essays in Politics and Social Development*, 4th ed. New York: McGraw Hill.

Kennedy, Roger G. 2000. *Burr, Hamilton and Jefferson: A Study in Character.* New York: Oxford University Press.

Kenyon, Cecilia M. 1985. *The Antifederalists*. Boston: Northeastern University Press.
Kolchin, Peter. 1993. *American Slavery, 1619–1877*. New York: Hill and Wang.
Kramnick, Isaac. 1990. *Republicanism and Bourgeois Radicalism: Political Ideology in Late Eighteenth-Century England and America*. New York: Cornell University Press.
Levine, Lawrence W. 2007. *Black Culture and Black Consciousness: Afro-American Folk Thought from Slavery to Freedom*. New York: Oxford University Press.
Lincoln, Abraham. 1989. 'Address to the Young Men's Lyceum of Springfield, Illinois', in *Abraham Lincoln: Speeches and Writings, 1832–1858*. New York: New York Library Classics of the United States.
Lockridge, Kenneth A. 1974. *Literacy in Colonial New England: An Enquiry into the Social Context of Literary in the Early Modern West*. New York: Norton.
Lynd, S., ed. 2009. *Class Conflict, Slavery, and the United States Constitution*. Cambridge: Cambridge University Press.
Main, Jackson Turner. 1965. *The Social Structure of Revolutionary America*. Princeton: Princeton University Press.
McDonald, Forrest. 1985. *Novus Ordo Seculorum: The Intellectual Origins of the Constitution*. Lawrence: Kansas University Press.
McPherson, James M. 1964. *The Struggle for Equality: Abolitionists and the Negro in the Civil War and Reconstruction*. Princeton: Princeton University Press.
Merrill, Walter M. 1998. *Against Wind and Tide: A Biography of William Lloyd Garrison*. Massachusetts: Harvard University Press.
Moore, Jr, Barrington. 1993. *Social Origins of Dictatorship and Democracy: Lord and Peasant in the Making of the Modern World*. Boston: Bacon Press.
Nevins, Allan. 1947. *Ordeal of the Union: Fruits of Manifest Destiny, 1847–1852*. New York: Scribner's.
———. 1971. *The War for the Union*, vol. 3: *The Organized War to Victory: 1863–1864*. New York: Scribner's.

Nisbet, Robert A. 1973. *The Social Impact of Revolution*. Washington: Institute for Public Policy Research.
Nobles, Gregory H. 1983. *Divisions Throughout the Whole: Politics and Society in Hampshire County, Massachusetts, 1740–1775*. Cambridge: Cambridge University Press.
Ojha, Archana. 2003. 'Federal Policies and Governance of First Nations in Canada', PhD diss. New Delhi: Jawaharlal Nehru University.
Onuf, Peter S. 1989. 'Reflections on the Founding: Constitutional Historiography in Bicentennial Perspective', *William and Mary Quarterly 46*, 3rd series.
Painter, Nell Irvin. 2006. *Creating Black Americans: African American History and its Meanings, 1619 to the Present*. New York: Oxford University Press.
Parish, Peter J. 1989. *Slavery: History and Historians*. New York: Harper and Row.
Patterson, Orlando. 1998. *The Ordeal of Integration: Progress and Resentment in America's 'Racial' Crisis*. Washington, DC: Civitas/Counterpoint.
Perdue, Theda. 2002. 'Trail of Tears: Removal of the Southern Indians in the Jeffersonian–Jacksonian Age'. In *'They Made Us Many Promises': The American Indian Experience, 1524 to the Present*, ed. Philip Weeks. Illinois: Harlan Davidson.
Pocock, J. G. A. 1975. *The Machiavellian Moment: Florentine Republican Thought and the Atlantic Republican Tradition*. Princeton: Princeton University Press.
Potter, David M. 1962. 'The Historian's Use of Nationalism and Vice Versa'. *The American Historical Review 67* (4), pp. 924–950.
———. 1976. *The Impending Crisis, 1848–1861*. New York, London: Harper & Row.
Remini, Robert V. 1984. *Andrew Jackson and the Course of American Democracy, 1833–1845*. New York: Harper and Row.
———. 1991 *Henry Clay: Statesman for the Union*. New York: W. W. Norton.
———. 2001. *Andrew Jackson and His Indian Wars*. New York: Penguin Viking.

Riley, Russell L. 2000. *Andrew Jackson, 1829–1837*. New York: Oxford University Press.
Ritcheson, Charles R. 1981. *British Policies and the American Revolution*. Westport: Greenwood Press.
Satz, Ronald N. 1975. *American Indian Policy in the Jacksonian Era*. USA: University of Nebraska Press.
Schlesinger, Arthur M. 2013. *The Colonial Merchants and the American Revolution, 1763–1776*. New York: Hardpress Publishing.
Schmitt, Gary J., and Robert H. Webking. 1979. 'Revolutionaries, Antifederalists, and Federalists: Comments on Godon Wood's Understanding of the American Founding'. *The Political Science Reviewer 9* (Fall).
Segal, Ronald. 1995. *The Black Diaspora: Five Centuries of Black Experience Outside Africa*. New York: Farrar, Straus and Giroux.
Stampp, Kenneth M. 1956. *The Peculiar Institution: Slavery in the Ante-Bellum South*. USA: Vintage Books.
———. 1976. 'Slavery: The Historian's Burden'. In *Perspectives and Irony in American Slavery: Essays*, ed. Carl Degler and Harry P. Owens. Jackson: Mississippi University Press.
Storing, Herbert. 2008. *What the Anti-Federalists Were for: The Political Thought of the Opponents of the Constitution*. Chicago: Chicago University Press.
Taylor, Alan. 2010. *The Civil War of 1812: American Citizens, British Subjects, Irish Rebels*. New York: Knopf.
Turner, Frederick Jackson. 1920. 'The Significance of the Frontier in American History'. In *Fronter and Sections: Selected Essays of F. J. Turner*, ed. Ray Allen Billington. New York: Holt.
United States Senate Historical Office. 2000. 'George Washington's Farewell Address: To the People of the United States', 106th Congress, 2nd session, Senate document no. 106–21. Washington: Superintendent of Documents, US Government Printing Office.
Urofsky, Melvin I. 2000. *The American Presidents*. New York and London: Taylor and Francis Group.

Vorenberg, Allen. 2001. *Final Freedom: The Civil War, the Abolition of Slavery, and the Thirteenth Amendment.* Cambridge, UK: Cambridge University Press.

Wertenbaker, Thomas Jefferson. 1940. *Torchbearer of the Revolution: The Story of Bacon's Rebellion and its Leaders.* Princeton: Princeton University Press.

White, Richard. 1997. *It's Your Misfortune and None of My Own: A New History of the American West.* Oklahoma: Oklahoma University Press.

Wilentz, Sean. 1994. *Chants Democratic: New York City and the Rise of the American Working Class, 1788–1850.* New York: Cambridge University Press.

Wood, Gordon S. 1969. *Creation of the American Republic, 1776–1787.* Chapel Hill: North Carolina University Press.

——. 2009. *Empire of Liberty: A History of the Early Republic, 1789–1815.* New York: Oxford University Press.

Woods, Michael E. 2012. 'What Twenty-First Century Historians Have Said about the Causes of Disunion: A Civil War Sesquicentennial Review of the Recent Literature'. *Journal of American History* 99 (2), pp. 415–439.

Woodworth, Steven E. 2000. *Cultures in Conflict: The American Civil War.* Westport: Greenwood.

Wright, Benjamin F. 1967. *Consensus and Continuity, 1776–1787.* New York: W. W. Norton & Co.

Zimmerman, Larry J., and Brian Leigh Molyneaux. 1996. *Native North America.* Oklahoma: Oklahoma University Press.

Index

49th degree parallel 157, 161
51st degree parallel 157
55th degree parallel 157
1828 90
1850 census 183

Aaron Burr Conspiracy 82
Abolitionist Movement 100, 188, 232, 235, 240
Acts of Trade and Navigation 20
Adams, John 11, 19, 35, 58, 76–79, 228
   midnight appointments 78
Adams, John Quincy 90, 95, 97, 157
Administration of Justice Act (1774) 34
adult enfranchisement 40
Africa 21, 42, 78, 87, 126, 164–65, 170–71, 199, 201, 203, 205, 213, 217
African American 164, 193, 198, 200–201, 203–04, 207–08, 217, 237–38, 255
   culture 198, 200–201, 208
agricultural
   capitalism 189
   economy 77, 91, 120, 122, 128, 146, 223, 229
   land(s) 87, 125, 149, 172, 182, 241
   products 74, 177, 228
agriculture 7–8, 13, 15, 106, 111–12, 115, 127, 130, 181
Albany Plan of 1754 54
alcohol 13, 101–02, 130, 137
   consumption of 101, 137, *see also* Temperance Movement
   provision of 102
alcoholism 79, 136
Alien and Sedition Acts (1798) 77–78, 228
American
   armed forces 119
   army 146
   capitalist system 191
   colonies 9–10, 18–30, 32, 38, 43, 45, 48, 52, 54–55, 109–10, 166–68, 170, 178, 226
   commerce 143, 146, 154, 160
   commercial liberties 150
   commercial rights 150
   constitutional law 79
   democracy 68, 99
   diplomacy 87
   economic order 15
   economy 74, 94, 119, 229
   enslavement system 192
   exceptionalism 159
   expansion 137–38, 153

expansionism 117
foreign policy 141
frontier settlements 138
industrial growth 151
institutions 123, 156, 159
legal system 79
mass culture 245
party system 11
political culture 117
political economy 240
settlers 43, 82, 100, 123–24, 136, 161
American Antislavery Society 235
American Baptist Movement 6
American Board of Customs Commissioners 32
American Civil War of 1861 84, 148
American Colonization Society 205, 216
American Constitution 11, 40, 52, 55, 65, 67, 69, 102, 227, *see also* US Constitution
  establishment of the 40
  formulation of the 55
  Formulation of the 11, 52
  interpretation of the 67, 69
  nature of the 65
American Declaration of Diplomatic Independence 156
Americanisation 118–19, 122–23
American Protestant Association 101
American Republican Party (ARP) 101–02
American Revolution 10, 14, 18–20, 26–27, 31, 37–44, 46–48, 52–53, 55, 65, 70, 85, 128–29, 160, 170, 172, 178, 215, 226, 242, 249
  aftermath of the 14
  beginning of the 20, 26
  causes of the 48
  consequences of the 43
  culmination of the 55
  evaluation of the 38
  nature of the 37

rise of the 27
roots of the 19
second 70
settlers 42
American Society of Free Persons 239
American Union 115, 147, 157
American War of Independence 47, 110, 207, *see also* American Revolution
American West 13–14, 119, 123, 125–26, 180
Anglo-American ties/union 157
Anglo-French Wars 38, 41
Anglo-Indian Wars 38, 41
Annapolis Convention (1786) 59
antislavery movement 244–45
Anti-Stuart revolution 22
Appalachians 1, 7, 228
armed rebellions 161
Article of Impeachment 62
Articles of Confederation Constitution 54, 57, 59, 65, 129
Asia 3, 42, 105, 165
assimilation 115, 128, 130, 151

Bank War 93, 99
Bastille Day 217
Battle of Bull Run (1861) 223
Battle of Horseshoe Bend 151, *see also* Battle of Tohopeka (1814)
Battle of New Orleans (1815) 89
Battle of Thames (1812) 138
Battle of Tippecanoe (1811) 138
Battle of Tohopeka (1814) 89
Battle of Trafalgar (1805) 145
Berlin Decree (1806) 144
Bible, the 101–02, 206, 216, 239
Bill of Rights 58, 63, 87
Black
  childhood 183
  church 205, 207
  communities 103, 200, 201, 206, 219, 235, 241
  labour 14, 164, 166, 169, 193

Black Holocaust 164
Black people
  enslavement of 111
  exploitation of 15
  oppression of 170, 198
Bleeding Kansas (1856) 224, 233
blockade 83, 144, 148
Board of Customs Commissioners 32
Board of Trade 25, 54
Board of Trade and Plantations 25
bondage 168, 175, 192, 208, 210, 216, 220, 255
Boston Massacre (1770) 26, 33
Boston News-Letter 8, 26, 43
Boston Port Act (1774) 34
Boston Tea Party (1773) 26, 33
Brazil 106, 156, 191, 212
Britain
  economic blockade 148
  events in 23
  imperialist control of 26
  industrial revolution 74, 178, 228
  policy of 147
  sanctions against 146
  US pressure on 84
British
  aggression 148
  army 32, 55
  colony(ies) 7–11, 22, 115, 147, 149, 161
  government 10, 22, 25, 31–34, 55
  marine merchant system 20
  monarch/monarchy 7–9, 20, 22
  policy/regulations 19, 26, 30, 35, 44–45, 137, 144, 147
  rule 35, 37, 41, 144, 162
British American colonies 10, 18, 22, 25, 32, 43, 48, 109–10, 168
British Civil War 41
British Crown 24, 27, 48
British Empire 7, 9, 20, 25, 38
British North American colonies 23
British Parliament 5, 29–32, 54–55, 170

Brown, John 224, 233, 235, 255
Bureau of Indian Affairs 117, 126–27
Bureau of Land Management 126
Bureau of Reclamation 126
Burr, Aaron, former Vice President 73, 82–83

Calhoun, John C. 97, 231–32
Canada 5, 82, 108, 110, 147, 149–51, 157, 159, 161, 217–18, 240
capital 6, 29, 34, 54, 66–67, 69, 74, 80, 122, 131, 177–82, 187–89, 192, 196–97, 223, 232, 254–55
  accumulation of 189
  supply of 180
capitalist
  classes 20, 41, 76, 84, 92, 196
  economy 177
cases
  case of Samuel Chase 79
  Cherokee Nation v. Georgia case 93, 116
  Dred Scott Case 231, 241
  Essex Case 144
  Worcester v. Georgia case 116, 134
Catholicism 23, 155
  conversion to 155
Catholics 6, 34, 101–02, 242
Charles II, British monarch 20, 22–23
chattel slavery 2, 166–67, 170, 178, 183
Cherokee removal crisis of 1806–1809 130
Cherokee resistance 131
Chesapeake–Leopard Affair 83–84, 145
Christianisation 117
Christianity 5, 127–28, 130, 137, 167, 175, 204, 206–07, 228
  conversion to 128, 130
churches 23, 27, 46, 101–03, 109, 160, 176, 186, 204–07, 218, 228
citizenship 16, 86, 235
civilisation/civilization 116–18, 121, 123, 127, 131, 204

Civil Rights Movement 103
Civil War 37, 183, 223
   beginning of the 71, 104, 148, 174, 213, 220, 255
   cause(s) of the 230, 245, 249–50
   course of the 223, 241
   interpretation of the 242
   nature of the 237
Civil War of 1813 131, *see also* Creek War
class(es)
   agrarian/agricultural 67, 68
   agricultural 65, 91
   capitalist 20, 41, 76, 84, 92, 196
   conflict 37, 39–40, 66, 68, 121
   enslaver 176–77, 179, 181, 186, 189, 215, 249, 251
   enslaver-planter 174, 177
   professional 26, 43, 45, 101
   social 30, 40, 66
   upper 28, 40, 75
   working 33, 102–03
Clay, Henry 90, 95, 98, 150–51, 155, 229–32
clergy 7, 101–02, 206
colonial
   assemblies 22, 24, 29–30, 33, 45
   goods 21
   period 66, 214, 226
   population 18–19, 42
   rule 155, 187
   system 26, 28
   trade 21, 43
colonialism 13, 167, 172
   settler 13
colonisation 1–2, 5, 7, 10, 13, 15, 18, 54, 109, 113, 121–22, 128, 156–58, 164, 168, 175, 192, 226
   internal 13, 109, 113, 128, 158
   process of 2, 5, 10, 13, 18, 122
colonisers 13, 110, 119, 137, 199
colony(ies) 4–11, 13, 18–34, 38–40, 42–46, 48, 52–55, 66, 80, 108–10, 115, 144, 147, 149, 154, 161, 166–68, 170–72, 176–78, 205, 214, 226
   control over the 21, 29, 31, 54
   proprietary 6, 8, 19, 27, 53
   royal 8, 19, 53–54
   types of 53
Colportage movement 101
Columbian Exchange 13, 126
Columbus, Christopher 3, 108
Commerce and Enslaved Person Trade Compromise 64
commercial revolution(s) 10, 20, 29, 44
commodity(ies) 6, 28–29, 83, 97, 144, 168, 175–78, 185, 190–91, 209–10
common law 24, 28, 127
Compromise of 1850 193, 224, 232, 254
Confederate States of America 223, 236, 241, 246
conflict(s)
   Anglo-French 28, 43
   British customs and American identity 43
   colonial powers and colonies 42
   colonists and Indigenous groups 45
   France and England 24
   Protestants and Catholics 242
   Puritans and Catholics 6
   racial 15, 187, 248
   sectional 242–43, 248–50, 253
   settlers and the British governor 7
   social 68, 85, 100, 241
Connecticut Compromise 61, *see also* Great Compromise
conscription scheme 225
constitutional amendment(s) 61–62, 64–65, 81–82, 87, 118, 220, 235, 240
   12th Amendment 82
   17th Amendment 61

Index

21st Amendment 62
first Amendment 63
thirteenth Amendment 220
Constitutional Convention, 1787 49, 58–60, 62–63, 250
constitutionalism 11, 104, 252
Constitution of 1787 227
Continental Army 55, 226
Continental Congress 26, 34–35, 46, 55, 75, 226
continental expansion 74, 119
Continental War 87, 143, 154
cotton 10, 47, 74, 97, 108, 111, 124, 132, 160, 166, 171, 173–75, 178, 180, 182, 184, 188–91, 195–96, 203, 211, 225, 228, 237–38, 249, 252
 cultivation 10, 111, 132, 173, 182, 249
 production 173, 180, 190, 238
counter-revolution 40, 66, 155
credit 80, 95, 130, 153–54, 174, 180, 191, 196
 facilities 80, 153
 system 130, 154
Creek Confederacy 128, 135
Creek War (1813) 89, 131
crop(s) 6, 10, 19, 45, 74–75, 106, 150, 166, 171–74, 179, 180, 186, 188, 190, 197, 203, 210, 228, 249
 cash 19, 45, 75, 150, 166, 171, 173, 197, 228
 commercial 172, 186
Cuba 155, 162, 165, 217, 248
culture(s) 1, 3–4, 8, 10–11, 13–14, 18, 23, 26–27, 43–45, 84, 103, 106, 113, 117, 121, 123, 125, 128, 135, 161, 167, 184, 193–95, 198–201, 208, 215, 242, 244–47
 American 4, 198, 200–201, 208
 political 10–11, 18, 23, 27, 43–44, 117, 242, 245
Currency Act 29

currency system 93
Cushing Treaty of 1844 160

Daniel Shay's Rebellion 58
Declaration of Independence 26, 35–36, 48, 56–57, 59, 68–69, 75, 77, 87, 158, 208, 215–16, 226–27
Declaration of War 22
Declaratory Act 31
democracy(ies)
 Jacksonian 12–13, 91, 99–100, 104, 159, 245
 Jeffersonian 82, 84, 86, 162, 228–29
Democratic Party 12, 92, 102, 148, 159, 229
Democrats 12, 56, 68, 162
development
 agricultural 132
 industrial 112, 180–81, 184
 internal 26, 179, 227
 westward 111
discrimination 169, 183, 202
disease(s) 6, 13, 109, 111, 126–27, 134, 136, 165, 197
displacement 14, 116, 118, 121, 124, 136, 138
dispossession 82, 92, 114, 129–30, 136, 153
Distribution Act 97
Distribution or Deposit Act 95
Doctrine of Nullification 97, *see also* nullification doctrine
Douglass, Frederick 234, 236, 240
Dred Scott Decision 224

East India Company 33
economic
 backwardness 177, 197, 244
 changes 154, 244
 development 74, 178, 189, 243
 expansion 158, 179
 growth 8, 19, 94, 168, 177, 181, 190, 229

independence 112, 145, 161
interest(s) 39–40, 66–68, 78, 94, 98, 176, 195–96, 251, 253
prosperity 22, 55, 174, 249
relations 44, 178, 243
systems 106, 127, 131, 166, 192
economy(ies)
  agricultural 45, 77, 91, 120, 122, 128, 146, 223, 229, 243
  colonial 29
  northern 181, 189, 254
  plantation 26, 29, 165, 176, 180, 182, 189, 192–93, 215
  southern 177, 179, 181–82, 190–91, 196
education 18, 27, 123, 130, 133, 178–79, 181, 192, 197, 200–202, 210, 219, 228, 238, 254
  denial of 202, 210
  Western 18, 130, 200
egalitarianism 15, 75, 161
electoral colleges 62, 82
emancipation 87, 172, 235, 238, 241–42
Emancipation Proclamation 225, 237, 247
Embargo Act of 1807 73, 84, 145, 148, 229, 250
England 3, 6–8, 19, 21–24, 28, 34–35, 42, 45–46, 52–55, 82, 84, 97–98, 109, 142, 149–50, 178, 214, 244, 251
Enlightenment 37, 85, 167
enslaved people(s) 2, 21, 45, 63, 70, 87, 110, 112, 124, 126, 128, 155, 165–67, 169, 171–88, 191–92, 194–203, 205–17, 219, 227, 230, 233, 235–42, 245–48, 252–53, 255
  demand for 173, 184
  importation of 166, 172
  movement of 174, 191
enslavement 10, 64, 109, 111, 164–68, 183, 186, 192–93, 195–96, 199, 203, 206–07, 216, 227, 240, 254–55

enslaver class 176–77, 179, 181, 186, 189, 215, 249, 251
  political ideology of the 182
enslaver-enslaved relationship 188
enslavers 43, 87, 124, 167–68, 171, 174–86, 188–91, 193, 195–98, 207, 209, 212–13, 215–17, 227, 229, 232–33, 235, 237, 239, 241–42, 245, 249–53, 255
equality 36, 41, 44–45, 56, 84, 87, 112, 119, 127, 192, 202, 238, 245, 253–54
Essex Decision (1805) 83
Europe 1, 6, 16, 19, 21, 42–43, 73, 83, 120–21, 124–26, 143–46, 155, 160–61, 165, 173, 196, 249
European
  affairs 154, 156–58
  nations 18, 70, 121, 143, 152, 158
  powers 2, 5, 18, 25, 84, 142, 151, 156, 158
exceptionalism 159
expansion
  frontier 119–21, 123–24, 149, 166, 209, 230
  policy of 82, 156
  westward 28, 70, 80, 82, 91, 95, 109, 111, 118, 120–21, 123, 127, 138, 153, 159, 173, 182, 234, 249
expansionism 13, 87, 117, 142, 156, 162, 252
exploitation 2, 10, 14–15, 97, 121, 166–67, 169–70, 175–76, 179, 183, 187, 193–95, 199–200, 207, 209, 212, 219–20

factories 145–46, 182, 234
farmers 12, 39, 45–46, 56, 66, 69, 74–77, 80, 84, 87, 90–91, 107, 112, 142, 146, 168, 173, 180–81, 186, 228, 241, 245, 253
  American 45, 74, 80, 228

small 56, 69, 75, 77, 80, 87, 90–91, 142
tenant 112, 186, 241
Federal Convention 60, 65
federal courts 61, 65, 78
federal government 59, 63–64, 74, 76–78, 80–81, 86, 90, 93, 99, 109–11, 114–16, 118–19, 124–26, 129–36, 143, 155, 158–59, 161, 226–34, 240, 246
federalism 69, 77, 159
Federalist era 84, 142
Federalist Party 73
Federalists 11, 14, 64, 67–70, 74–76, 78–80, 84–85, 142, 150–52, 227, 244, 251
feminist movement 103
First Bank 76, 93
First Confiscation Act of 1861 237
First Continental Congress 26, 34, 55
five-nation confederacy 107
Foote Resolution 93
Force Bill 98, 230
foreign policy 84, 141, 156, 158
forgotten war 147
France 3–4, 11, 22, 24–25, 60, 73, 76, 82–83, 119, 141–46, 158, 217, 225, 228, 230, 234, 237
Free African Society of Philadelphia 205
freedom 1, 19, 27, 34, 36, 38–39, 43, 46–47, 55, 86, 99, 102, 109, 112, 120, 122, 128, 141, 154–55, 159–61, 168, 172, 187, 192, 197, 203–06, 208, 216–17, 219, 225–26, 231, 235–38, 240, 244–45, 248, 255
  complete 55, 99, 238
  economic 19, 109, 112, 160, 244
  religious 34, 46, 102, 160–61
Free-Soil agitation 188
Free-Soil Party 219, 224, 240
French and Indian War 25
French civil law 34
French colony(ies) 34, 80

French Revolution 42, 75, 85, 142
French Revolutionary Wars 83
frontier
  expansion 119–21, 123–24, 149, 166, 209, 230
  theory 120, 123
frontier theory 123
Fugitive Slave Act /Law of 1850 218–19, 224, 227, 231–33, 237

Gabriel Rebellion 215
Gadsden Purchase 13
gag rule 12
Glorious Revolution 23, 54
Gold Rush 118
governance structure(s) 2–3, 22, 122, 126, 190
government(s)
  federal 59, 63–64, 74, 76–78, 80–81, 86, 90, 93, 99, 109–11, 114–16, 118–19, 124–26, 129–36, 143, 155, 158–59, 161, 226–34, 240, 246
  national 12, 14, 49, 56–61, 64–65, 67, 119, 122, 159, 191, 226–28, 234, 244, 252
  republican 47, 56, 70, 132, 155
  state 48, 56, 58, 64, 92–93, 95, 97, 99, 114, 115, 124
Grant, Ulysses S. 225
Great Awakening 23, 27
Great Britain 14, 25, 31, 141, 237
Great Compromise 61
Great Depression 62
Great Lakes 1, 107, 110, 118, 150, 160
Great Plains 117, 127
Great Water 136
Gulf of Mexico 5, 107, 126, 171, 182

Haitian Revolution 248, 250
Hamilton, Alexander 73–74, 76, 82, 85, 142, 227
Hartford Convention (1814–1815) 229

Henry VII, English king 5
Homestead Act 226
House of Representatives 61–62, 64, 79, 90, 227, 231
Hunters' Lodge 162

identity(ies) 19, 25, 37, 43–44, 103, 117, 126, 128, 135, 158, 164, 168, 174, 176–77, 187, 194–95, 199–200, 241, 246–47, 251–52
ideology(ies) 1, 15, 24, 27, 30, 44–45, 54, 56, 69, 73, 75, 143, 159, 162, 166, 170, 173, 175, 182, 185, 188, 192, 199, 202–03, 253
immigrants 1–3, 10, 16, 18–19, 29, 42, 45, 52, 55, 100–102, 118–19, 121, 124, 128, 165, 169, 179, 243
immigration 19, 120, 124, 165, 242
imperialism 18, 27, 121, 192
Indian
    affairs 115–17, 126–27
    agent(s) 130–31, 135
    policy 117, 129
Indian Intercourse Act of 1796 111
Indian Removal Act of 1830 93
Indian War 25
Indigenous
    communities 13, 45, 82, 92, 99, 106, 109–15, 118, 124–28, 130, 136, 138, 151
    groups 28, 45, 47, 54, 58, 64, 82, 105–06, 109, 111, 113, 115, 117, 128, 130–33, 137, 149, 153, 173
    land(s) 7, 13, 114–15, 131–33, 138
    nations 4–6, 10, 13–14, 115–16, 121, 129, 157
    resistance 10, 127, 135, 138
    societies 24, 44, 92, 105, 115–16, 125–26, 129, 137, 159
Indigenous people 2–4, 11, 14, 16, 24, 27, 34, 43–45, 82, 92, 105, 108, 109–11, 113–17, 120, 124, 126–27, 129–30, 133–36, 147–49, 168, 214, 245
    decimation of 16, 120
    expulsion/removal of 127, 129
Indigenous Revitalisation Movement 135
indigo 8, 19, 21, 45, 97, 171, 203
individualism 27, 44, 70, 84, 113, 119–23, 172, 177, 189, 220
industrial
    expansion 15, 226, 242
    growth 151, 230
industrialisation 10, 29, 44, 73, 92, 119–20, 123, 152, 180, 189–90, 192, 226, 230, 243, 245
Industrial Revolution 74, 178, 196, 228
industry(ies) 20–21, 45, 47, 84, 111, 117–20, 145, 148, 150, 173, 178–81, 184, 226, 229, 234
    American 118–19, 229
    growth and expansion of 120
    rudimentary 20, 47, 184, 234
injustice 117, 195, 198, 201
innovation(s) 2, 12, 52, 121
Intolerable Acts 26, 34, 55
Intolerable or Repressive Acts 34
invention(s) 111–12, 160, 173, 178, 191, 254

Jackson, Andrew, US President 12, 14, 68, 89–99, 113–18, 133, 135, 148, 151–53, 155, 159, 162, 229–30
    administration 12
    autocratic approach 91
    'Indian Policy' 115
    military achievements 90
    presidency of 12, 113
    style of governance 104
    success in 1828 90
    unilateral military action 155
Jacksonian democracy 12, 91, 99–100, 104, 159, 245
Jacksonian era/Jackson's era 12, 92, 113, 187, 230, 250
Jamaica 165

Jeffersonian Age/era 11, 75, 84, 111, 132
Jefferson, Thomas, US President 11, 14, 35, 56, 73–87, 91–92, 110, 114, 117, 130, 132, 142–43, 145–46, 154, 159, 202, 223, 227–29, 236, 247, 250
   administration 11
   controversial 86, 89, 90
   democratic political agenda 87
   diplomatic policy 142
   electoral campaigns 143
   electoral triumph 85
   foreign policy 84
   moderate actions 86
   policies of 77
   policy(ies) of 114, 146
   political philosophy 86, 145, 229
   presidency of 75
   removal policy 130, 132
   weakness 87
judiciary 22, 56, 60–61, 78–79, 153, 231, 240
Judiciary Act of 1789 79
Judiciary Act of 1801 78
justice 2, 34, 36, 76–78, 199, 203, 232

Kansas-Nebraska Act 224
Kentucky and Virginia Resolutions of 1798 77
Know-Nothing Party 224

labour/labourer
   Black 14, 164, 166, 169, 193
   bonded 172, 183, 190, 192
   enslaved 8, 20, 26, 45, 169, 174, 179, 181–82, 223
   free 12, 15, 240, 244, 252–53
   indentured 10, 166, 168–69
   system 10, 15, 29, 44, 108, 126, 164, 166–69, 173–74, 177, 181, 190–91, 193, 196, 208, 223, 229, 234, 252
   urban 12, 178

   wage 29, 44, 124, 223, 229, 234
land cession treaties 131–32
land hunger theory 150
Land Ordinance Act of 1785 136
Land Ordinance Act of 1787 136, 172
land-plantation system 207
Land Policy of 1820 93
land(s)
   agricultural 87, 125, 149, 172, 182, 241
   ancestral 109, 113–14, 128, 132–33, 135–36, 138
   free 118–20, 123–24
   prices 93, 154, 179
   sacred 115, 128
   'virgin'/virgin 121, 124, 129, 173, 177, 180
land surrender treaties 109, 129
Large State Plan 60
Latin America 42, 155–58
law and order 100, 103
liberalism 3, 29, 46, 104, 156, 162, 187
libertarian 245
Lincoln, Abraham, US President 40, 100, 159, 223–25, 233–34, 236–37, 242–45, 247
Lincoln-Douglas debates 224
literacy 44, 206
Lords of Trade 25
Lost Cause 246–47
Louisiana Purchase of 1803 13, 80–82, 111, 130, 142–43, 173, 230
Lower House 53, 61, 65
Loyal Nine 30

Macon's Bill No. 2 146
Madison, James 14, 60, 73, 75, 77–79, 146–47, 150, 154, 187, 228
Maine 7–8, 62, 166, 230
mandate from Heaven 119
Manifest Destiny 82, 112, 119, 156, 159–61

marginalisation 2, 13–14, 82, 109, 117, 120, 129, 135–36, 138
maritime rights 148–49
market(s)
  economy 12, 14, 122, 124, 196
  external 74–75, 125, 171, 191, 228
  new 29, 44, 124, 160, 179
  revolution 12, 87, 153, 160, 243
Massachusetts Government Act 34
master-slave relationship 174, 180, 186, 192
mercantilism 18, 20, 25, 39, 47, 70
Mexican–American War (1848) 248
Middle Passage 165, 191
migration 105–06, 112, 118, 125, 133, 154, 160, 192
Milan Decree (1807) 83, 144
Militia Act of 1862 237
minority(ies) 42, 99, 126, 134, 183
missionary(ies) 109, 121, 130–31, 138, 167, 169, 218
  zeal 167, 169, 218
Mississippi River 4–5, 25, 48, 81, 92, 112, 130, 133, 155
Missouri Compromise of 1820 148, 154, 173, 230, 232–33, 249–50, 254
mobility 27, 40, 112, 122, 154, 178, 186, 190, 244
  economic 122, 178, 244
Molasses Act (1733) 21
monarchy 22–23, 43, 45, 55, 95, 160
monocropping 74, 179, 181
Monroe Doctrine 119, 141, 154, 156, 158
Monroe, James, US President 119, 141, 154, 156–58
Mount Vernon Conference 59

Napoleon Bonaparte, French emperor 11, 143–45, 150
  Continental System 144–45
Napoleonic War 83, 142–43
National Bank 74, 91, 93, 95, 153, 228

nationalism 3, 41, 99, 115, 119, 121–22, 152–54, 156, 159, 161–62, 192, 248, 251–52
National Negro Convention 239
Native American Riots 100
Nat Turner's Rebellion 239
Navigation Acts 20–22, 24–25, 27–28, *see also* Acts of Trade and Navigation
Nebraska-Kansas Act 233
Negro Act of 1740 170
neutrality 83–84, 143, 145–47
New Deal 75
New England Confederation 54
New Jersey's plan 60–61
New York City Vigilance Committee 218
New York Restraining Act (1767) 32
Non-Importation Acts 87
Non-Intercourse Act (1809) 83, 146
non-wage system 178
North America 3, 5–7, 16, 18–19, 24–25, 27, 29, 37, 60, 105–06, 112, 119, 129, 149, 151, 157–58, 165, 183, 232
North American colonies 23–25, 43, 52
northern colonies 26, 45, 171, 177
Northwest Land Ordinance Act of 1787 172
Northwest Ordinance of 1785 75, 111
Nullification Crisis 12, 97, 99, 135, 230
nullification doctrine 98–99
nullification ordinance 98

one-drop rule 167
one-party system 92
Order(s)-in-Council 144, 148
Oregon Treaty 113, 161
original peoples 82, 105, 135
Ostend Manifesto 162

Panic of 1837 97
paper money 22, 29, 94

Paris Treaty 54
partisan appointments 78, 92
paternalism 169, 176, 188–89, 195–96, 198
Paterson Plan 61
Peace Treaty of Amiens 143
Pennsylvania Abolition Society 172
Pequot War 109
persecution 6, 18, 202, 216
Philadelphia Convention 59, 67
Philadelphia Nativist Riots 100
plantation 15, 26, 29, 59, 165, 173–74, 176, 179–80, 182, 189–93, 195, 198, 207, 209–11, 215–16, 239
    economy 26, 29, 165, 176, 180, 182, 189, 192–93, 215
    system 173–74, 192, 207
planter(s) 27, 45, 56, 89, 91, 97, 112, 126, 153–54, 173–74, 176–82, 186, 188–89, 191–92, 195–96, 215, 236, 241, 245
pocket veto 92
policy(ies)
    federal 91–92, 113, 119, 179
    Indigenous removal 113
    isolationist 156–57
    land 91–93, 119
    of denial of education to enslaved people 202
    of forcefully removing Indigenous groups 132
    removal 113, 115, 130, 132
    trade 84, 170, 249
political
    culture 10–11, 18, 23, 27, 43–44, 117, 242, 245
    differences 250
    group/groupings 15, 75, 150–51, 229, 251
    institutions 2, 30, 52, 121–22, 127, 131, 251
    movement 30, 101
    party(ies) 62, 75, 85, 154, 187
    rhetoric 12, 68, 244
    systems 36, 99, 106, 114, 128, 131, 226, 242–43
popular vote 62, 64, 90, 227
populism 12, 120
poverty 18, 44, 76, 102, 134, 178, 185
power(s)
    balance of 43, 99, 143, 149, 232
    economic 22, 122, 186, 230, 252
    executive 57–58, 187, 230
    naval 143, 145, 252
    political 22, 75, 90, 122, 151, 186, 253
Powhatan Confederacy 108
prejudice 195, 200
Privy Council 25, 54
property
    private 23, 70, 115, 137, 190–91
    rights 65, 67, 70, 84, 87
Protestantism 122, 156
Protestants 23, 34, 101–02, 242
protests 28–30, 103, 132, 230, 233, 245
provisional removal treaty 134
Pueblo Revolt 109
punishment(s) 168, 196, 199, 208–13, 215
Purification movement 137

Quaker(s) 6, 42, 45–46, 172, 216, 218
Quartering Act (1765) 31–32, 34
Quebec Act (1774) 34

race(s) 10, 15, 45, 103, 117, 124, 126, 159–60, 164, 167, 170, 176, 183, 188, 197, 204, 247–48
    mixed- 167, 176, 183
racism 15, 127, 173, 188, 198–99, 207, 241
railroads 112, 118–19, 160, 181–82, 228
Randolph Plan 60
rebellion(s) 7, 11, 22, 35, 37, 47, 59, 66, 161, 170, 176, 186, 194, 198, 201, 212–17, 219, 239, 248

colonial 22, 37, 66
  slave 186, 212–13, 215–16, 219, 239, 248
Re-charter Bill 95
religion(s) 19, 34, 45–46, 86, 101, 114, 117, 130, 204, 206–07
religious conversion 115, 130
removal treaty 134–35
republicanism 70, 77, 82, 89, 102, 104, 155, 158–59, 252
Republican Party 87, 95, 101–02, 148, 187, 190, 224, 226, 233, 236, 244, 251–53, 255
Republicans 11, 14, 73–76, 78–80, 87, 142, 145, 150, 152–53, 225, 228–29, 243
  Jeffersonian 75, 150
Republican war 146
resistance(s) 2, 4, 10, 13, 30, 33–35, 99, 127, 131, 135, 137–38, 168, 170, 176, 187, 192–94, 197, 201, 203, 206, 211–13, 215–17, 225, 253
  forms of 192–93, 203, 215
revolt(s) 42, 59, 168, 172, 193–94, 213–14, 216, 219, 235, 239
revolutionary era/revolutionary period 11, 40, 66, 68, 192
Revolutionary War(s) 56, 58–59, 78, 83, 196
Revolution of 1800 75, 85
revolution(s) 2, 10, 12, 20, 22–23, 29, 35, 37, 39–40, 42, 44, 46–48, 56, 66, 74, 76, 85, 87, 100, 118, 121, 153, 155, 160, 172, 180, 243–44, 248
  market 12, 87, 153, 160, 243
right(s)
  civil 103, 235
  individual 42, 86, 153, 183
  land 13
  neutral 142–43, 146–48, 158
  political 19, 40, 116
  state 11, 75, 91, 99, 160–61, 225, 247

to self-determination 109, 151
to tax 24, 30, 32
to vote 12, 67, 69
riot(s) 30, 100, 103
royal
  appointments 25
  charter 8
  decrees 22
rule of law 190
Russia 156–57, 225

Sabbatarian movement 101
secession 12, 39, 82, 150, 187, 230, 234, 236, 246–47, 251–52, 255
Second Bank of the United States 91, 93, 95, 148, 152–53
Second Confiscation Act of 1862 237
Second Continental Congress 35, 55
Second Middle Passage 191
Second Seminole War 135
Second Slavery 191–92
Second War for Independence 146–47
sectional crisis 71, 154, 242
sectionalism 70, 98–99, 121–22, 148, 161, 223, 246, 248–49, 251–52
Sedition Act of 1798 79
self-determination 48, 109, 128, 151
self-government 24, 39, 41, 54, 157, 160
Seminole Confederacy 131
Senate 61–62, 64, 135, 146, 227, 231
servitude 44
settlement(s) 2, 4–7, 9–10, 13–14, 19, 22, 80, 106, 111, 117–18, 121, 123–24, 126, 128, 133–34, 138, 171, 173, 227, 242
settler(s) 1–3, 4, 6–7, 9–11, 13–14, 16, 18–20, 22–25, 27, 34, 42–43, 45, 52–55, 75, 82, 92, 100, 105–06, 109–11, 113–14, 117–18, 120–30, 132–36, 138, 151, 153, 155, 161, 166–69, 175, 202, 208, 214
  European 13, 16, 105–06, 128
  immigrant 18, 52, 55, 121

White 14, 54, 109–11, 113–14, 124, 126–27, 129–30, 132–34, 136, 138, 151, 153, 155, 166–68, 175, 202, 208
Seven Years War 25
ship rebellions 213
six nations' alliances 110
slaveholders 186, 196, 207, 239–40, 252
slavery 2, 10, 12–15, 44, 46, 63, 74, 84, 87–88, 120, 122, 126, 132, 135, 149, 153, 159, 162, 164, 166–68, 170–79, 182–97, 199, 201–02, 205, 207–10, 212, 214–17, 219–20, 223, 225, 227, 229–55
  abolition of 187, 244, 255
  American 189, 207
  development of 242
  expansion of 14–15, 120, 153, 173, 182, 216, 219, 233–34, 236, 244, 253
  institution of 10, 46, 63, 87–88, 120, 126, 167, 172, 175, 178–79, 185, 187, 189–90, 192–94, 197, 210, 212, 219, 227, 231, 236, 250, 252–53, 255
  issue of 84, 230, 236, 240–41, 243–44
  Lincoln's views 243–44, 247
  spread of 122, 162, 170, 173, 235, 238, 255
slavery and American Revolution 172
slave(s) 2, 10, 14–16, 27, 46, 56, 108–09, 149, 165–72, 174–84, 186, 189–99, 201–04, 206–07, 209–19, 227, 230–37, 239–41, 248–50, 253, 255
  codes 168, 170, 217, 219, 233, 255
  rebellions 186, 212–13, 215–16, 219, 248
  social-cultural life of the 192
slave trade 2, 46, 109, 165, 171, 174–75, 181–82, 196–97, 209, 213, 219, 227, 249–50

abolition of the 46
constitutional ban on the 165
domestic 209, 250
internal 171, 174–75, 181–82, 197, 219
transatlantic 2, 165, 213
slavocracy 240, 253
Small State Plan 61
social/societal
  groups 12, 16, 40–41, 241
  order 40–41, 85, 207
  relations/relationships 11, 189, 196
  status 186, 198, 204
  structures 15, 106, 121, 125, 177, 196, 246
society(ies)
  colonial 27, 40
  settler 10, 23, 42, 109, 111, 136, 167–68
Society of Filibusters 162
Sons of Liberty 26, 30, 33
Southampton Insurrection 239
South Carolina Ordinance of Nullification 98
sovereignty 30, 32, 47, 52, 57, 64, 68, 71, 77, 86, 112, 116, 132, 145, 147–48, 151, 161, 232
Spain 3–4, 21–22, 25, 60, 90, 141, 143, 151, 154–56, 157, 162, 214
Spanish colony(ies) 48, 80, 108, 144
Specie Circular 96
Spoils System 12, 92
squatters 89, 124, 135–36
Stamp Act (1765) 26, 29–31
state(s)
  slave 16, 149, 230–32, 234–35, 237, 240, 250
  southern 14, 80, 93, 97, 127, 132, 135, 166, 172, 177, 182, 187, 189, 199, 218–19, 234–36, 239, 242
  western 14, 82–83, 93, 95, 118, 148, 150–51, 217, 234, 254

Stono Rebellion/Stono Uprising 170, 214
Sugar Act (1764) 26, 28–30, 55
Supreme Court of US 60, 62, 64–65, 78–79, 93, 95, 116, 134, 217, 231, 234, 240

tariff(s) 67, 76–77, 93, 97–99, 118–19, 135, 142, 148, 151–52, 154, 179, 229–30, 247, 252
    rates 93, 97–99, 135, 152, 154, 230
tax/taxation 11, 21, 24–25, 29–33, 38–39, 45, 53, 55, 58, 64–65, 67, 73, 75–77, 142, 180, 215, 228, 241
Tea Act (1773) 26, 33–34
Tecumseh 135–38, 151
Temperance Movement 102, 242
Tenure of Office Act (1820) 92
territorial expansion 45, 74, 80, 87, 114, 135, 147–48, 151, 159–60, 192, 197
Thanksgiving Day 6
Thirteen (13) Colonies 8–10, 14, 19–20, 52, 141, 226
Three-Fifths Compromise 63
Townshend Acts (1767) 31
trade and commerce 20, 34, 43, 58, 64, 66, 74, 77, 84, 142–44, 146, 154, 157, 160, 228, 254
    American 28, 143, 146–47, 154, 158, 160
    foreign 47, 157, 229
    free 74, 84, 142–43, 170, 228, 249
Trade and Intercourse Act (1834) 117
Trade with Africa Act (1698) 170
trading 4–5, 45, 67, 110, 119, 128, 142, 144, 147, 171, 191
    posts 4–5, 110
    slave ports 171
tradition(s) 6, 24, 28, 45, 56, 68, 84, 118, 121, 128, 130, 137, 167, 174, 190, 199–203, 206–07, 228

Trail of Tears 99, 127, 134
Treaty of Dancing Rabbit Creek 133
Treaty of Doak's Stand 131
Treaty of Echota 134
Treaty of Fort Wayne 138
Treaty of Ghent 147
Treaty of Greenville, 1795 111, 136
Treaty of Guadalupe Hidalgo, 1848 113, 224, 231, 248
Treaty of Paris 26, 48, 54, 58
Treaty of Pontotoc 134
Tribal Confederacy 138
tripartite power sharing 56
Tripoli pirates 78, 86
Tubman, Harriet 218–19, 239–40
Turner's frontier theory 120–24
Tuscarora War 109
two-party system(s) 85, 92

Uncle Tom's Cabin (Stowe) 233, 240
Underground Railroad movement 240
Union Army 236–38, 240–41
United States of America (USA)
    colonisation of 18, 121, 128, 156, 175
    commercial prosperity 20, 144
    creation of, as a republican state 38
    economic interests of 78
    expansionist programme 155
    expansion of 45, 70, 80, 148
    foreign policy 84, 141, 156, 158
    geographical expansion of the 126
    impact of Europe on 120
    independence of the 14
    lifting all sanctions against 146
    political structure 226
    post-war 153
    progress of the 153
    revolutions in 121
    rise as a world power 152
    territorial expansion of the 159
    territorial integrity 145
    trade policy 84

violation of the sovereignty of the 147
Upper House 53, 61, 65, 227
urbanisation 9, 15, 73, 100, 120, 125, 145, 152, 180, 230, 243
US Constitution, 97, 132, 233, *see also* American Constitution
   Article I 61, 63
   Article V 63
   federal 66
   Necessary and Proper Clause 63
   opposition to the 67, 70
   principles of the 64
   ratification of the 64, 67
   Reserved Powers Clause 63
US–Mexican War/Mexican-American War 224, 231, 248
US President's election 11–12, 73–74, 76, 82, 90, 92, 94
   elections of 1800 11, 73
   elections of 1804 82
   elections of 1824 90
   elections of 1828 90, 92, 94

Vesey, Denmark 216–17
Vespucci, Amerigo 3
violence 100–103, 134, 137–38, 191, 209, 211–12, 217, 233
Virginia Plan 60–61
Virginia Statute for Relation of Freedom 46

vote/voting 12, 16, 40, 53, 57, 62–65, 67, 69, 90, 102, 227, 253

War Hawks 150
War of 1812 14, 89, 111–12, 141–43, 146, 148, 150–55, 162, 173, 191, 216, 229, 249–50
War of Independence 37, 42, 47, 110, 147, 207
Western hemisphere 3, 119, 141, 154–56, 158, 160, 162, 225
Whig Party 12, 95
Whigs 12, 42, 95, 148, 151, 159, 229–30
White(s)
   enslavers 168, 184, 193, 209, 239, 250
   groups 44, 245, 253–54
   settlements 111, 117, 133–34, 173
Wilmot Proviso of 1846 224, 231
women 33, 43, 46, 120, 124, 165, 184, 191, 204–06, 209, 212–13, 219, 234, 255
   enslaved 165, 191, 204, 209, 212–13, 219
World War II 2, 62, 125, 194
Writ of Assistance Act 27
writ of mandamus 79

Yamasee War 109